MW00654087

THE MYSTERY
of
PREDESTINATION

THE MYSTERY
of
PREDESTINATION

According to Scripture, the Church, and
St. Thomas Aquinas

By
John Salza

TAN Books
Charlotte, North Carolina

© 2010 John Salza

All rights reserved. With the exception of short excerpts used in articles and critical reviews, no part of this work may be reproduced, transmitted, or stored in any form whatsoever, printed or electronic, without the prior written permission of the publisher.

ISBN: 978-0-89555-905-0

Cover design by Milo Persic, milo.persic@gmail.com.

Front cover image: Guariento di Arpo (fl. 1338-d.1367/70). Angel weighing souls and combating a devil. Photo credit: Cameraphoto Arte, Venice/Art Resource, NY. Musei Civici, Padua, Italy. Back cover image: Osvaldo Bignami (1856-1936), Thomas Aquinas Fresco (1909), in the Chapel of Our Lady of Pompei, in the church of Santa Maria del Carmine, Italy. Picture by Giovanni Dall'Orto.

Printed and Bound in the United States of America

TAN Books
Charlotte, North Carolina
2010

TABLE OF CONTENTS

To my dear friend:
Fr. Thomas Scott
Thank you for encouraging me to address this most difficult topic, and to find the truth in the teachings of St. Thomas, Universal Doctor of the Catholic Church.

PREFACE

Predestination is a doctrine clearly revealed in Scripture and taught by the Catholic Church for 2,000 years. However, the doctrine is rarely explained in modern catechisms and almost never addressed in the Sunday sermon.[1] This is in part because predestination is one of the most sublime of all the doctrines of the Catholic faith. But its omission in sermons and catechism classes is seemingly not due to its sublimity alone. After all, the doctrine of the Blessed Trinity is equally mysterious. We don't understand how God can be three Persons and still be one God. Yet it is the subject of many sermons and catechisms.

Unlike the doctrine of the Trinity, which reveals who God is, the doctrine of predestination reveals *how God chooses*. Specifically, it states how God chooses to infallibly direct certain people (whom Scripture calls the "elect")[2] to salvation, and how God chooses to allow certain other people (the "reprobate") to fall way from salvation. Many people would rather talk about our freedom to choose God rather than God's freedom to choose us. Sermons and catechesis seem more pleasant when they focus on God's love and goodness for humanity rather than His complete sovereignty over His creatures. Nevertheless, God's plan of predestination exists precisely *because* of His love and goodness.

As this book demonstrates, God loves all men and grants all sufficient grace to be saved in Jesus Christ. Even though God predestines His elect to heaven, God makes it really possible for all men to follow His precepts and

---

1. The current Catechism of the Catholic Church (CCC) mentions "predestination" only once in paragraph 600: "To God, all moments of time are present in their immediacy. When therefore he establishes his eternal plan of 'predestination,' he includes in it each person's free response to his grace."

2. The scriptures use the term "elect" (Greek, *eklektos*) in 2 Kg. 22:27; Tob. 13:10; Ps. 17:27; 88:4; Wis. 3:9; Eccles. 11:33; 24:4, 13; 46:2; 47:24; Isa. 42:1; 45:4; 65:9, 15, 23; Zach. 9:17; Matt. 24:22, 24, 31; Mark 13:20; Luke 18:7; 23:35; Rom. 8:33; 16:13; Col. 3:12; 1 Tim. 5:21; 2 Tim. 2:10; Titus 1:1; 1 Pet. 1:1; 2:6; 2 John 1:1, 13; Apoc. 17:14.

never commands the impossible. Those who are saved are saved by God's special grace, and those who are condemned are condemned *by their own choosing*. Thus, God communicates His goodness by saving the elect in His mercy, and by condemning the reprobate in His justice. This means the elect must give all the glory to God for their salvation, and the reprobate must blame only themselves for their condemnation. God has implemented His plan of predestination so that the elect have nothing to boast about, and the reprobate have nothing to complain about.

The doctrine of predestination—which seeks to reconcile God's sovereign liberty with human free will—is an incomprehensible mystery. We cannot understand how God wills all men to be saved and yet chooses His elect for salvation. Although we can comprehend these truths in isolation, they appear contradictory when we attempt to reconcile them. It seems impossible that they could coexist. This is because both of these truths proceed from the inscrutable and unfathomable God, in whom infinite mercy, infinite justice, and infinite sovereignty reside. As St. Paul says, "How incomprehensible are his judgments, and how unsearchable his ways!" (Rom. 11:33).

Because the reconciliation of these truths surpasses our understanding, we must be careful not to emphasize one of the truths—God's sovereignty or man's free will—at the expense or exclusion of the other. For example, when Scripture emphasizes God's sovereign action over man, one cannot exclude human free will, which is moved by that action. Likewise, when Scripture emphasizes the human capacity to repent and come to God, one cannot dismiss that the act of repentance is brought about by God's grace. Excluding or minimizing one of these truths is the cardinal error of bad exegesis, particularly when addressing predestination. This book attempts to hold both truths in balance while concluding in no uncertain terms that "Salvation is of the Lord" (Ps. 3:9) and "Destruction is thy own, O Israel" (Hos. 13:9).

God has not revealed the doctrine of predestination to scare us (although a holy fear of God is good)[3] but to move us to completely abandon ourselves to His providence and holy will. As we say in the Our Father, "Thy will be done." This self-abandonment to God should not only humble us but should also give us comfort as we "work out our salvation with fear and trembling" (Phil. 2:12). We should be comforted in knowing that whenever we do any good that is

---

3. In fact, Scripture says "fear of the Lord" is the beginning of wisdom (Ps. 110:10; Prov. 1:7; 9:10) and one of the seven gifts of the Holy Ghost (Isa. 11:3). This means that a holy fear of God is one of the effects of predestination.

beneficial to our salvation (prayer, good works), *it is God* who is working in us "both to will and to accomplish" that good (Phil. 2:13). Thus, our salutary acts are a great sign from God that He is predestining us to the glory of His heaven, where we will gaze in wonder on the Blessed Trinity for all eternity.

"All the works of the Lord are exceedingly good. There is no saying: What is this, or what is that? For all things shall be sought in their time" (Ecclus. 39:21, 26).

John Salza, J.D.
7 March 2009, *Anno Domini*
Feast of St. Thomas Aquinas

1

Predestination and Divine Predilection

Predestination is the process by which God by His grace directs man to eternal life. This plan to direct man to eternal life is part of God's providence over all His creation. As the Catechism says, "[P]rovidence consists of the dispositions by which God guides all his creatures with wisdom and love to their ultimate end."[1] Indeed, God's providence over all things is one of the most powerful proofs of His existence. The Book of Wisdom teaches that God's providence "reacheth therefore from end to end mightily, and ordereth all things sweetly" (8:1); "but thou has ordered all things in measure, and number, and weight" (11:21); "But thy providence, O Father, governeth it: for thou hast made a way even in the sea, and a most sure path among the waves" (14:3).[2]

---

1. The current Catechism of the Catholic Church (CCC) mentions "predestination" only once outside of a few direct Scripture or Patristic quotations, in paragraph 600.

2. For this book, I have chosen the Douay-Rheims (DR) translation of Scripture for the following reasons: (1) it is the only traditional Catholic Bible in the English language (for over 300 years, the DR was the only Catholic English translation of Scripture used) and does not suffer from the defects of many modern Bibles (e.g., non-literal, dynamic translations; inclusive language); (2) it is a word-for-word translation of the Latin Vulgate (compiled by St. Jerome from the original Hebrew and Greek under Pope St. Damasus), which is the official translation of the Catholic Church (the Vulgate has been universally used in the Latin Rite for over 1,600 years); (3) the Council of Trent declared that "the old Latin Vulgate Edition, which, in use for so many hundred years, has been approved by the Church, be in public lectures, disputations, sermons and expositions held as authentic, and that no one dare or presume under any pretext whatsoever to reject it" (4th Session, April 8, 1546); (4) Pope Pius XII declared that the Latin Vulgate is "free from any error whatsoever in matters of faith and morals" (*Divino Afflante Spiritu* (1943), no. 21); (5) the DR has been repeatedly approved by great churchmen throughout the ages, such as Bishop Challoner (who made important revisions from 1749 to 1752) and Cardinal Gibbons (1899); (6) the English translations of the primary sources used in this book (St. Thomas Aquinas' *Summa*

1

Because God's providence governs all things, God is in control of all things and can do all things, for He says, "Is there any thing hard to God?" (Gen 18:14) and "Behold I am the Lord the God of all flesh: shall any thing be hard for me?" (Jer. 32:26). Job confessed to God, "I know that thou canst do all things, and no thought is hid from thee" (Job 42:2). God has "absolute sovereignty over the course of events" and "is the sovereign master of his plan."³ God's control over His entire creation means that His purpose in ordering things to their final end is always accomplished. God says through Isaiah, "Surely as I have thought, so shall it be: and as I have purposed, [s]o shall it fall out" (14:24-25); and, "My counsel shall stand, and all my will shall be done" (46:10). St. Paul confirms that God predestines man "according to the purpose of him who worketh all things according to the counsel of his will" (Eph. 1:11).

God's providential plan to order all things to their final end pre-exists in His mind, just as our plans pre-exist in our minds before we carry them out. As St. Thomas Aquinas teaches, because God is the cause of all things by His intellect, the ordering of those things toward their final end must also exist in His intellect.⁴ Hence, the word "predestination" is composed of the prefix *pre*, which means "before," and *destine*, which means "direct" or "send."⁵ This means that God decided prior to creating the universe how He would direct all things in His creation to their final end.

It is clear to us that unintelligent things—such as plants and animals—act toward their good end. Plants grow and bear fruit; animals reproduce and feed

---

Theologica; Denzinger's *The Sources of Catholic Dogma*) rely upon the DR translation of the Latin Vulgate; (7) the Protestant King James Version (KJV) is based on the DR translation, which helps Catholics convict Protestants of the correct interpretation of God's Word using their own hallowed KJV translation (this means the DR is older than the KJV; the DR New Testament was completed in 1582 and the Old Testament in 1609; the KJV was completed in 1611); (8) the DR provides the best translation of the scriptures concerning the study of predestination, with all the relevant subtleties and nuances that bear upon the verses' true meaning; (9) I want those unfamiliar with the DR to discover this most faithful and accurate translation of the original languages and experience the true joy of reading such a translation (and to discourage them from using the many modern, liberal translations that distort and fabricate God's Word); and (10) it is my favorite English translation!

3. CCC 303 and 306. The Catechism also says, "God is master of the world and of its history" (CCC 314).

4. *Summa Theologica* (ST), Pt I, Q 22, Art 1.

5. The word "predestination" comes from the Greek *proorizo* and is used six times in the New Testament to describe a predetermining knowledge or decree (Acts 2:25; 4:28; Rom. 8:29-30; 1 Cor. 2:7; Eph. 1:5, 11). Generally, when we use the word "predestination," we mean to refer to the fact that we are oriented to the glory of salvation, although, as we will see, one can also be predestined to grace but not to final glory (that is, some are not given the grace of final perseverance).

their young. It is evident that these things are directed to their end by an intelligent cause. But what about human beings? If humans have an intellect and a free will, then why is it necessary for God to order us to our final end? The answer: because God created *heaven* as our final end, and attaining heaven is above our nature and the nature of every creature.

We would never see God unless He granted us this supernatural privilege. Eternal beatitude surpasses our natural capacities. As St. Thomas teaches, "[E]verlasting life is an end exceeding the proportion of human nature."[6] The Catechism also states, "The vocation to eternal life is *supernatural* . . . It surpasses the power of human intellect and will, as that of every other creature."[7] Because man cannot attain to eternal life by his own natural efforts, he must be predestined to that end by God. St. Thomas says that "if a thing cannot attain to something by the power of its nature, it must be directed thereto by another; thus, an arrow is directed by the archer towards a mark."[8] Because we cannot attain the Beatific Vision by the power of our nature, God must direct us to this end by His power and grace. Thus, predestination is a certain and infallible truth, revealed by Scripture and taught by the Catholic Church.

Schools of Thought

How does God choose to predestine His elect to glory? How does He choose to permit the reprobate to fall away? Does He grant and withhold graces according to His own good will and pleasure? Or does He base His acts on man's foreseen merits and demerits? The remainder of this section presents a brief synopsis of the major competing schools of Christian thought dealing with predestination. This background is important as we dig more deeply into the mystery of predestination and attempt to discern truths and identify errors.

In Catholicism, the two major schools on predestination are Thomism and Molinism.[9] Thomists believe that God gives man both sufficient and efficacious graces according to His divine decree. With efficacious grace, God infallibly moves man to freely choose the spiritual good. Man is infallibly moved because the grace is intrinsically efficacious to produce the salutary act. Even though

---

6. ST, Pt I-II, Q 109, Art 5.

7. CCC 1998.

8. ST, Pt I, Q 23, Art 1.

9. Thomists are followers of St. Thomas Aquinas (1225-1274), who developed the doctrines of grace first propounded by St. Augustine (354-430) and the Second Council of Orange (529). Molinists are followers of Luis de Molina (1536-1600).

man remains free under the influence of efficacious grace, God is the first and primary cause of the good act. With sufficient grace, God provides man with the power to choose the good, but man resists, and so the power remains in potency and is never actualized.[10] Because sufficient grace is truly sufficient to apply man to act, the defect (the resistance or sin) is attributable to man, not God. The distinctions between these graces reveal that God is responsible for man's salvation, and man is responsible for his damnation.

Although God grants man both sufficient and efficacious graces, He grants the efficacious grace of perseverance *only to His elect*. God causes the elect to persevere in grace because He lovingly wills them a greater good, even though He gives all men the grace to be saved.[11] This is called the principle of predilection: No one thing would be better than another unless it were loved more by God. Because God's love is the cause of all goodness in things, God favors the elect because He gives them more, and not because of anything independently in them. We will explore this principle in greater depth in the next section.

Because God does not depend on man for anything, Thomists reject the notion that God predestines certain men based on their future merits. Rather, God grants the elect the intrinsically efficacious grace of perseverance out of pure benevolence. If God were to base His decision to grant grace on man's foreseen merits (that is, how man would respond to the grace), this would render God passive and dependent upon the will of man. This is impossible for the Supreme Being who, as St. Thomas says, is pure Act.[12] Because God's choice to predestine certain men is not conditioned upon man's future efforts, Thomists believe in what is called "unconditional election." At the same time, however, Thomists maintain that a man's demerits (namely, the sins he commits by rejecting sufficient grace) are the reason for his reprobation.

Molinists, named after the Spanish Jesuit Luis de Molina, have difficulty reconciling the Thomist position of the absolute gratuity of predestination with the freedom of the will. Thus, Molinists believe that God establishes His plan

---

10. The term "potency" in Thomism refers to the ability or capacity to be changed. The term "actualized" refers to the principle of change whereby something is completed or perfected. Because God is unchanging (Mal. 3:6; Num. 23:19; Jas. 1:17), He is pure Act with no potency. This is why God's will is never contingent upon the will of man.

11. Every salutary act is a product of efficacious grace, and thus the reprobate also receive efficacious graces to the extent they perform such acts. However, God grants only the elect the efficacious grace of perseverance.

12. "Act" means both "existence, being, actuality," and "fully real, complete, perfect." God is pure Act because He is the first and only perfect Being who is undetermined and unchanging.

of predestination based upon His foreknowledge of man's future cooperation with His grace, which is called "conditional election."[13] For example, God decides to give someone the grace of perseverance because He foresees that the person will freely persevere with the help of the grace. In this system, the person's cooperation is essential to the granting of the grace and the final result. The grace is not intrinsically efficacious (as it is for Thomists), but rather is made efficacious by the person's consent and cooperation (often referred to as extrinsically efficacious grace).[14]

In fact, Molinists generally believe that one person may receive a lesser grace than another person, and yet the person with the lesser grace may be converted while the person with more grace may not be converted. Thus, unlike Thomists, Molinists believe that one who makes a greater effort has not necessarily received a greater grace (and hence greater love from God). Although the Church has allowed Catholics to hold either the Thomist or Molinist position, I maintain that the Thomist position on predestination best reflects the teaching of Scripture and the Magisterium, and will attempt to demonstrate the same throughout this book.[15] As Pope Pius XII declared, "Theology, which is concerned with the interpretation of dogmas, also found in St. Thomas by far the richest of all commentators; for nobody ever more profoundly penetrated or expounded with greater subtlety all the august mysteries, as, for example . . . the obscurity of eternal predestination."[16]

In Protestantism, the two major schools on predestination are Calvinism and Arminianism.[17] Calvinists believe that God by eternal decree gratuitously

---

13. Molinists refer to this knowledge as "middle knowledge" (Latin, *scientia media*). St. Robert Bellarmine and Francisco Suarez were two Molinists who believed in unconditional election but not in the intrinsic efficacy of grace.

14. There is a "middle" system called Congruism that lies between Thomism and Molinism; it holds that intrinsically efficacious grace is required only for difficult salutary acts, while sufficient grace is required for common acts like prayer.

15. After nearly two centuries of heated debate, Pope Clement VIII (1592-1605) appointed the congregation known as *De Auxiliis* (1598-1607) to investigate these questions. Although the congregation favored Thomism and censured 42 propositions of Molinism, Pope Paul V concluded the investigation on August 28, 1607 without rendering a definitive judgment. On July 13, 1748, Pope Benedict XIV confirmed Pope Paul V's decision that the Thomist, Molinist, and Augustinian schools can promote their positions without accusations of heresy until the Church resolves the controversy. I speculate that the Church did not condemn Molinism at that time because of the rise of Calvinism. A condemnation of Molinism may have confused the faithful into believing in the legitimacy of Calvinism (because of some of the latter's similarities with Thomism).

16. Pope Pius XI, *Studiorem Ducem* (1923), No 19.

17. Calvinists are followers of John Calvin (1509-1564), and Arminians are followers of Jacob Arminius (1560-1609). Calvinism is found in Reformed, Presbyterian, and some Baptist com-

grants the grace of salvation to the elect, but does *not* grant salvific grace to the reprobate. In Calvinism, God gives the elect irresistible grace which they never refuse, similar to the efficacious grace of Thomism. However, although Calvinists maintain that God does not save a sinner against his will, they do not admit that the person has the actual power to resist God's "irresistible" grace. Thomists, on the other hand, maintain that the sinner has the power to resist efficacious grace, but that this power to resist remains in potency, and is never actualized, because God infallibly moves man to freely choose the good by such grace.

Further, in Calvinism, the reprobate are never offered sufficient grace for salvation, whereas in Thomism the reprobate are offered this grace but reject it. This means that in Calvinism God's constant pleadings with sinners to repent and be converted serve only to glorify His mercy in saving the elect and vindicate His justice in punishing the reprobate. Thus, Calvinism supports the notion of a "double predestination," whereby God leads the elect to salvation and the reprobate to damnation. Because God is directing the reprobate to their final end, Calvinism practically makes God responsible for man's sin—an idea at odds with Scripture and God's supreme goodness.[18] Double predestination is incompatible with the truth that God loves all men and desires all to be saved. We examine Calvinism in greater depth throughout this book.[19]

Arminians, like the Molinists, believe that God uses His foreknowledge to determine who will cooperate with His grace and receive salvation. Based on this foreknowledge, God pronounces who He will predestine to heaven. Thus, like the Molinists, Arminians deny the intrinsic efficacy of grace and believe that man's cooperation renders the grace efficacious. Also like the Molinists, Arminians believe that man can resist salvific graces, and like the Molinists (and Thomists) they generally believe that those who cooperate with saving grace can still fall away from salvation through sin. Calvinists, on the other

---

munities. Arminianism is found in Methodist, Pentecostal, Wesleyan, Congregational, and most Baptist communities. Protestants also contend that there are different traditions within each of these schools (e.g., "extreme" and "hyper" versus "moderate" Calvinism and Arminianism).

18. Although Calvinists generally deny that God is responsible for man's sin (see, for example, Canons of Dort, Article V), their theology demands this conclusion if God doesn't give man the power to obey His commandments. In fact, Huldrych Zwingli, the leader of the Reformation in Switzerland, declared that "God is the sinless author of sin."

19. Most Calvinists are known for believing in the five doctrines called the "Five Points of Calvinism." They are: Total Depravity, Unconditional Election, Limited Atonement, Irresistible Grace, and Perseverance of the Saints (forming the acronym T-U-L-I-P). We examine these points throughout the book. See also the Appendix.

hand, like many Reformed and Evangelical traditions within Protestantism, believe in "eternal security." That is, once a person accepts Christ, he is assured of his salvation.

DIVINE PREDILECTION

Having summarized the various schools of thought, we now set forth what we maintain is the true and correct motive for predestination: *Divine predilection.* The word "predilection" is used to describe God's special love for His elect and the divine favor He bestows upon them. This is the most foundational principle for apprehending the mystery of predestination and should be the guiding light for our analysis and reflections. Because God is love and "first hath loved us" (1 John 4:19), all discussions concerning predestination should hinge upon this fundamental truth.

As we will see below, the principle of predilection is revealed in the teachings of Scripture. It was also formulated by the Church at the Second Council of Orange (a regional council held in 529). Canon 12, entitled *God loves such as us*, states: "God loves us, as we shall be by the gift of His grace, not as we are by our own merit."[20] In other words, the Council teaches that the more we are loved by God, the more we will be aided by His grace. The Catechism also says, "Justification is the *most excellent work of God's love.*"[21] The truth that God's love is the reason for divine favor and election was developed in great detail by St. Thomas.

In the *Summa*, St. Thomas explains that the will of God is the cause of things. A thing has existence, or any kind of good, only insofar as it is willed by God.[22] Because love is the willing of good for another, this means that God's love is the cause of goodness in things. We see this at the beginning of divine revelation, where each time God creates He sees that His creation is "good."[23] From these basic truths, St. Thomas concludes that "no one thing would be better than another, if God did not will greater good for one than for another."[24] St. Thomas further says that "the reason why some things are better than others,

---

20. Denz., 185. The council based this canon on St. Prosper's 56th sentence.
21. CCC 1994 (emphasis in original). The Catechism also says, "*The charity of Christ is the source in us of all our merits* before God" (2011; emphasis in original).
22. See ST, Pt I, Q 19, Art 4, and Q 20, Art 2.
23. Gen. 1:4, 10, 12, 18, 21, 25, 31.
24. ST, Pt I, Q 20, Art 3.

is that God wills for them a greater good. Hence it follows that He loves more the better things."[25]

As we said in the beginning, God's providence, of which predestination is a part, is the plan existing in His intellect that directs the order of things to their end. Nothing, however, is directed toward an end unless the will for that end already exists. Because good is the essential object of the will, and love is the willing of good for another, love is the *first* movement of the will.[26] St. Thomas says, "Whence the predestination of some to eternal salvation presupposes, in the order of reason, that God wills their salvation; and to this belong both election and love: love, inasmuch as He wills them this particular good of eternal salvation . . . election, inasmuch as He wills this good to some in preference to others."[27] This means that *God's love is the motive for election and predestination.*

Although the principle of predilection means that God chooses to save the elect because He loves them more, we are not to confuse God's predilect love for His elect with our love for God and others. This is a key to understanding the Thomist position. We choose whom we love because of the goodness that exists in them. However, God chooses whom He loves because of the goodness that His love thereby *creates* in them. St. Thomas says that "the love of God creates and infuses goodness" in His creatures.[28] The Council of Orange II also says, "Although we were displeasing we were loved, so that there might be produced in us [something] by which we might please."[29] Thus, the way humans love and choose is ordered differently in God. St. Thomas explains:

> Election and love, however, are differently ordered in God, and in ourselves: because in us the will in loving does not cause the good, but we are inclined to love by the good which already exists; and therefore we choose someone to love, and so election in us precedes love. In God, however, it is the reverse. For His will, by which in loving He wishes good to someone, is the cause of that good possessed by some in preference to others. Thus it is clear that love precedes election in the order of reason, and election precedes predestination. Whence all the predestinate are objects of election and love."[30]

25. ST, Pt I, Q 20, Art 4.
26. See ST, Pt I, Q 20, Art 1.
27. ST, Pt I, Q 23, Art 4.
28. ST, Pt I, Q 20, Art 2.
29. Denz., 198.
30. ST, Pt I, Q 23, Art. 4. St. Thomas says "in the order of reason" presumably because there

That there are distinctions, if you will, in God's love is certainly not inconsistent with the truth that God is all-loving. If we are ever tempted to question God's eternal love for each one of us, we need only to look at a crucifix. Although Jesus loves all men so much that He shed His blood for them, His love for the Father exceeds His love for any man. Likewise, the Father loves Jesus more than anyone or anything, and He loves the Blessed Virgin Mary more than any other human being or any angel. Jesus had a special love for John the Apostle vis-à-vis the other apostles (see John 19:26), and has a unique love for His Church in preference to those outside His Church (see Eph. 5:25).

Although certainly not a perfect comparison, we can relate to the distinctions in God's love in light of our own love for others. For example, we are called "to work good to all men, but especially to those who are of the household of the faith" (Gal. 6:10). Men are to sacrificially love their wives "as Christ also loved the church" (Eph. 5:25). Men are also "to love their wives as their own bodies" (Eph. 5:28). However, men are not to love their neighbors' wives or bodies the same way. Parents have a greater and more intense love for their children than for the children of other parents. Parents also love some attributes in their children more than other attributes. Grades of intensity within the act of loving do not negate the fact that the love exists.

In summary, St. Thomas teaches that God's love is the cause of goodness in all things. This means that one thing would not be better than another unless it were loved more by God. God the Supreme Good is not a spectator of good; He is the author of all good. Even though God loves all men and thus wills them good, God loves the elect more because He gives them more. God loved St. Peter more than Judas Iscariot because He gave St. Peter more grace and help than Judas (even though He gave Judas sufficient grace to avoid sin and repent of his sins). As St. John the Baptist says, "A man cannot receive anything unless it be given him from heaven" (John 3:27). St. James also says, "Every best gift, and every perfect gift, is from above, coming down from the Father of lights" (Jas. 1:17).

Hence, where there are two sinners, the one who converts is loved and helped more by God than the one who does not, even though God loves both sinners and gives them both sufficient grace for conversion. St. Augustine says the same regarding the angels: "If both were created equally good, then, while some fell

---

is no chronological sequencing of events in eternity and God does not have discursive knowledge. However, we maintain that God's decrees in eternity must precede His foreknowledge of future events because future events exist only because of His decrees.

by their evil will, the others were more abundantly assisted, and reached that high degree of blessedness from which they became certain they would never fall."[31] All good, whether it's the grace of profound conversion or the grace of resisting temptation, comes from God through Jesus Christ. As St. Paul says, "Or what hast thou that thou hast not received?" (1 Cor. 4:7). Jesus also says, "Without me you can do nothing" (John 15:5). St. Thomas further says, "For a man receives all his power of well-doing from God, and not from man. Hence a man can merit nothing from God except by His gift."[32]

Romans 8: "For Whom He Foreknew, He Also Predestinated"

St. Thomas's teaching on divine predilection is clearly supported by Sacred Scripture. For example, in his letter to the Romans, St. Paul reveals that predilection is the motive for predestination. In chapter 8, St. Paul writes:

> And we know that to them that love God, all things work together unto good, to such as, according to his purpose, are called to be saints. For whom he foreknew, he also predestinated to be made conformable to the image of his Son; that he might be the firstborn amongst many brethren. And whom he predestinated, them he also called. And whom he called, them he also justified. And whom he justified, them he also glorified (vv. 28-30).

In verse 28, St. Paul says that "all things work together unto good" for those who are called to be saints. Because God's love is the cause of the "good" in verse 28, St. Paul is teaching that God elects His saints according to His predilection. In verse 29, St. Paul reveals a sequence of five active verbs that have God as the subject and the elect as the object: God "foreknew," "predestinated," "called," "justified," and "glorified."[33] Calvinists refer to Romans 8:29 as "the golden chain of redemption."

---

31. *De civitate Dei*, XII, 9.

32. ST, Pt I-II, Q 114, Art 2.

33. We note that Paul in Romans 8:28-30 is referring to the elect because they are ultimately glorified (they received the efficacious grace of final perseverance). However, this doesn't mean that everyone in Scripture who is "predestined," "called," and "justified," receives final glory. As we mentioned and will see in greater detail in the last chapter, God permits those who resist sufficient grace to fall away.

The first verb in the chain is "foreknew," which comes from the Greek *progi-nosko*. In the two other instances of the use of this verb in the New Testament in the context of predestination, it likewise refers to predilection. For example, St. Paul uses *proginosko* two chapters later, in Romans 11:2, when he says, "God hath not cast away his people which he foreknew [*proginosko*]. Know you not what the scripture saith of Elias; how he calleth on God against Israel?"

In this verse, St. Paul is revealing that God grants a special love to His elect that secures their salvation. St. Paul could not have chosen a better Old Testament example than Elias (Elijah). God had a very special and unique love for Elias, for Scripture says that "the Lord would take up Elias into heaven by a whirlwind."[34] A few verses later, St. Paul confirms that he is discussing divine election when he says, "Even so then at this present time also, there is a remnant saved according to the election of grace. And if by grace, it is not now by works: otherwise grace is no more grace" (vv. 5-6). In this last verse, St. Paul affirms that God does not base His election on "works" or future merits but chooses out of His pure benevolence and gratuity.

St. Peter also uses *proginosko* in the context of divine predilection. In 1 Peter 1:19-20, he says that we have been redeemed "with the precious blood of Christ, as of a lamb unspotted and undefiled, foreknown (*proginosko*) indeed before the foundation of the world." In this passage, St. Peter is clearly referring to the love that the Father had for Christ before He sent Him into the world. In fact, in St. John's gospel, Jesus refers to the Father's predilect love for Him in almost the same words: "Father . . . thou hast loved me before the creation of the world" (17:24).[35]

Notwithstanding these examples, Molinists and Arminians insist that St. Paul's use of "foreknew" in Romans 8:29 means that God chose His elect based on His foreknowledge of their future merits (even though the verse says nothing about the elect's future merits), and not His predilection. It is true that when *proginosko* is used as a noun, it refers to knowledge of future events. For example, after St. Peter warns how private interpretation of Scripture can lead to one's own destruction, he says, "[T]herefore, brethren, knowing these things before (*proginosko*), take heed."[36]

Moreover, Scripture is clear that God knows all things, for the Psalmist says,

---

34. 4 Kg. 2:1; see also 4 Kg. 2:11; Ecclus. 48:13; 1 Mac. 2:58.
35. The Greek for "before the foundation/creation of the world" in these verses is identical (*pro katabole kosmos*).
36. 2 Pet. 3:17; see also Acts 26:5.

"Behold, O Lord, thou hast known all things, the last and those of old" (138:5). God's knowledge includes knowledge of future events, as He says through Isaias (Isaiah), "[B]efore they spring forth, I will make you head them" (42:9). Daniel also reveals, "But there is a God in heaven that revealeth mysteries, who hath shown to thee ... what is to come to pass in the latter times" (2:28). St. Peter also declared at the council of Jerusalem, "To the Lord was his own work known from the beginning of the world" (Acts 15:18).

However, when *proginosko* is used as a verb, as it is in Romans 8:29 and 11:2 and in 1 Peter 1:20, it does not refer to God's knowledge of future events but rather God's *action* of arranging those events in advance, according to His divine plan. Love is an act of the will. This means that God is not predestining those in Romans 8:29 based on His "passive" foreknowledge of their future merits (the Molinist and Arminian position) but is actively foreordaining those events that will infallibly fulfill His plan of predestination based on His predilection (the Thomist and Calvinist position).

St. Peter's use of *proginosko* in 1 Peter 1:20 could not possibly refer to the Father's knowledge of Christ's foreseen merits. St. Thomas explains that the human nature in Christ was united to the Son of God "without any antecedent merits."[37] Further, because Christ had an impeccable free will, His obedience to the Father was certain to occur. St. Thomas further adds that "Christ's predestination is the exemplar of ours."[38] As St. Paul says, Jesus "was predestinated the Son of God in power" (Rom. 1:4). This means that we, who are "predestinated to be made conformable to the image of his Son," are also predestined by God in Christ, irrespective of our foreseen merits. Moreover, St. Thomas says that Christ "was predestinated to be the natural Son of God, whereas we are predestinated to the adoption of sons, which is a participated likeness of natural sonship."[39] Thus, if Christ's predestination is the exemplar of ours, and He was predestinated as a *natural* Son without regard to foreseen merits, much more are we predestinated as *adopted* sons without regard to foreseen merits.

St. Augustine agreed that Scripture's use of God's foreknowledge in the context of predestination referred to His divine prearrangement of the elect to glory and the means by which they will infallibly attain it. St. Augustine says, "By predestination, God foreknew those things which He was going to do."[40]

---

37. ST, Pt III, Q 24, Art 3.
38. Ibid.
39. Ibid.
40. *De praed. sanct.*, chapter 10.

The Doctor of Grace equates foreknowing with divine action. God foreknew the special love and goodness He would freely give man. Similarly, St. Augustine refers to the "foreknowledge and preparation of those gifts whereby whoever are liberated are most certainly liberated."[41] Once again, Augustine connects foreknowledge with preparation, both of which are divine actions that cause the liberation of the elect. In short, Augustine says that predestination is the foreknowledge of God's benefits, not man's merits.[42]

The Church at the Third Council of Valence (a regional council held in 855) also attributes action to foreknowledge in regard to God's punishment of the reprobate. The third canon says: "But God foreknew the malice of the wicked, and because it was their own and He was not the cause of it, He did not predestine it. The punishment, of course, following their demerit, this He foreknew and predestined."[43] In this canon, we clearly see that God's foreknowledge of future demerits is not part of predestination. However, God's punishment of the wicked is a foreordained (or "foreknown") divine action that is part of His plan of predestination.

St. Thomas teaches in no uncertain terms that divine election is not based upon foreseen merits. In fact, in a departure from his usual calm and objective tone, St. Thomas says that "nobody has been so insane as to say that merit is the cause of divine predestination as regards the act of the predestinator."[44] St. Thomas's position that election is exclusive of human effort is clearly supported by Scripture and the teachings of the Church. For example, in his second letter to Timothy, St. Paul reveals that God "hath delivered us and called us by his holy calling, not according to our works, but according to his own purpose and grace, which was given us in Christ Jesus before the times of the world" (1:9). St. Paul is clear that God calls us independently of our works according to His purposes and before time began.

In his letter to Titus, St. Paul says, "Not by works of justice, which we have done, but according to his mercy, he saved us, by the laver of regeneration, and renovation of the Holy Ghost" (3:5). St. Paul also writes to the Ephesians, "For by grace you are saved through faith, and that not of yourselves, for it is the gift of God; not of works, that no man may glory" (2:8-9). He also says to the Romans, "[T]here is a remnant saved according to the election of grace. And

---

41. *De dono persever.*, chapter 14.
42. This is St. Thomas's interpretation of St. Augustine. See ST, Pt I, Q 23, Art 2.
43. Denz., 322.
44. ST, Pt I, Q 23, Art 5.

if by grace, it is not now by works: otherwise grace is no more grace" (11:5-6). These and other verses demonstrate that God saves us through grace and not works (current or future merits), according to His purpose and election.

Canon 18 of the Council of Orange II says: "*That grace is preceded by no merits. A reward is due to good works, if they are performed; but grace, which is not due, precedes that they may be done.*"[45] The council further says that "in every good work we do not begin, and afterwards are helped by the mercy of God, but He Himself, with no preceding good services [on our part], previously inspires us with faith and love of Him."[46] Pope Boniface, in confirming the Council of Orange, says that "the beginning of all good will, according to Catholic truth, is inspired in the minds of individuals by the preceding grace of God."[47] In fact, the pope states that all blessings, including faith in Christ, are conferred upon us by the preceding grace and mercy of God, and not because of our merits.[48] Canon 3 of the Council of Valence III says that "in the election, moreover, of those who are to be saved, the mercy of God precedes the merited good."[49] For those who are justified by grace, the Ecumenical Council of Trent says, "[W]hereby without any existing merits on their part they are called."[50]

St. Thomas also explains that God's purported reliance on foreseen merits confuses the effects of grace with the effects of free will, as if both effects didn't come from God. Attributing our free-will acts to man and not to God suggests that our acts are outside the effect of predestination. This is not possible. St. Thomas says:

> Now there is no distinction between what flows from free will, and what is of predestination; as there is no distinction between what flows from a secondary cause and from a first cause. For the providence of God produces effects through the operation of secondary causes ... Wherefore, that which flows from free will is also of predestination.[51]

---

45. Denz., 191. The Catechism also says, "The divine initiative in the work of grace *precedes*...the free response of man" (CCC 2022) and "We can merit in God's sight *only* because of God's free plan to associate man with the work of his grace" (CCC 2025).

46. Ibid., 200.

47. Ibid., 200a.

48. Ibid., 200b.

49. Ibid., 322.

50. Ibid., 797.

51. ST, Pt I, Q 23, Art 5. The Catechism also says, "God is the first cause who operates in and through secondary causes" (CCC 308).

St. Thomas further says that "whatsoever is in man disposing him towards salvation, is all included under the effect of predestination; even the preparation for grace."[52] The Catechism similarly says, "The *preparation of man* for the reception of grace is already a work of grace."[53] This is because acquiring God's divine life of grace surpasses our natural abilities. Jesus affirmed the same when He said, "No man can come to me, except the Father, who hath sent me, draw him" (John 6:44). This is also why in the Preface we said that our salutary acts should give us great humility and comfort, for they are a sign that God is "disposing us toward salvation," which is an effect of predestination. St. Thomas beautifully summarizes his thoughts on this issue by saying that "God preordained to give glory on account of merit, and . . . He preordained to give grace to merit glory."[54]

Thus, God's "foreknowledge" refers to the special favor He gives to the elect that causes them to freely choose salvation. This favor includes even the secondary causes that will bring about His plan of predestination, such as our free-will decisions. This is why Jesus at the end of time will tell the reprobate, "Depart from me, I never *knew* you." When Christ will say that He never *knew* the reprobate, this doesn't mean He didn't personally know them or their future merits and demerits. Rather, it means that He did not love them the way He loved the elect. Even though Jesus loved them enough to die for them, He permitted them to resist His grace by their own free will (whereas He caused the elect to freely choose salvation). No one thing can be better than another thing unless it is loved more by God.

More Problems with Molinism (and Arminianism)

In addition to denying the truth of God's predilection as the basis for predestination, Molinism (as well as Arminianism) raises other serious objections. By claiming that God bestows grace on account of future merits, one renders God passive by making the salutary act dependent upon man, not God. God is no longer the author of our good acts but a spectator of them. But as St. Thomas teaches, there is no passivity or potentiality in God. God is Pure Act who

---

52. Ibid. See also Pt I-II, Q 109, Art 6.
53. CCC 2001 (emphasis in original).
54. Ibid. In Catholic theology, "merit" means "deserving justly." Man can merit under the influence of grace because the grace causes man to act freely, without coercion. See CCC 2006-2011.

does not change. This must be the case because, absolutely speaking, actuality is prior to potentiality. That is, something can change from potentiality to actuality only by a being in actuality, and God is the First Being. If God ever had potentiality, then something would have had to precede Him to move Him to actuality, which is impossible.[55] As the Catechism says, God is "the first cause of all that exists" (CCC 300).

This also means that Molinism (along with Arminianism) denies the intrinsic efficacy of grace. Grace becomes efficacious only because of our foreseen consent. Grace becomes dependent upon human will. This position is untenable *because it is circular*: God grants grace because of our foreseen consent, but our foreseen consent happens only because of grace. As St. Paul says, "[W]hat hast thou that thou hast not received?" (1 Cor. 4:7). Thus, God cannot bestow grace on account of foreseen merits because those merits are the product of the very grace He has decreed to bestow, and from all eternity. Without the grace of Christ, one can do nothing beneficial for his salvation (see John 15:5). St. Paul says, "Not that we are sufficient to think any thing of ourselves, as of ourselves: but our sufficiency is from God" (2 Cor. 3:5).

The Molinist position also depreciates the gift of grace. As we have said, in Molinism, one who receives a lesser grace may convert, while one who receives a greater grace may not convert. It seems entirely implausible to conclude that one who has died in a state of grace has received less from God than one who has not. To say that God loved less and helped less the person who lived a better life and went to heaven is to denigrate the gift of grace and salvation, and the truth that God is the cause of goodness in things. St. Thomas says, "He who makes a greater effort, has received a greater grace; but that he makes a greater effort, he needs to be moved by a higher cause, according to the text: 'Convert us, O Lord, to Thee, and we shall be converted'" (Lam. 5:21).[56]

Another problem with Molinism is the notion of the "middle knowledge" (*scientia media*), which refers to God's knowledge of how man will respond to His grace. As we have explained, Molinists argue that God grants graces based on what He foresees a man would freely choose. This would mean that man would not be dependent upon God's knowledge and will, but God's knowledge

---

55. The author acknowledges the different systems of metaphysics, but maintains the superiority of Thomism, based on the teachings of Scripture and the Church. Scripture (from revelation) and metaphysics (from reason) are not inconsistent with each other, but teach the same truths about God (e.g., God is the first cause, all good comes from God, etc.).

56. *Commentary on Matthew 25:15.*

and will dependent upon man. Man's action would come outside the purview of God's intention and causality. This eliminates God's sovereign independence over the created order. As St. Thomas says, "The knowledge of God is the cause of all things. For the knowledge of God is to all creatures what the knowledge of the artificer is to the things made by his art."[57] In addition, middle knowledge cannot exist prior to God's divine decree. That is, prior to any divine decree, there cannot be any conditionate future that is determined.[58] There exists only an undetermined contingent future. For example, God can foresee that St. Peter will either be faithful to Jesus or betray Jesus, but God cannot know which one St. Peter will infallibly choose because St. Peter's will is undetermined in the absence of God's divine decree. St. Thomas also teaches this truth when he says, "Contingent futures, the truth of which is not determined, are not in themselves knowable."[59] Again, Molinism renders God's decrees dependent upon man's will, which means that God's determining decrees are really not determining, but determined. This position denigrates God's omnipotence and sovereignty over His created order.

Thus, just as Molinism denies the intrinsic efficacy of God's grace, it also denies the infallibly efficacious nature of God's decrees. By decrees, we mean those effects that proceed from God's perfect intellect and will. St. Thomas defines them by saying, "Determined effects proceed from His own infinite perfection, according to the determination of His will and intellect."[60] St. Thomas also says, "God's knowledge is the cause of things, insofar as His will is joined to it."[61] Regarding the decree of the atonement, St. Peter says Jesus was "delivered up, by the determinate counsel and foreknowledge of God" (Acts 2:23). Jesus also says, "And the Son of man indeed goeth, according to that which is determined" (Luke 22:22). Although Jesus laid His life down freely, God decreed from all eternity the events that were necessary to procure His atoning death. God's decree of Jesus' death did not depend upon Jesus' foreseen merits, for Jesus' merits were the result of God's decree.

---

57. ST, Pt I, Q 14, Art 8.
58. See Garrigou-LaGrange, *Predestination*, p. 147.
59. ST, Pt II-II, Q 171, Art 3. St. Thomas teaches that God has "practical knowledge" or the "knowledge of vision" of all things that He brings about by His divine causality, and "speculative knowledge" or "simple intelligence" of things that are not, nor will be, nor were that He has never planned to make (ST, Pt I, Q 14, Art 9; *De veritate*, 2.8.c.). This knowledge includes future contingents (ST, Pt I, Q 14, Art 13).
60. ST, Pt I, Q 19, Art 4.
61. ST, Pt I, Q 14, Art 8.

Just as Christ's death was decreed by God, all of the graces that flow from His death—and that produce the salutary acts in us—have also been decreed by God. These decrees most certainly include whom God chooses to elect to eternal salvation, and whom He permits to fall away from salvation. Moreover, God's decrees include not only those things God wills to be done but also the way in which they are to be done. St. Thomas says, "Since the divine will is perfectly efficacious, it follows not only that things are done which God wills to be done, but also that they are done in the way that He wills. Now God wills some things to be done necessarily, some contingently, to the right ordering of things, for the building up of the universe."[62] Thus, all things happen by God's efficacious decrees, which precede His "middle knowledge" of our future merits and demerits.

Scripture also defeats the idea that "middle knowledge" is the basis for conferring grace. For example, in Matthew's gospel, Jesus makes an extraordinary statement to the Jews as He upbraids them for their unbelief:

> Woe to thee, Corozain, woe to thee, Bethsaida: for if in Tyre and Sidon had been wrought the miracles that have been wrought in you, they had long ago done penance in sackcloth and ashes. But I say unto you, it shall be more tolerable for Tyre and Sidon in the day of judgment, than for you. And thou Capharnaum, shalt thou be exalted up to heaven? thou shalt go down even unto hell. For if in Sodom had been wrought the miracles that have been wrought in thee, perhaps it had remained unto this day. But I say unto you, that it shall be more tolerable for the land of Sodom in the day of judgment, than for thee. At that time Jesus answered and said: I confess to thee, O Father, Lord of heaven and earth, because thou hast hid these things from the wise and prudent, and hast revealed them to the little ones. Yea, Father; for so hath it seemed good in thy sight (11:21-26).

This passage tells us that Jesus performed many miracles among the Jews living in the cities of Corozain, Bethsaida, and Capharnaum, but the Jews remained obstinate unbelievers. Jesus tells the Jews that if the wicked cities of Tyre, Sidon, and Sodom had witnessed these same miracles, they would have repented of their wickedness. Yet we know that God did not convert these

---

62. ST, Pt 1, Q 19, Art 8.

sinners through miracles, but destroyed them with brimstone and fire for their evil ways (see Gen. 19:24-25). This account demonstrates that God did *not* grant the grace of conversion to the Sodomites even though God foresaw that the Sodomites would have responded favorably to this grace through miracles (disproving Molinism/Arminianism).[63]

This, however, does not mean that God predestined the Sodomites to destruction. As we have said and will continue to explain, God gives all men sufficient grace to be saved, and men are able to respond freely to this grace by an act of their will. Because man's resistance to grace is not a good but rather a defect, it necessarily comes from man, not from God. God grants only the divine permission to sin. Just as the Sodomites were able to respond to the graces they were given (but refused them), the Jews were also able to respond to God's grace (but most refused). Jesus can compare the Jews with the Sodomites because they both had free will and sufficient grace to believe. If the Sodomites weren't capable of believing, then Jesus could not say that they would have responded to the miracles. In fact, Jesus is indicting the Jews for this very reason—for failing to respond to God, unlike the Sodomites who would have responded had they been given the great graces and miracles that God gave the Jews.[64] This means that God had given the Jews sufficient grace for belief, for God cannot command the Jews to do the impossible.

We do not comprehend God's reasons for granting and withholding graces, and Jesus completes His admonition of the Jews by keeping the mystery in front of us. He says that God "has hid these things from the wise and prudent, and hast revealed them to the little ones" (v. 25). "These things" refers to the mysteries of infallible graces that God chooses to give His elect, the "little ones," in preference to the sufficient grace He gives to others. How God determines who is among His "little ones," we don't know. But as we have seen and will further examine below, God's choice of election is based on His love of the "better things" of which He is the cause. God loves the "little ones" more because He has given them more. God is the cause of all goodness, and no

---

63. This scenario proves that there is a distinction between sufficient grace (which man freely resists) and efficacious grace (which man does not resist), which we will further examine throughout the book.

64. Of course, the Sodomites would have repented only if God had eternally decreed to grant them the efficacious grace of repentance. Because God did not decree this result, it is an undetermined contingent future that God knows only speculatively. Thus, it is no surprise that the Greek of Matthew 11:23 is not definitive about the Sodomites' repentance, and that the Douay-Rheims translation says that Sodom "perhaps" would have remained unto this day.

thing would be better than another unless it were loved more by God. As Jesus concludes, "Yea, Father, for so hath it seemed good in thy sight" (v. 26).

Romans 9: "Jacob I Have Loved"

After revealing God's plan of predestination in Romans 8:28-30, St. Paul provides further insights into the motives for God's plan in chapter 9 (remember, the chapter divisions are not part of the original text). St. Paul opens this chapter by grieving for the unbelief of the Jews with "great sadness" and "continual sorrow" (v. 2). St. Paul refers to the Jews as "my brethren" and "my kinsmen" (v. 3), and even says that he would be willing to be separated from Christ if that would save the Jews (v. 3). St. Paul affirms that the Israelites had received the promises of salvation from God (v. 4), but then states: "Not as though the word of God hath miscarried. For all are not Israelites that are of Israel" (v. 6). St. Paul goes on to say:

> Neither are all they that are the seed of Abraham, children; but in Isaac shall thy seed be called: That is to say, not they that are the children of the flesh, are the children of God; but they, that are the children of the promise, are accounted for the seed. For this is the word of promise: According to this time will I come; and Sara shall have a son. And not only she. But when Rebecca also had conceived at once, of Isaac our father (vv. 7-10).

What is St. Paul's point? He is responding to those who were accusing him of preaching a false gospel. St. Paul was being so accused because many Jews, who were still thought by some to be God's chosen people, had rejected St. Paul's gospel. St. Paul reveals that their understanding is erroneous. The Jews were rejecting Christ because God saves "the children of the promise," not "the children of the flesh."[65] That is, not all who are the physical seed of Israel are the spiritual seed of Abraham and "the children of God" (v. 8). Thus, St. Paul reveals that the national identity of a person is irrelevant to God's plan of salvation. In fact, as St. Paul later explains, only a fraction of the nation of

---

65. The "promise" refers to the covenant of grace that God inaugurated through Abraham (Gal 3:18, 29), and not the covenant of law that came through Moses. The Abrahamic covenant of grace has been fulfilled in the New Covenant of Christ (Rom. 4:16; Gal 3:14), and the Mosaic covenant of law has been abolished (Rom. 7:4; 1 Cor. 3:14; Gal 3:10-13; Eph. 2:15; Col 2:14; Heb. 7:12, 18; 8:13; 10:9).

Israel would be saved, which Paul describes as "a remnant saved according to the election of grace" (Rom. 11:5).[66]

If the Jews were wrong and national identity is irrelevant to God's saving plan, then how does God determine who are "the children of God"? How does He determine who is saved according to "the election of grace"? St. Paul further explains: "For when the children were not yet born, nor had done any good or evil (that the purpose of God, according to election, might stand,) Not of works, but of him that calleth, it was said to her: The elder shall serve the younger. As it is written: Jacob I have loved, but Esau I have hated" (vv. 11-13).

Once again we see God's election based on divine predilection. In referring to an example of divine election in Malachias 1:2, St. Paul says, "Jacob I have *loved*, but Esau I have hated." St. Paul could have just as easily said, "Jacob I have predestined, but Esau I have reprobated."[67] Hence, St. Paul in Romans 9:13 is expressly connecting God's election *with His love for the elect*. Just as God chose Isaac before Ishmael, He chose Jacob over Esau *because He loved him more*. God loved Jacob more because He gave Him more. Jacob would not have been better than Esau unless he had been given more and loved more by God.

On what basis did God love Jacob and hate Esau?[68] In no uncertain terms, St. Paul says that it was *not* because of their future merits or demerits. God made His decision before the twins "were not yet born, nor had done any good or evil (that the purpose of God, according to election, might stand)" (v. 11). St. Paul also excludes merits in the next verse when he says, "Not of works, but of him that calleth, it was said to her: *The elder shall serve the younger*" (v. 12). The phrase "not of works, but of him that calleth" literally means "not *out* of acts *but out* of the One calling."[69]

---

66. Scripture indicates that only a remnant of all Jews throughout history will convert to Jesus Christ. See, for example, 4 Kg. 19:31; 2 Para. 34:21; Isa. 10:20-22; 37:32; 46:3; Jer. 31:7; Rom. 9:27; 11:14; Apoc. 1:7. Because God saves the elect Jews and the Gentiles in the same manner (through Christ and the Catholic Church), the "all Israel" of Romans 11:26 that will be saved refers to the Church, "the Israel of God" (Gal. 6:16).

67. In Hebrews 12:16-17, St. Paul intimates that Esau was reprobated because he says, "Lest there be any fornicator, or profane person, as Esau; who for one mess, sold his first birthright. For know ye that afterwards, when he desired to inherit the benediction, he was rejected; for he found no place of repentance, although with tears he had sought it."

68. God's hatred for Esau can be explained in two ways. First, God eternally decreed to permit Esau to reject His grace through his own free will, knowing that he would do so. Second, God eternally decreed to punish Esau for his final impenitence. Although Scripture says that God "hatest none of the things which thou hast made" (Wis. 11:25), it also says that God "hatest all workers of iniquity" (Ps. 5:7).

69. The Greek transliteration is *"ou ek ergon alla ek ho kaleo."*

Turning to the original Greek, the double use of the preposition "out" (*ek*), which is separated by the conjunction "but" (*alla*) forcefully distinguishes between man's acts and God's call. St. Paul's usage reinforces the truth that God's decree to prefer Jacob over Esau is made independently of anything in them and proceeds "out" of the complete sovereignty of God. God loved Jacob before He created him and before he had any opportunity to respond to God's graces. It is not what Jacob did, but what God *gave* Jacob, that determined his election.

In an effort to deny God's sovereign election of individuals independently of future merits, some Protestants (generally Arminians and other non-Calvinists) argue that Romans 9 is not about the individual Jacob, but about the nation of Israel, which Jacob fathered.[70] They base this argument on St. Paul's reference to Genesis 25:23, where God reveals to Rebecca that she is having twins and says, "Two nations are in thy womb, and two peoples shall be divided out of thy womb, and one people shall overcome the other, and the elder shall serve the younger." According to the Protestant argument, since Jacob represents Israel and Esau represents Edom, the verse speaks only to the corporate election of God's chosen Israel, but not to individual people (such as Jacob himself).

Catholics (and Calvinists) strongly disagree with this interpretation. First, even if Jacob did represent Israel, God's basis for choosing Israel was because He loved Israel more (e.g., "Israel I loved, but Edom I hated"). Thus, the Protestant argument does not deny predilection. Secondly, St. Paul denies a corporate election of the nation of Israel when he grieves over their unbelief (Rom. 9:2-3) and says that only a remnant of Israel will be saved (Rom. 9:27; 11:5). In fact, the reprobation among the Israelites was so obvious that St. Paul had to declare the Word of God had not miscarried (Rom. 9:6). Thirdly, one cannot reconcile a corporate election of Israel with St. Paul's statement, "For all are not Israelites that are of Israel" but "the children of the promise, are accounted for the seed" (Rom. 9:6, 8). St. Paul is clear that God's election was *not* based on the Israelites' national identity but on the spiritual identity of His chosen ones.[71]

To deny any eternal decree of predilection, Arminians also argue that God is expressing His love for Jacob (Israel) and hate for Esau (Edom) not before, but

---

70. Protestant apologist Norman Geisler makes this argument in his book *Chosen But Free.* Catholics and most Calvinists rightfully reject this Arminian interpretation.

71. To deny individual election, some Protestants also say because "the elder" (Esau) did not actually serve "the younger" (Jacob), Romans 9 must be about nations and not individuals. Not only does such an argument completely overthrow St. Paul's argumentation, but Esau did serve Jacob by reversing the birth order in selling his birthright to him (Gen. 25:33).

after they were born. To support this argument, Protestant apologist Norman Geisler emphatically states, "The citation in Romans 9:13 is not from Genesis when they were alive (c. 2000 B.C.) but from Malachi 1:2-3 (c. 400 B.C.), long after they died!"[72] Because God is purportedly speaking about the post-natal twins, their respective nations and their role in salvation history, the Arminian argues that God in Romans 9:13 is condemning the Edomites *for their conduct*, and not in consequence of His eternal decree. This is a silly argument for a number of reasons.

First, the argument presupposes that God is referring to the nations of Israel and Edom, which we have demonstrated is not true. Secondly, although God surely hated the Edomites for their evil ways, God hardly had good things to say about Israel during their persecution by the Edomites. In fact, God allowed the Edomites to kill many of the Jews precisely because of the Jews' unfaithfulness. Thus, it doesn't follow that God would connect His love for Israel and His hatred for Edom in a single verse in Scripture, when both nations were guilty of faithlessness and idolatry at the same time. This is especially true given that Israel continued to reject God in the New Covenant, as St. Paul so clearly and regretfully expresses.

Thirdly, while the Prophecy of Malachias was written about 1,600 years after Jacob and Esau were born, this doesn't mean that Malachias 1:2-3 is about the *post-natal* Jacob and Esau! In fact, the Hebrew phrase "[b]ut have hated Esau" (*oshu shnathi*) in Malachias 1:3 includes a past-tense verb which means that God's hatred for Esau is not limited to the time the verse was penned (c. 400 B.C.) but can go back indefinitely, even prior to Esau's birth. Fourthly, although Romans 9:13 cites Malachias 1:2-3, which was written after the twins' death, the preceding verse cites Genesis 25:23, which refers to the time period *before* the twins' birth! God determined that Esau would serve Jacob before they were born, and that is because God loved Jacob more than Esau from all eternity.

Finally, St. Paul in Romans 9:11 refers to "the children . . . not yet born." These pre-born children (not adults or nations) are none other than Jacob and Esau. Because both verses 11 and 12 are about the pre-natal Jacob and Esau, St. Paul in verse 13 interprets Malachias 1:2-3 to *also* be about the pre-natal Jacob and Esau. St. Paul, in three consecutive verses, is revealing that God's plan of election is not determined by anything in man. Rather, God's predestination

---

72. Geisler, *Chosen But Free*, p. 85.

plan is conceived in the divine mind from all eternity, and executed in time according to God's good will and pleasure.

If God made this decision before Jacob and Esau were born, without any consideration of their future response to His grace, one might think that God was acting arbitrarily. Does this mean that God acts unjustly? St. Paul was certainly aware of this inquiry and the potential allegations of injustice in God. To preempt any such arguments, St. Paul says in the very next verse: "What shall we say then? Is there injustice with God? God forbid. For he saith to Moses: I will have mercy on whom I will have mercy; and I will show mercy to whom I will show mercy. So then it is not of him that willeth, nor of him that runneth, but of God that sheweth mercy" (vv. 14-16).[73]

Obviously, St. Paul's answer does not include a detailed list of criteria that God uses for determining divine predilection. Rather, St. Paul reveals that God's predilection is based purely *on His mercy*. After referring to the statement that God made to Moses in Exodus 33 ("I will have mercy on whom I please"), St. Paul eliminates any possibility that predilection is based on human effort (will or action) when he says that it is not "of him that willeth" and not "of him that runneth" (v. 16)[74] In other words, God does not base His decision on any foreseen merits or demerits, but sees all involved in sin, in the common "mass of perdition."[75] Therefore, whoever God delivers from condemnation, He delivers in His mercy, and whoever God leaves in condemnation, He leaves in His justice. Such was the interpretation of both St. Augustine and St. Thomas.

WHAT IS THE BASIS FOR PREDESTINATION/REPROBATION?

The question still remains: On what basis did God prefer Jacob over Esau? On what basis does God choose to save some in His mercy, and to leave others in their condemnation? St. Augustine believed that any attempt to answer this question would be fraught with so much potential error that it was best not to form a judgment: "Why He draws one, and another He draws not, seek not

---

73. The Greek verbs for "I will have mercy" (*eleao*) and "I will show mercy" (*oiktiro*) are singular future active verbs and literally mean "I will mercy" and "I will pity." These verbs emphasize that God *actively*, not passively, bestows His mercy, that is, independently of foreseen merits.

74. The Greek verbs for "willeth" (*thelo*) and "runneth" (*trecho*) are two singular present active participles that underscore that the personal and individual actions of man are not considered in God's eternal decrees (but rather flow from those decrees). They also demonstrate that the passage is about individual people, not "nations."

75. Council of Quiersy (853), Denz., 316.

to judge, if thou dost not wish to err."[76] St. Thomas says, "Yet why He chooses some for glory, and reprobates others, has no reason, except the divine will."[77] But St. Thomas also says that any effort to understand the divine will on this matter must focus on the goodness of God: "The reason for the predestination of some, and reprobation of others, must be sought for in the goodness of God."[78] As we will see in the next chapter, God desires to communicate His goodness in the greatest measure possible, and He accomplishes His desire by communicating both His mercy to the elect, and His justice to the reprobate, according to His will.

St. Paul reveals this truth about predilection and reprobation in the next two verses. Specifically, St. Paul refers to the hardening of Pharao's heart in Exodus 33. Pharao was the evil ruler of Egypt who persecuted the Israelites during the time of Moses. St. Paul says, "For the scripture saith to Pharao: To this purpose have I raised thee, that I may show my power in thee, and that my name may be declared throughout all the earth. Therefore he hath mercy on whom he will; and whom he will, he hardeneth" (vv. 17-18). Thus, St. Paul expands the discussion to include God's action in hardening the hearts of sinners. There is a clear parallel between God's sovereign will to have mercy and His sovereign will to harden hearts.

Because of this parallel, many Calvinists contend that God hardened Pharao's heart without regard to Pharao's free will. In fact, most Calvinists don't believe that God gave Pharao sufficient grace to be saved but created him for destruction in order to achieve God's plans.[79] In other words, if God doesn't consider future merits in granting mercy, the Calvinist argues that He doesn't consider future demerits in hardening hearts. Moreover, the Book of Exodus is clear that God did harden Pharao's heart, when He reveals: "See that thou do all the wonders before Pharao, which I have put in thy hand: I shall harden his heart, and he will not let the people go" (4:21); "But I shall harden his heart, and shall multiply my signs and wonders in the land of Egypt, [a]nd he will not hear you" (7:3-4); "And the Lord hardened Pharao's heart, and he hearkened not unto them, as the Lord had spoken to Moses" (9:12).[80]

Although it is true that God decrees to permit certain people to reject His

---

76. ST, Pt I, Q 23, Art 5, citing Augustine, *Homilies on the Gospel of John*, 26:2.
77. Ibid.
78. Ibid.
79. Protestant apologist James White says that Pharao "is but a servant, one chosen for destruction." *The Potter's Freedom*, p. 212.
80. See also Ex. 10:1, 20, 27; 14:4, 8.

grace without regard to future demerits, there are a number of problems with the Calvinist argument. First, Scripture says that Pharao also hardened his own heart, for example: "And Pharao seeing that rest was given, hardened his own heart, and did not hear them, as the Lord had commanded" (Ex. 8:15); "And Pharao seeing that the rain and the hail, and the thunders were ceased, increased his sin. And his heart was hardened, and the heart of his servants, and it was made exceeding hard" (9:34-35).[81]

Secondly, if the Calvinist attributes the hardening exclusively to God (without regard to Pharao's free will), he denies the verses that reveal that Pharao also played a part in the hardening. Clearly, these verses need to be reconciled. Thirdly, attributing the hardening to God alone makes God responsible for Pharao's sin, even though "to God the wicked and his wickedness are hateful alike" (Wis. 14:9). God doesn't cause the things He hates but rather permits hateful deeds for a greater good. This truth is lost in the Calvinist position.

So how do we reconcile God's hardening of Pharao with Pharao's hardening of himself? If God doesn't consider future demerits when He decrees to permit sin, then what role do sinners play in their spiritual blindness? Further, if God is not determined by man's sin, then how can God's hardening not be the cause of his sin? The Thomist answer: God's eternal decree includes both the permission to sin *and* the punishment of sin without regard to future demerits, but God is not the cause of sin, as Scripture teaches. This means that the permission and the punishment come from God, but the defect (the sin) comes from man. In other words, God in His eternal decree permitted Pharao to reject His graces (Pharao hardened his heart), and God predestined Pharao's punishment for rejecting these graces (God hardened Pharao's heart).

Because hardheartedness is a punishment from God (which St. Thomas teaches),[82] it is predestined by God without regard to future demerits, just like the punishment of the reprobate in hell is predestined without regard to future demerits. These principles are set forth in the teachings of the Catholic Church. For example, the Council of Quiersy (a local council held in 853) teaches that, of those God left in the mass of perdition, "He did not predestine that they would perish because He is just; however, He predestined eternal punishment for them."[83] The Council of Valence (855) also says that "God, who

---

81. See also Ex. 7:13-14, 22; 8:19, 32; 9:7, 35; 13:15.
82. See ST, Pt I-II, Q 79, Art 3.
83. Denz., 316. The council condemned the views of a Saxon monk named Gottshalk (d.868) who believed that God predestined the reprobate to hell irrespective of their free will acts (a view

sees all things, foreknew and predestined that their evil deserved the punishment which followed, because He is just."[84] This punishment is the withholding of grace, which leads to both spiritual blindness in this life and eternal damnation in the next life.

Thus, the teachings of these councils, as further expounded by St. Thomas, hold in balance two fundamental truths regarding reprobation: (1) God is not the cause of man's sin, and (2) God is not determined by man's sin (He is unmoved). This position maintains that God is completely in control of the salvation/reprobation process while also maintaining that man sins through the use of his free will. Mercy and justice come from God, whereas sin comes from man. We will look at the mystery of reprobation in greater detail later in the book.

Because God permits sin but is not the cause of sin, St. Paul is clear that no sinner can accuse God of "forcing" him to sin. St. Paul poses the hypothetical objection: "Thou wilt say therefore to me: Why doth he then find fault? for who resisteth his will?" (Rom. 9:19). In other words, the sinner may be inclined to retort: "Why does God blame me for my sin? Who resists His will?" St. Paul provides the following stern reply to those who would make such an accusation:

O man, who art thou that repliest against God? Shall the thing formed say to him that formed it: Why hast thou made me thus? Or hath not the potter power over the clay, of the same lump, to make one vessel unto honor, and another unto dishonor? What if God, willing to show his wrath, and to make his power known, endured with much patience vessels of wrath, fitted for destruction, [t]hat he might show the riches of his glory on the vessels of mercy, which he hath prepared unto glory? (vv. 20-23).

With this reply, St. Paul forcefully rejects the suggestion that God is to blame for one's sin. In fact, the purpose of St. Paul's raising this hypothetical objection was to assert this very truth. No man has any business making such a reply against God. He is not only blameless when it comes to man's sin but He does not even tempt man to sin. St. James says, "Let no man, when he is tempted, say that he is tempted by God. For God is not a tempter of evils, and

of "double predestination").
84. Denz., 322.

he tempteth no man. But every man is tempted by his own concupiscence, being drawn away and allured. Then when concupiscence hath conceived, it bringeth forth sin. But sin, when it is completed, begetteth death" (1:13-15).

St. Paul uses the metaphor of the potter and the clay to underscore God's sovereignty in choosing who are the objects of His mercy (predilection), and who are the objects of His justice (reprobation). St. Paul uses the same metaphors of "vessels" of "honor" and "dishonor" elsewhere in Scripture, for example: "But we have this treasure in earthen vessels, that the excellency may be of the power of God, and not of us" (2 Cor. 4:7); "But in a great house there are not only vessels of gold and of silver, but also of wood and of earth: and some indeed unto honor, but some unto dishonor" (2 Tim. 2:20).

God applied the same metaphor to the Israelites through the prophet Jeremias: "Cannot I do with you, as this potter, O house of Israel, saith the Lord? Behold as clay is in the hand of the potter, so are you in my hand, O house of Israel" (18:6). God also said through Isaias: "And now, O Lord, thou art our father, and we are clay: and thou art our maker, and we all are the works of thy hands" (Isa. 64:8).[85] We also read in Ecclesiasticus, "As the potter's clay is in his hand, to fashion and order it: All his ways are according to his ordering: so man is in the hand of him that made him, and he will render to him according to his judgment" (33:13-14).

Of course, the potter determines the clay; the clay does not determine the potter or force the potter's hand. Moreover, the criteria that the potter uses to determine the clay are known to the potter alone. There is nothing inherent in the "same lump" of clay that determines how the potter will use it. Thus, the metaphor teaches us that God simply chooses, according to His secret purposes, those on whom He desires to have mercy ("vessels of mercy"), and those whom He will permit to reject Him ("vessels of wrath"). Scripture never says that God bases this decision on any foreseen merits or demerits, which, as we have said, would imply potentiality in God, and which would not exist in the absence of His divine decree.

Calvin interpreted Romans 9:22-23 as evidence that God determines whom He will condemn before man ever commits sin. Whereas Catholics believe that God merely *permitted* the vessels to become fitted for destruction by their sins, most Calvinists argue that God actually *made* the vessels for destruction. Calvin even labeled God's purported decision the "dreadful decree" (*decretum*

---

85. See also Isaias 29:16.

horribile). However, if Calvin's position were true, then all things would happen of necessity, and free will would be sham. Moreover, the Greek verb St. Paul uses to describe the vessels "fitted for destruction" is in the passive voice, whereas the verb that describes the vessels "prepared unto glory" is in the active voice.[86] This usage further underscores God's causality in determining the final end of the elect, and His mere permission in allowing the fate of the reprobate. As the Catechism teaches, "God predestines no one to go to hell" (CCC 1037).

Because mercy is a free gift from God, He can bestow it in the proportion He deems fit, without offending justice. As St. Paul states, "Is there injustice with God? God forbid" (v. 14). St. Thomas teaches, "Neither on this account can there be said to be injustice in God, if He prepares unequal lots for not unequal things ... In things which are given gratuitously a person can give more or less, just as he pleases (provided he deprives nobody of his due), without any infringement of justice."[87] God bestows mercy on His elect out of pure gratuity, according to His good will. As Jesus said in the parable of the master of the house: "Take what is thine, and go thy way ... Or, is it not lawful for me to do what I will?" (Matt. 20:14-15).

As we noted in the very beginning, God bestows mercy on sinners in proportion to how much He loves them and wills their good, which is called predilection. God loves all men, but loves some more than others, because He creates more goodness in one sinner than in another. One sinner would not be better than another unless he were loved more and given more by God. St. Thomas says, "In the justification of the ungodly justice is seen, when God remits sins on account of love, though He Himself has mercifully infused that love. So we read of Mary Magdalen: *Many sins are forgiven her, because she hath loved much* (Luke 7:47)."[88]

---

86. The Greek phrase "fitted for destruction" (*katartizo eis apoleia*) uses a perfect passive participle that can be translated has "having been made." Catholic apologist Robert Sungenis also notes that the verb could be in the middle voice, which would be translated as "having made themselves for destruction" (*Not By Faith Alone*, p. 461). This is in stark contrast to the aorist, active voice of "prepared unto glory" (*proetoimazo eis doxa*), which emphasizes the divine causality of the preparation, before future merits.

87. ST, PT I, Q 23, Art 5.

88. Ibid., Pt I, Q 21, Art 4.

FR. MOST AND ROMANS 8-9: A "TRADITIONAL" OR "NOVEL" INTERPRETATION?

In his influential book *Grace, Predestination, and the Salvific Will of God* (*GPS*), Catholic theologian Fr. William Most rejects the traditional interpretation of Romans 8 and 9. In fact, Fr. Most denies that Romans 8-9 is about individual election at all. Moreover, Fr. Most says that Sts. Augustine and Thomas had "erroneous interpretations" of these passages. As we have seen, because all men are condemned (part of the *massa damnata*), Sts. Augustine and Thomas held that God rescues some in His mercy, and permits others to be damned in His justice, according to His will and before foreseen merits and demerits (see Rom. 9:16, 18). For example, St. Thomas says, "Since all men because of the sin of the first parents are born exposed to damnation, those whom God frees through His grace, He frees out of mercy alone. And so He is merciful to certain ones whom He delivers, but to certain ones He is just, whom He does not deliver."[89]

Fr. Most claims "that the interpretation of Romans 8-9 which St. Thomas inherited from St. Augustine is erroneous,"[90] and he emphatically states, "All exegetes today reject this interpretation."[91] It is important to address Fr. Most's claims for a number of reasons. First, Fr. Most is a worthy scholar whose opinions have influenced the views about predestination of a significant number of Catholics, and we are not aware of any meaningful scholarship that has challenged his unique positions. Secondly, Fr. Most's rejection of the traditional interpretation of Romans 8-9 is the basis for many of his novel interpretations of St. Thomas and his theories on grace (more on this later). Thirdly, interacting with Fr. Most's argumentation helps us see more clearly the principles that St. Thomas has left us. These principles help us build our spiritual lives upon a necessary, dogmatic foundation and give the greatest glory to God.

We first note that Fr. Most in *GPS* does not provide any meaningful exegesis of Romans 8 or 9. He engages in no contextual, grammatical, or lexical analysis of the applicable texts. This is uncharacteristic of Fr. Most's otherwise thorough scholarship. One would expect more from a renowned scholar, particularly when he is criticizing a position shared by the two greatest minds of the Church. Yet Fr. Most repeatedly claims that St. Augustine, St. Thomas, and other theologians who followed them "were severely hampered by a formerly

---

89. *Commentary on Romans 9* (Lesson 3, comments on v. 15; lesson 2, comments on v. 13).
90. GPS, p. 307.
91. GPS, p. 24.

current misinterpretation" of the passages.[92] Fr. Most says, "Today we know that these interpretations of Scripture were all erroneous for they are rejected with unanimity by all good exegetes of all schools."[93] Fr. Most continues by saying, "[E]xegetes of all schools teach a different interpretation of the passage from the Epistle to the Romans."[94] And again, he says, "[T]his interpretation . . . is now rightly abandoned, as false and lacking in foundation, by all good exegetes of all schools."[95] Fr. Most makes these kinds of sweeping statements throughout his nearly 700-page book.

After summarily dismissing the views of St. Augustine and St. Thomas, Fr. Most appeals to the "modern scholarship" of Père Lagrange, J. Huby, and A.M. Dubarle. Based on this modern scholarship, Fr. Most says, "As a result, we are able to know clearly that which was hidden in the days of St. Thomas, namely: St. Paul, in Romans 8-9, was not speaking about the infallible predestination of individuals to eternal glory, but about the plans of God for the call of peoples to be members of the Church, in the Old or New Testament, in the full sense, and about the divine plans for those who already are members of the Church in the full sense."[96]

Notwithstanding Fr. Most's assertions, the Council of Valence authentically teaches that Romans 9 *is about individual predestination and election*! After citing both Romans 9:21 (about the potter's power over the clay) and Romans 9:22 (about the vessels of mercy and wrath), the council offers its interpretation of those verses: "[F]aithfully we confess the predestination of the elect to life, and the predestination of the impious to death; in the election, moreover, of those who are to be saved, the mercy of God precedes merited good. In the condemnation, however, of those who are to be lost, the evil which they have deserved precedes the just judgment of God."[97] In short, Fr. Most's interpretation of Romans 8-9 is expressly rejected by the Council of Valence as well as the constant teaching tradition of the Church espoused by Sts. Augustine and Thomas.

---

92. GPS, p. 3. In this statement, Fr. Most specifically refers to Romans 8:28-9:24 and 1 Corinthians 4:7.
93. Ibid.
94. GPS, p. 4.
95. GPS, p. 55. Notice that Fr. Most uses the all-inclusive adjective "all" when he says "all exegetes," "all erroneous" and "all schools." With due respect to Fr. Most, authors have a tendency to use such all-encompassing adjectives when their case is weak. Not only do "all" exegetes not reject the traditional interpretation of Romans 8-9, but most theologians before Vatican II adhered in some way to the traditional interpretation (whether Thomist or Molinist).
96. GPS, p. 4.
97. Denz., 322.

Continuing with his novel theory about Romans 9, Fr. Most sees a distinction between what he calls the "internal economy" that regards individual salvation (whether a man will go to heaven or hell) and the "external economy" that regards the external order (whether a man or a nation will belong to the Church). Fr. Most applies this concocted paradigm to any verse he thinks speaks of individual predestination (e.g., Rom. 8-9; 1 Cor. 4:7; Acts 13:48). Fr. Most argues that Romans 9 is about the external economy, not the internal economy. Specifically, Fr. Most advances the Arminian argument that St. Paul is speaking about the predestination of "nations" and not individuals.[98]

We have already demonstrated that Fr. Most's interpretation is at odds with the Council of Valence. We have also refuted the "nations" argument with an exegesis of the text, and so will not repeat that analysis here. We remind the reader that St. Paul's teaching in Romans 9 flows directly from his explicit teachings about *individual* predestination in Romans 8:28-30, which St. Thomas also emphasizes.[99] We also remind the reader that St. Paul was specifically *rejecting* the idea that God predestines nations and not individual persons. The Jews were using their place in the "external economy" (as the nation of Israel) to claim that they were the beneficiaries of God's election (Rom. 9:4-5), and St. Paul said they were wrong. To emphasize that God predestines individuals and not nations, St. Paul says, "For all are not Israelites that are of Israel," but are "the children of the promise" (Rom. 9:6, 8). To further emphasize individual predestination, St. Paul brings it down to the level of *individual persons*: Jacob and Esau (vv. 11-13). St. Paul's references to individual man's "works" and "will" (see Rom. 9:12, 16) vis-à-vis God's gratuitous election also underscore that St. Paul is talking about individuals and not nations.

When Fr. Most reveals his two categories, he also includes the Church in the category of the "external economy." However, St. Paul never mentions the "Church" in Romans 8 or 9. Rather, he is focused on the nation of Israel and the Jews' erroneous understanding of how God determines His election. Moreover, we fail to understand Fr. Most's distinction between individual election (internal economy) and membership in the Church (external economy). God

---

98. GPS, p. 28.

99. In the *Summa*, St. Thomas quotes from both Romans 8:29-30 (Q 23, Art 1-2, 5-7) and Romans 9:11-13, 22-23 (Q 23, Art 3 and 5) in his articles on individual predestination, showing the continuity between the chapters. In these articles, St. Thomas also quotes from 2 Mac. 6:20; Mal. 1:2-3; Osee 13:9; Lam. 5:21; Job 34:24; Eph. 1:4; Titus 3:5; 2 Cor. 3:5; 2 Tim. 2:20; and Matt. 20:14-15 to prove individual predestination. Fr. Most does not say whether he believes St. Thomas also interpreted these verses incorrectly.

predestines people (internal economy) to eternal salvation precisely by bringing them into the Catholic Church (external economy). In light of this truth, we must also disagree with Fr. Most's assertion that "God has freely decided upon different fundamental principles for the two economies. These principles are quite incompatible with one another."[100]

This assertion is problematic because individual salvation is one effect of predestination, and membership in the Church is another effect of predestination. In fact, one effect (Church membership) may be called the cause of the other effect (salvation). As St. Thomas remarks, "[T]here is no reason why one effect of predestination should not be the reason or cause of another."[101] Even if there were two economies as Fr. Most maintains, this does not mean that God would govern them by different principles, since both economies flow from God's single decree of predestination. This is why St. Thomas says that all the effects of predestination proceed "from its first moving principle," which is God.[102] If God really governed the "external economy" differently than the "internal economy," one could argue that God wills to save some people (internal economy) but doesn't will them to be Catholic (external economy). Nevertheless, we do not assume that Fr. Most's distinction was motivated by any dissent from the Church's infallible dogma: *Extra ecclesia nulla salus est* (outside the Church there is no salvation).[103]

Fr. Most contends that modern scholarship refutes the *massa damnata* interpretation of Romans 9. He even implies that the Church has overturned this long-standing interpretation. After claiming that "the obstacles that arose from the erroneous interpretations of the Epistle to the Romans (and a few other passages in St. Paul) have been removed," he says that "the Church, benefiting from the cumulative light which the Holy Spirit has now sent through so many centuries, teaches many truths more clearly, especially the salvific will of God."[104] Fr. Most gives his readers the impression that the teachings of the

---

100. GPS, p. 30, cf. pp. 35-36.

101. ST, Pt I, Q 23, Art 5.

102. Ibid.

103. The Church teaches that Christ saves man through the Catholic Church, which is His Mystical Body. If one is invincibly ignorant of his obligation to be a member of the Catholic Church, he may still have the possibility of salvation if he obeys the natural and moral law. In this way, such a man would be inside the Catholic Church through the charity of Christ. Those who are culpable of their rejection of the Church have no hope of salvation. Only God—not the Church—is the judge of these matters. For more on this topic, see my books *The Biblical Basis for the Papacy* (pp. 203-211) and *Why Catholics Cannot Be Masons* (pp. 9-10; 62-63).

104. GPS, p. 5.

modern Church are at odds with the Augustinian and Thomistic interpretation. However, not only has the Church never criticized the traditional interpretation but she essentially adopted it at the Council of Quiersy in 853![105] In addition, the Church has not issued any other interpretation of Romans 8-9 in the context of grace and predestination since Quiersy and Valence, Fr. Most's opinions notwithstanding.

The council of Quiersy explicitly teaches St. Augustine's view of the *massa damnata* ("mass of perdition"), even referring to the Doctor of Grace's works. The council proclaimed:

> Omnipotent God created man noble without sin with a free will, and he whom He wished to remain in the sanctity of justice, He placed in Paradise. Man using his free will badly sinned and fell, and became the "mass of perdition" of the entire human race. The just and good God, however, chose from this same mass of perdition according to His foreknowledge those whom through grace He predestined to life [Rom. 8:29ff; Eph. 1:11], and He predestined for these eternal life; the others, whom by the judgment of justice he left in the mass of perdition, however, He knew would perish, but He did not predestine that they would perish, because He is just.[106]

Fr. Most appears to reject the traditional interpretation of Romans 9 because he incorrectly believes it promotes positive reprobation (God wills some to be damned) and not negative reprobation (God wills to permit some to damn themselves). For example, Fr. Most says, "Now if God were to reject a man from eternal salvation as He rejected Esau, that is, before considering anything that the man would or would not do . . . the rejected man could not 'distinguish himself' in regard to being reprobated or not: then he could not simultaneously say sincerely that He willed all men—including those reprobated—to be saved."[107] However, as we will further examine, God does not "reject a man"

---

105. We acknowledge that Quiersy was a regional council only (not an ecumenical council). Nevertheless, the teachings of Quiersy have never been reformed by the Church, and can be easily harmonized with the teachings of the regional Council of Orange (confirmed by Pope Boniface II) as well as Sts. Augustine and Thomas.

106. Denz., 316. Although Quiersy was not a dogmatic council, its condemnation of double predestination (God predestines some to heaven and others to hell) is considered part of the Church's ordinary and universal Magisterium. Thus, the council's teachings on the *massa damnata* carry significant dogmatic weight. We believe it is unfortunate that Fr. Most holds "modern scholarship" above the authentic teachings of the Magisterium.

107. GPS, p. 31.

and will his damnation; He only permits man to choose it. St. Thomas defines reprobation as "the will to permit a person to fall into sin, and to impose the punishment of damnation on account of that sin."[108] Moreover, whereas Fr. Most thinks one man should be able to "distinguish himself" from another by his positive response to grace, St. Paul tells man that nothing "distinguisheth thee" except the will and intention of God (1 Cor. 4:7).

Although it is true that God determines whom He will reprobate before they do any good or evil (see Rom. 9:11),[109] we know that God gives all men sufficient grace to be saved. By using his free will to reject this grace and commit sin, man is responsible for his own damnation. St. Thomas further says, "Reprobation by God does not take anything away from the power of the person reprobated . . . he that falls into this or that particular sin comes from the use of his free-will."[110] Fr. Most's rejection of the traditional interpretation of Romans 9 results in his erroneous understanding of sufficient grace. As we will see later in the book, Fr. Most holds that sufficient grace (in the Thomistic understanding) is actually insufficient for salvation, contrary to what St. Thomas and his adherents teach.

Fr. Most's misunderstanding of Romans 9 also results in his rejection of the principle of divine predilection and causality (God's will is the cause of all good). Fr. Most not only twists the meaning of Romans 9 to deny predilection ("Jacob I have *loved*") but also does the same with 1 Corinthians 4:7: "Or what has thou that thou hast not received? And if thou hast received, why dost thou glory, as if thou hadst not received it?" Fr. Most says that "in these words St. Paul is simply not speaking of the graces of the internal economy. He was merely rejecting the pride of the Corinthians who thought they had been called into the Church because of their special good qualities."[111] Fr. Most's interpretation is not only a-Thomistic but also contrary to the official interpretation of the Council of Orange (529), which issued canons on the Church's doctrines of grace and predestination.

In canon 6, the Council of Orange clearly equated St. Paul's teaching in 1 Corinthians 4:7 with the spiritual graces of the "internal economy:"

---

108. ST, Pt I, Q 23, Art 3.
109. In reading Fr. Garrigou-Lagrange's interpretations of ST, Pt I, Q 23 Art 4-6, Fr. Most says, "He wants to prove by these passages that St. Thomas teaches predestination before consideration of merits. We grant that it is *at least probable* that St. Thomas does teach this" (GPS, p. 190, emphasis added). "At least probable"! It seems that certainty on this question is eliminated for Fr. Most when the proper interpretation of Romans 9 is eliminated.
110. Ibid.
111. *GPS*, p. 201, cf. p. 34.

If anyone asserts that without the grace of God mercy is divinely given to us when we believe, will, desire, try, labor, pray, watch, study, seek, ask, urge, but does not confess that through the infusion and the inspiration of the Holy Spirit in us, it is brought about that we believe, wish or are able to do all these things as we ought, and does not join either to human humility or obedience the help of grace, nor agree that it is the gift of grace that we are obedient and humble, [he] opposes the Apostle who says: 'What have you, that you have not received?' [1 Cor. 4:7]; and: 'By the grace of God I am that, which I am' [1 Cor. 15:10; cf. St. Augustine and St. Prosper of Aquitaine].

Although Fr. Most ignores the Council of Orange's interpretation of 1 Corinthians 4:7, he admits that "because of the special confirmation given it by Pope Boniface II, the canons of this council have the force of a solemn definition."[112]

Ephesians 1 — "He Chose Us in Him before the Foundation of the World"

We conclude this discussion by taking a brief look at the beginning of St. Paul's letter to the Ephesians:

Blessed be the God and Father of our Lord Jesus Christ, who hath blessed us with spiritual blessings in heavenly places, in Christ. As He chose us in Him before the foundation of the world, that we should be holy and unspotted in His sight in charity. Who hath predestinated us unto the adoption of children through Jesus Christ unto Himself, according the purpose of His will, unto the praise of the glory of His grace ... That he might make known unto us the mystery of his will, according to his good pleasure, which he hath purposed in him ... In whom we are also called by lot, being predestinated according to the purpose of Him who worketh all things according to the counsel of His will that we may be unto the praise of His glory (Eph. 1:3-6, 9, 11).

---

112. GPS, p. 39. Although Fr. Most may have dismissed the Council of Valence's interpretation of Romans 9 because it was a particular council (we don't know, because he never addresses its interpretation), he acknowledges the dogmatic authority of the Council of Orange.

In this classic passage, St. Paul reveals many truths about God's plan of predestination that we have seen in other scriptures. St. Paul first blesses God, because God has blessed us with spiritual blessings in heavenly places. This blessing in "heavenly places" refers to nothing less than eternal salvation. The verb that St. Paul uses in the phrase "hath blessed us" in verse 3 (Greek, *eulogeo*) is in the aorist tense. The aorist tense describes an action in the past that has ceased; it does not describe the effects that the action may have on the future. This usage reveals that God has *already* decreed who will be predestined to eternal life, and it underscores that God's plan of predestination is a certainty.

In verse 4, St. Paul continues the thought by revealing that God "chose us" in Christ. Again, St. Paul uses the aorist tense for the verb "to choose" (Greek, *eklego*), emphasizing that God has already decreed the number of His elect in eternity. Scripture elsewhere uses the verb "chose" in connection with God's elect. For example, in John's gospel, Jesus uses the same tense verb (*eklego*) three times when He identifies His elect by saying, "I speak not of you all: I know whom I have chosen" (13:18); "You have not chosen me: but I have chosen you; and have appointed you" (15:16); "If you had been of the world, the world would love its own: but because you are not of the world, but I have chosen you out of the world, therefore the world hateth you" (15:19).[113] In Matthew's gospel, Jesus says, "For many are called, but few are chosen (*eklektos*)."[114] In Mark's gospel, Jesus also refers to "the elect which he hath chosen" (13:20).

St. Paul reveals that God chooses His elect "before the foundation of the world" (Greek, *pro katabole kosmos*). This phrase confirms the usage of the aorist tense for "chose." God chose His elect in eternity and predestines them to heaven in time. God chooses before He brings us into being, before "we were not yet born, nor had done any good or evil" (Rom. 9:11). The Greek phrase "foundation of the world" is often used in the New Testament in connection with God's bestowing favors upon His chosen ones before their existence. For example, Jesus says, "Come, ye blessed of my Father, possess you the kingdom prepared for you from the foundation of the world" (Matt. 25:34). Note also that both Jesus and St. Paul call the elect "blessed" (*eulogeo*) for the great grace God has given them.

---

113. The verb *eklego* in John 13:8; 15:16, 19 and Mark 13:20 is identical to the verb in Ephesians 1:4 (aorist tense, middle voice, singular).

114. Matt. 22:14; see also Matt. 20:16. Further, see 1 Cor. 1:27-28, where St. Paul repeatedly affirms that God has chosen (*eklego*) that which is foolish, weak, and contemptible (the "little ones") to shame the wise and strong.

In His high priestly prayer to the Father, Jesus prays that His chosen ones "may see my glory which thou hast given me, because thou hast loved me before the creation of the world."[115] Here, Jesus reveals God's predilect love for Him before time began, and it was because of this love that God glorified Jesus in His human nature (as we have learned, love precedes election and predestination). St. Peter also says that Christ was "[f]oreknown indeed before the foundation of the world" (1 Pet. 1:20). Like Jesus, St. Peter is referring to the love that God had for Christ before the Incarnation. Because God loved Christ independently of His future merits, He predestines us in Christ before our future merits as well.

St. Paul continues the theme of predilection by stating "that we should be holy and unspotted in his sight in charity" (v. 4). God didn't choose us because of our holiness (future merits) but chose us so that we might *become* holy by His election and love. Because God chose us "*in charity*," His election is gratuitous and inspired by the love He has given us, and it is not because of anything in us or from us. In Romans 9:13, we saw how God predestined Jacob because He loved (*agapao*) him. Now, in Ephesians 1:4, we see how God chooses His entire elect people in love (*agape*). God's plan of predestination is inspired completely by His love for us, and not because of anything we do.

In verse 5, St. Paul says that God "hath predestinated us unto the adoption of children through Jesus Christ unto himself: according to the purpose of his will." By using "predestination" in the past tense,[116] St. Paul reveals once again that God has already established His plan of predestination. Moreover, God has established it according to His will and not according to anything we have done. St. Paul emphasizes this again in verses 9 and 11 when he refers to "the mystery of his will according to his good pleasure" (v. 9) and to how we are "called by lot ... according to the counsel of His will" (v. 11).

St. Paul is clearly emphasizing God's sovereignty in His plan of election. God chooses His elect according to His secret purposes, which St. Paul rightly calls a "mystery." St. Paul even says that God takes "pleasure" (*eudokia*) in His plan, and that is because God has a special love for His elect. Jesus uses this same word when He describes the Father's predilect love for His "little ones" and says, "Yea, Father; for so hath it seemed good (*eudokia*) in thy sight" (Matt. 11:26). In Luke's gospel, Jesus also says, "Fear not, little flock, for it hath pleased

---

115. John 17:24; Jesus uses the exact same phrase "before the foundation of the world" (*pro katabole kosmos*) that St. Paul uses in Eph. 1:4 and St. Peter uses in 1 Pet 1:20.

116. *Proorizo* is an active verb in the aorist tense.

(*eudokeo*) your Father to give you a kingdom" (12:32). The "little ones" and the "little flock" are those whom God was pleased to choose in love for eternal life.

In verse 11, St. Paul also says that those who are predestinated are "called by lot." This phrase reminds us of St. Thomas's statement that God "prepares unequal lots for not unequal things." Elsewhere, St. Paul uses "call" in connection with God's choice of election. For example, in his letter to the Galatians, St. Paul says, "But when it pleased him, who separated me from my mother's womb, and called me by his grace" (Gal. 1:15). To Timothy, St. Paul says, "Who hath delivered us and called us by his holy calling, not according to our works, but according to his own purpose and grace, which was given us in Christ Jesus before the times of the world" (2 Tim. 1:9). In both verses, St. Paul affirms that God calls us by His grace before we were born, and even before He created the world.

St. Peter refers to the call of the elect when he says, "As all things of his divine power which appertain to life and godliness, are given us, through the knowledge of him who hath called us by his own proper glory and virtue" (2 Pet. 1:3). St. John also says, "Behold what manner of charity the Father hath bestowed upon us, that we should be called, and should be the sons of God" (1 John 3:1).[117] Like St. Paul, St. John reveals that God calls us in "charity" (predilection). St. Jude also says, "Jude, the servant of Jesus Christ, and brother of James: to them that are beloved in God the Father, and preserved in Jesus Christ, and called" (Jude 1). Like St. Paul, the apostles Peter, John, and Jude were also inspired to reveal God's special call of the elect in the grace of Jesus Christ.

A Brief Summary of Our Introduction to Predestination

In this chapter, we have learned about the incredible and profound truth of divine predilection as taught by Scripture, the Church, and St. Thomas: God's love is the cause of goodness in things, and one thing would not be better than another unless it were loved more by God. Because God created us in love, He loves all men and desires all to be saved. Yet because God loves "the better

---

117. The verb for "called" (Greek, *kaleo*) in Gal. 1:15; 2 Tim. 1:9; 2 Pet. 1:3; 1 John 3:1 is in the aorist tense, which demonstrates that God's calling of the elect occurred in the past.

things," He chooses to infallibly save His elect because He has made them "better" and thus loves them more. Moreover, God chooses His elect according to His secret counsel and not because He foresees that the elect will cooperate with His grace.

Because grace is a gratuitous gift of God, He gives it according to His good will and pleasure, and not because He owes us anything. Further, because God gives all men sufficient grace to be saved, He doesn't offend justice by giving more grace to some than to others. Those who are predestined to salvation have nothing to boast about because their salvation is a work of grace. Those who reject God's grace have nothing to complain about because their reprobation is their own fault. Those who are saved are saved by God's mercy, and those who perish are allowed to perish by God's justice.

We continue to explore the great mystery of God's universal will to save sinners, and His plan of divine election, in the next chapter.

2

God's Will to Save Sinners

oth Old and New Testament scriptures reveal that God wills to save all men. In the Old Testament, God reveals through Eze-chiel, "Is it my will that a sinner should die, saith the Lord God, and not that he should be converted from his ways, and live? ... For I desire not the death of him that dieth, saith the Lord God, return ye and live" (18:23, 32). God also says, "Say to them: As I live, saith the Lord God, I desire not the death of the wicked, but that the wicked turn from his way, and live. Turn ye, turn ye from your evil ways: and why will you die, O house of Israel?" (33:11). The Book of Wisdom also says, "For God made not death, neither hath he pleasure in the destruction of the living" (13:1).

In the New Testament, Jesus says that "it is not the will of your Father, who is in heaven, that one of these little ones should perish" (Matt. 18:14). St. Paul also says, "For this is good and acceptable in the sight of God our Savior, Who will have all men to be saved, and to come to the knowledge of the truth" (1 Tim. 2:3-4). St. Peter further says, "The Lord delayeth not his promise, as some imagine, but dealeth patiently for your sake, not willing that any should perish, but that all should return to penance" (2 Pet. 3:9).

Although Scripture asserts very strongly that God wills all men to be saved, Scripture also says that no one can resist God's will. As we have seen in Ro-mans 9, St. Paul says, "Thou wilt say therefore to me: Why doth he then find fault? For who resisteth his will?" (v. 19). In the Book of Esther, Mardochai prays, "O Lord, Lord, almighty king, for all things are in thy power, and there is none that can resist thy will, if thou determine to save Israel" (Esth. 13:9). He further says, "Thou art Lord of all, and there is none that can resist thy majesty (Esth. 13:11). The Book of Proverbs also says, "As the divisions of waters, so the heart of the king is in the hand of the Lord: whithersoever he will he shall turn it" (21:1).

These scriptures present us with an obvious dilemma: If God wills all men to be saved, and no one resists God's will, then why isn't everyone saved? Why do some people go to hell? Isn't this a contradiction? Does God fail in His effort to save? Protestants have very different ways of addressing this issue. Calvinists try to resolve this dilemma by saying that God's will to save "all men" really means all *kinds* of men, but not every single person who ever lived. Because Christ's atonement is perfectly efficacious but not all people are saved, Calvinists also believe that Christ died only for the elect, but not for all people. With this position, the Calvinist wishes to show that God has the final decision regarding salvation and damnation, and is not determined by man's decisions. This position preserves God's complete sovereignty over man in His plan of unconditional election.

Arminians, on the other hand, say that God's will to save "all men" really means all men, not just the elect—thereby upholding the plain meaning of Scripture and God's universal will to save all. Since all men are not saved, however, Arminians conclude that God leaves the ultimate decision to man, based upon man's free-will response to grace. This position preserves the Arminian view of conditional election based on God's evaluation of foreseen future merits. Calvinists argue that the Arminian position denies God's sovereignty by making God determined by man, and His salvation plan a failure (because Christ will have died for those who go to hell). Arminians argue that Calvinism denies man's free will and makes God a tyrannical despot because He reprobates man without giving him a chance to respond to His grace. We will look at both of these positions in greater detail later, in chapters 4 and 5.

What does the Catholic Church say? In her typically balanced fashion, the Catholic Church holds that God's universal will to save all men *and* His divine election to save some men are *both true*. That is, Christ's atoning death was sufficient for all, but only efficacious for some, according to the eternal will of God. This means that God's will is achieved (not frustrated or resisted) through His eternal decree and the free-will acts of man. This position holds in perfect balance God's complete sovereignty over His plan of salvation and man's free-will actions within the divine plan. God's sovereignty and irresistible will *include* man's free-will actions, because God's providence governs all things as He orders all things to their final end.

St. Thomas Aquinas provides us with the best methodology for reconciling the seemingly irreconcilable truths of God's sovereignty and human free will. Based on Scripture and the teachings of the Church, St. Thomas explains that

God has an *antecedent* will and a *consequent* will.[1] In his antecedent will, God wills to save all men (consistent with Scripture). In his consequent will, God wills to save only the elect and to permit the non-elect to be damned (also consistent with Scripture).[2] God provides for both outcomes for the greater good of His entire creation according to His "wills." As Scripture says, "Great are the works of the Lord: sought out according to all his wills" (Ps. 110:2). Let us explore this profound distinction in greater detail. In doing so, it is necessary to quote from St. Thomas at some length.

THE ANTECEDENT AND CONSEQUENT WILLS

St. Thomas teaches that God's antecedent will concerns what He wills for a thing in isolation, before any other considerations. Thus, when God considers each individual absolutely, without regard to the totality of His predestination plan, He antecedently wills the person's salvation. In His antecedent will, God considers only the individual parts of His plan (a single person) and not the entire plan (all people). This understanding can be applied to St. Paul's statement that God wills "all men to be saved, and to come to the knowledge of the truth" (1 Tim. 2:4).

However, unlike truth, which is the object of the intellect, goodness is the object of the will. For human beings, the intellect moves the will to the good only after it considers all of the accompanying circumstances. Good is not formally in the mind but in things as they actually exist.[3] This means that our will is directed to the good as it currently is, according to the whole of reality. St. Thomas explains:

A thing taken in its primary sense, and absolutely considered, may be good or evil, and yet when some additional circumstances are taken into account, by a consequent consideration may be changed into the

---

1. St. John Damascene was the first to refer to the antecedent and consequent wills of God, which St. Thomas later developed with unparalleled clarity and precision.

2. Reformed (and some Evangelical) Protestants also have a concept of "two wills" in God, which they often call the perceptive or revealed will (what should happen) and the decretive or saving will (what will happen), although both camps contradict Catholic teaching. Arminians generally deny the distinction between "two wills" in regard to salvation, although they admit that God must will to permit some to fall away more than He wills to save all. Arminians often say that God wills to preserve free will more than He wills to save all, but this argument also makes a distinction between "two wills" in God.

3. See Garrigou-LaGrange, *Predestination*, p. 74.

contrary. Thus that a man should live is good; and that a man should be killed is evil, absolutely considered. But if in a particular case we add that a man is a murderer or dangerous to society, to kill him is a good; that he live is an evil. Hence it may be said of a just judge, that antecedently he wills all men to live; but consequently wills the murderer to be hanged ... Hence we will a thing simply inasmuch as we will it when all particular circumstances are considered; and this is what is meant by willing consequently.[4]

Thus, the judge doesn't evaluate the murderer as an individual absolutely. Rather, he judges the murderer in light of all the people that he has killed, and could continue to kill, if he were not hanged. In other words, the judge considers his decision in light of the effect on the whole. This analogy helps us understand predestination. Even though humans respond to goodness, and God actually creates goodness, God wills His decrees to produce the best goodness *as a whole*, not in the individual parts. St. Thomas explains:

It is the part of the best agent to produce an effect which is best in its entirety; but this does not mean that He makes every part of the whole the best absolutely, but in proportion to the whole; in the case of an animal, for instance, its goodness would be taken away if every part of it had the dignity of an eye. Thus, therefore, God also made the universe to be best as a whole, according to the mode of a creature; whereas He did not make each single creature best, but one better than another.[5]

Because God's will is the cause of goodness in things and some things are better than others, it necessarily follows that God wills different grades of goodness in His universe. God wills this variety of goodness in His universe because it is befitting for the Supreme Good to communicate His goodness to the greatest extent possible. St. Thomas says, "Hence, if natural things, insofar as they are perfect, communicate their good to others, much more does it appertain to the divine will to communicate by likeness its own good to others *as much as possible*."[6] This is achieved by a diversity of created goodness, for if

---

4. Pt I, Q 19, Art 6.
5. ST, Pt I, Q 47, Art 2. Thus, when God created the individual components of the universe, He declared that they were "good" (Gen. 1:4, 10, 12, 18, 21, 25). However, when God "saw all the things that he had made," according to the whole, He declared that "they were *very* good" (Gen. 1:31; emphasis added).
6. ST, Pt I, Q 19, Art 2. The Catechism also teaches that "God's plan" includes "the existence

God created all things with the same grade of goodness, He would not be communicating His goodness to the greatest extent. For example, the existence of one type of flower is good, but the existence of many types is a greater good. Further, the diversity of colors in roses, for example (red, pink, white, yellow), is a greater good than if roses were only red. St. Thomas elaborates on this cosmological principle:

> Hence we must say that the distinction and multitude of things come from the intention of the first agent, who is God. For He brought things into being in order that His goodness might be communicated to creatures, and be represented by them; and because His goodness could not be adequately represented by one creature alone, He produced many and diverse creatures, that what was wanting to one in the representation of the divine goodness might be supplied by another. For goodness, which in God is simple and uniform, in creatures is manifold and divided; and hence the whole universe together participates [in] the divine goodness more perfectly, and represents it better than any single creature whatever.[7]

Because God creates different grades of goodness in His universe to communicate His goodness in the greatest measure, it follows that God is the cause of the inequality of creatures. This inequality reveals the manifold goodness of God. Again, St. Thomas explains:

> Hence in natural things species seem to be arranged in degrees; as the mixed things are more perfect than the elements, and plants than minerals, and animals than plants, and men than other animals; and in each of these one species is more perfect than others. Therefore, as the divine wisdom is the cause of the distinction of things for the sake of the perfection of the universe, so is it the cause of inequality. For the universe would not be perfect if only one grade of goodness were found in things.[8]

St. Thomas also says that "the principal good in things themselves is the perfection of the universe; which would not be, were not all grades of being found in

---

of the more perfect alongside the less perfect" (310) and "God created the world to show forth and communicate his glory" (319).

7. ST, Pt I, Q 47, Art 1.
8. ST, Pt I, Q 47, Art 2.

things,"[9] and that "each and every creature exists for the perfection of the entire universe."[10]

The inequality that God wills in creatures includes not only different grades of goodness, but also that some things *fail in their goodness*. This, too, God wills for the perfection of the universe. St. Thomas says:

> Now, one grade of goodness is that of the good which cannot fail. Another grade of goodness is that of the good which can fail in goodness, and this grade is to be found in existence itself; for some things there are which cannot lose their existence as incorruptible things, while some there are which can lose it, as things corruptible. As, therefore, the perfection of the universe requires that there should be not only beings incorruptible, but also corruptible beings; so the perfection of the universe requires that there should be some which can fail in goodness, and thence it follows that sometimes they do fail. Now it is in this that evil consists, namely, in the fact that a thing fails in goodness.[11]

God wills to permit things to fail in their goodness—and thus evil to result—to manifest His goodness to the greatest extent possible. If God did not permit evil in the universe, then much good would not exist. St. Thomas remarks, "Hence many good things would be taken away if God permitted no evil to exist; for fire would not be generated if air was not corrupted, nor would the life of a lion be preserved unless the ass were killed. Neither would avenging justice nor the patience of a sufferer be praised if there were no injustice."[12] In another article, he similarly says, "[I]t belongs to His providence to permit certain defects in particular effects, that the perfect good of the universe may not be hindered, for if all evil were prevented, much good would be absent from the universe. A lion would cease to live, if there were no slaying of animals; and there would be no patience of martyrs if there were no tyrannical persecution."[13]

---

9. ST, Pt I, Q 22, Art 4.
10. ST, Pt I, Q 65, Art 2.
11. ST, Pt I, Q 48, Art 2. St. Thomas also says, "And the whole itself, which is the universe of creatures, is all the better and more perfect if some things in it can fail in goodness, and do sometimes fail, God not preventing this" (Ibid.).
12. Ibid.
13. ST, Pt I, Q 22, Art 2. The Catechism also says, "Faith gives us the certainty that God would not permit an evil if he did not cause a good to come from that very evil, by ways that we shall fully know only in eternal life" (CCC 324; see also CCC 311-314).

As we stated, these cosmological principles apply to divine predilection and God's plan of predestination. God's love is the cause of goodness in things, and no one thing would be better than another unless it were loved more by God. Because God created man in love, He wills all men some good. But in order to communicate His goodness to the greatest extent, God wills different grades of goodness in men. St. Paul reveals this diversity when he says, "But to every one of us is given grace, according to the measure of the giving of Christ" (Eph. 4:7); "Now there are diversities of graces, but the same Spirit; And there are diversities of ministries, but the same Lord; And there are diversities of operations, but the same God, who worketh all in all" (1 Cor. 12:4-6).

These different grades of goodness, whether in grace or ministries or operations, mean that some men achieve their goodness (the elect) and other men fail in their goodness (the reprobate). Through this diversity of goodness, the perfection of the universe is achieved. This is why St. Thomas says, "Now God wills some things to be done necessarily, some contingently, to the right ordering of things, for the building up of the universe."[14] He also says, "But it is manifest that the form which God chiefly intends in things created is the good of the order of the universe. Now, the order of the universe requires . . . that there should be some things that can, and do sometimes, fail."[15] He similarly says, "That which is the greatest good in the things that are caused by [by God] is the good order of the universe . . . So the good of the order of things . . . is that which is chiefly willed and caused by God. . .Therefore that which God cares for most greatly in created things is the order of the universe."[16] With incredible clarity and simplicity, St. Thomas further explains these principles:

Thus He is said to have made all things through His goodness, so that the divine goodness might be represented in things. Now it is necessary that God's goodness, which in itself is one and undivided, should be manifested in many ways in His creation; because creatures in themselves cannot attain to the simplicity of God. Thus it is that for the completion of the universe there are required different grades of being; some of which hold a high and some a low place in the universe. That this multiformity of grades may be preserved in things, God allows some evils, lest many good things should never happen . . . Let us then consider the

---

14. ST, Pt I, Q 19, Art 8.
15. ST, Pt I, Q 49, Art 2.
16. *Contra Gentiles* (CG), 3.64.

whole of the human race, as we consider the whole universe. God wills to manifest His goodness in men; in respect to those who He predestines, by means of His mercy, as sparing them; and in respect of others, whom He reprobates, by means of His justice, in punishing them. This is the reason why God elects some and rejects others.[17]

Thus, to communicate His goodness to the greatest extent, God wills to manifest *both* His mercy *and* His justice (and not His mercy alone). In His mercy, He saves. In His justice, He punishes. Jacob He loves, but Esau He hates (see Rom. 9:13). He has mercy on whom He will, and He hardens whom He will (see Rom. 9:18). If God were merciful only, He would not communicate the good of His justice, for both mercy and justice are good. If God did not permit evil, then the universe would be deprived of the good of God's avenging justice. The universe would be lacking good. This is why St. Thomas says, "The reason for the predestination of some, and reprobation of others, must be sought for in the goodness of God."[18]

In fact, God "endures the vessels of wrath" precisely so that he might show to all creation "the riches of his glory on the vessels of mercy" (see Rom. 9:22-23). God allows the reprobate to fall away so that the elect "may be unto the praise of his glory" (Eph. 1:12). God's goodness and glory are more greatly manifested when He not only saves the elect in His mercy, but also when He condemns the reprobate in His justice. St. Thomas says, "God antecedently wills all men to be saved, but consequently wills some to be damned, *as His justice exacts.*"[19] Both predestination and reprobation are for the greater glory of God, who orders all things to their final end.

Fr. Most rejects the Thomist position that God permits some men to fall away for the perfection of the universe. He points to St. Thomas's teaching that "the final perfection, which is the end of the whole universe, is the perfect beatitude of the Saints at the consummation of the world."[20] Although Fr. Most is correct to say that the final perfection of the universe is the beatitude of the saints, the diversity of creatures (the first perfection) exists *precisely for* the saints' beatitude (the final perfection). They are not disconnected, but connected. As

---

17. ST, Pt I, Q 23, Art 5.

18. ST, Pt I, A 23, Art. 5.

19. ST, Pt I, Q 19, Art 6 (emphasis added). The truth of reprobation and divine justice is an unfathomable mystery, as Scripture says, "For many of his works are hidden: but the works of his justice who shall declare?" (Ecclus. 16:22).

20. ST, Pt I, Q 73, Art 1.

St. Thomas says, the reprobate "seem to be preordained by God for the good of the elect, in whose regard *all things work together unto good* (Rom. 8:28)."[21] St. Thomas also says that God "extends His providence over the just in a certain more excellent way than over the wicked."[22] Thus, in God's plan of predestination, the reprobation of some is preordained for the good of the elect, and this *for the greater good of the whole.*

Thus, the saints' perfection in beatitude is derived from the diversity of creatures, just as a building's perfection is derived from the diversity of its component parts: "For just as an architect, without injustice, places stones of the same kind in different parts of a building, not on account of any antecedent difference in the stones, but with a view to securing that perfection of the entire building, which could not be obtained except by the different positions of the stones; even so, God from the beginning, to secure perfection of the universe, has set therein creatures of various and unequal natures, according to His wisdom, and without injustice, since no diversity of merit is presupposed."[23] In other words, the diversity of the means (graces/stones) is intended to bring about the perfection of the end (beatitude/building). This is not to say that God wills the reprobates' damnation like He wills the elect's salvation. He doesn't; He only permits it. Nevertheless, because God in His providence orders all things to their end, He uses the free-will decisions of the reprobate to achieve His plan of election.[24]

Fr. Most also argues that reprobation cannot be for the good of the universe because St. Thomas teaches that the universe would be more perfect without certain evils. St. Thomas says that "there are certain evils such that if they did not exist, the universe would be more perfect . . . as is chiefly the case in moral faults."[25] However, in this teaching St. Thomas is referring to the *means* of perfecting the universe, and not its *final* perfection. That is, St. Thomas is referring to moral fault where, "even without it, the ultimate perfection could be had; just as one can come to eternal life without the act of patience in persecutions . . . he

---

21. ST, Pt I, Q 23, Art 7 (emphasis in original). See also CCC 313.
22. ST, Pt I, Q 22, Art 2.
23. ST, Pt I, Q 65, Art 2. See also Pt I, Q 23, Art 6, where St. Thomas says, "[F]rom the simple will of the artificer it depends that this stone is in this part of the wall, and that in another; although the plan requires that some stones should be in this place, and some in that place. Neither on this account can there be said to be injustice in God, if He prepares unequal lots for not unequal things."
24. The Catechism also teaches that God "makes use" of His creatures' free-will decisions "in the accomplishment of his plan" (CCC 306).
25. 1 Sent. d. 46, Q 1, Art 3.

could attain salvation without the fault [of the other]."²⁶ This is because, as St. Thomas says, "[E]vil is not of itself ordered to good, but accidentally" and "Evil does not operate towards the perfection and beauty of the universe, except accidentally . . ."²⁷ Thus, St. Thomas is not teaching that God doesn't reprobate for the greater good of the universe. Rather, he is teaching that God could have achieved the same, final perfection of the universe without permitting certain moral faults.

In disputing the Thomist position that reprobation is for the good of the universe, Fr. Most also points to St. Thomas's statement: "In created things, nothing can be greater than the salvation of a rational creature."²⁸ Fr. Most appears to confuse the *nature* of the universe with the *grace* of salvation. When Thomists refer to the good of the universe in the context of reprobation, we are not referring to the natural elements of the universe. Rather, we are referring to human beings, in the order of grace, who make up the universe. There is a clear distinction between the good of nature and the good of grace. Grace is a greater good than nature because it is a direct sharing in God's divine life. As St. Thomas says, "[T]he good of *grace* in one is greater than the good of *nature* in the whole universe."²⁹

However, St. Thomas also says, "The good of the universe is greater than the particular good of one, if we consider both in the same genus."³⁰ In Thomism, a *genus* is "the aspect of a thing's essence which is common to it and other members of its species; a broader class to which a thing essentially belongs."³¹ As applied here, because the universe refers to the totality of all rational creatures, it is of the same genus as each individual rational creature in that universe. In the words of St. Thomas, this means that the good of the universe (all men considered) is *greater* than the particular good of one man. This is why St. Thomas doesn't say "nothing can be greater than the salvation of every single rational creature who ever lived." Of course, if God consequently willed all men to be saved, they would be saved. Yet, in God's inscrutable judgments, He achieves

---

26. Ibid.
27. ST, Pt I, Q 19, Art 9.
28. CG, 4.55.
29. ST, Pt I-II, Q 113, Art 9.
30. Ibid. St. Thomas's statement is a reply to the same type of objection that Fr. Most is advancing: "But the good of the universe is greater than the good of one man . . . Hence the creation of heaven and earth is a greater work than the justification of the ungodly." We have explained why St. Thomas says this objection is false.
31. Peter Kreeft, *Summa of the Summa*, p. 26.

the greater good by predestining some in order to communicate His mercy, and reprobating others in order to communicate His justice.

Thus, God creates diversity in the natural order for the same reason that He creates diversity of graces in the supernatural order—for the greater good of the universe. The natural order reflects the supernatural order. Just as God permits defects in the natural order to perfect the whole, He likewise permits defects (sin) in the supernatural order to perfect the whole. This is why St. Thomas directs us to "consider the whole of the human race, as we consider the whole universe." God directs *both* to their final end by making some achieve the ultimate goodness (heaven) and allowing others to fail in attaining that goodness. While Fr. Most says that "the formal glory of God is diminished by their [the reprobates'] existence," it is impossible for the reprobates to take away from God's glory. God's glory is eternal and lasts "before all ages, and now, and for all ages of ages. Amen" (Jude 1:25).[32] The reprobates reveal the glory of God's justice while the elect reveal the glory of God's mercy.

MORE ON REPROBATION

Let's recap what we have learned thus far. Reprobation, properly speaking, is the truth that God permits certain people to go to hell, just as predestination means God elects certain people to heaven. When speaking of reprobation, we reaffirm the truth that God does not cause people to sin, but neither does He prevent their sins. Rather, God *permits* people to sin, and He does so for the greater good of His creation. God is in complete control of the end of every creature, and permits only what He wills for the greater good of the whole. St. Thomas is clear on this point: "God therefore neither wills evil to be done, nor wills it not to be done, but wills to permit evil to be done; and this is a good."[33]

Just as God does not choose the elect based on their foreseen merits, neither does God choose whom He reprobates based on their foreseen demerits. God simply chooses "according to the purpose of his will" (Eph. 1:5). As we have also learned, without God's decrees in eternity, nothing would take place in time. Thus, God's choice to reprobate logically precedes a person's demerits, for the demerits would not exist without God's divine permission. This truth

---

32. See also Eph. 3:21; 1 Pet. 4:11; 5:11; 2 Pet. 3:18; Apoc. 1:6; 7:12.
33. Pt I, Q 19, Art 9.

highlights the Thomist position that God determines man, and is not determined by man.

However, there seems to be a greater mystery with reprobation than with
predestination. When God predestines the elect to heaven, God produces all
the results (that is, all salutary acts and the gift of perseverance) through His
efficacious grace. God wills the rewards of the elect before foreseen merits,
because both the works and rewards are God's gratuitous gifts to man. In other
words, both the cause and effect of predestination are the work of God.[34] This
is why David proclaims that "the salvation of the just is from the Lord" (Ps.
36:39). The Catechism also says, "Salvation comes from God alone" (CCC
169). St. Thomas confirms that predestination "is the cause both of what is
expected in the future life by the predestined—namely, glory—and of what is
received in this life—namely, grace."[35]

We cannot say the same thing with reprobation. Although the permission to
sin comes from God, the sin comes from man. In His providence, God orders
all things to Himself as their last end, and sin is a departure from this order.
Thus, it is impossible that God should be the cause of the departure from the
order that He ordains to Himself.[36] Of God, Scripture says, "[T]hou . . . hatest
none of the things which thou hast made" (Wis. 11:25), but also says, "[T]hou
hatest all the workers of iniquity" (Ps. 5:7). That God doesn't hate anything He
has made but does hate evil doers means that God does not make men evil or
cause sin.[37]

As we have seen, Fr. Most incorrectly believes that the Thomist system requires God to desert man before he sins, and precisely so he *can* sin. He calls
it the "desertion" theory. Fr. Most says, "Hence, in their theory, God wants to
desert certain men, so that they sin, so that He may have someone to punish, so
as to be able to manifest vindictive justice."[38] This statement does not describe

---

34. As we will see in the next chapter, this assertion is not a denial of free will, for God causes
the will to act freely, and not by necessity, by means of His efficacious grace.

35. ST, Pt 1, Q 23, Art 3.

36. See ST, Pt I-II, Q 79, Art 1. These teachings remind me of the great spiritual axiom: "*A
Deo ad Deum*" (From God to God).

37. Although God is not the cause of sin, St. Thomas teaches that God is the cause of the *act*
of sin. This is because God as Prime Mover is the cause of every action, and sin is an action. This
action, however, has a defect that cannot be attributed to God, for God orders all things to Himself
and sin departs from this order. Hence, sin is a defect with a created cause (human free will), just
like limping is a defect with a crooked leg as its cause and not the power of movement. See ST, Pt
I-II, Q 79, Art 1 and 2.

38. GPS, p. 50. Fr. Most's belief that the Thomist system requires man to sin is based on his

the Thomist position but rather the Calvinist heresy of double predestination. The Thomist position is that God decrees the permission to sin before it occurs (otherwise it would never happen), and deserts man only after he sins. Just because God wills to permit sin in order to manifest His divine justice does not mean that God wills the sin itself. Fr. Most confuses God's will to *permit* sin with His will to *punish* sin. While evil is not a good, God's will to permit evil *is a good* insofar as it communicates God's infinite justice and right to be loved above all things. God's will to justly punish those who do evil is also a good. This is why St. Thomas says, "God therefore neither wills evil to be done, nor wills it not to be done, but wills to permit evil to be done; *and this is a good.*"[39]

Because Fr. Most interprets the Thomist position to mean that God deserts certain men before they sin, he says that in this system God "is *not directly concerned with individuals*, but with *the whole*."[40] Once again, this distorts the Thomist position. God's concern for the whole does not mean that He is not directly concerned with individuals as well. As we shall see in chapter 4, Christ died for all men and gives all men sufficient grace to be saved. However, the fact that some individuals are reprobated shows that God's concern for the reprobate includes His respect for their freedom to reject His grace. As the Catechism says, "He permits it [evil], however, because he respects the freedom of his creatures and, mysteriously, knows how to derive good from it" (CCC 311). As St. Thomas explains, this permission manifests God's will to communicate His goodness and glory to men—for the predestined, His mercy; for the reprobate, His justice.

In defense of his position, Fr. Most attempts to turn the tables on Thomists by contending thusly: "Thomists need to prove not only that the manifestation of vindictive justice is necessary, but they must prove that it must be done by reprobation, and further, by reprobation before consideration of demerits. They surely have not proved this."[41] Yet God's vindictive justice is "necessary" only because God wills to manifest it to His creatures. In Thomistic terminology,

---

faulty understanding of sufficient grace (that is, that sufficient grace is insufficient to prevent man from sinning). We examine this issue in detail in chapter 4.

39. ST, Pt I, Q 19, Art 9 (emphasis added). Because of his erroneous understanding of both necessity and sufficient grace, Fr. Most also accuses the Thomist position of making God the author of sin.

40. GPS, p. 50 (emphasis in original).

41. GPS, p. 54, cf. pp. 644-645. Fr. Most also says that "it would not follow that God would necessarily have to desert any creature, because without desertion there can be reprobates" (p. 54). This is true insofar as sufficient grace is concerned, but it is not the case with efficacious grace.

we say that it is not *absolutely* necessary (because God is free to manifest His attributes however He sees fit), but it is necessary *by supposition* (supposing that God wills to manifest His justice, which He does).[42] To prove that reprobates aren't "necessary," Fr. Most points out that God "hath no need of wicked men" (Ecclus. 15:12). But God "hath no need" of creatures at all, and yet they exist. Thomists don't say that God *needs* to reprobate man absolutely. Rather, God wills to reprobate certain men because He wills to manifest His justice for the greater good of the universe, for "the order of justice belongs to the order of the universe."[43]

Furthermore, it is disingenuous for Fr. Most to claim that Thomists haven't proven that God reprobates before foreseen demerits.[44] Thomists take this position based on St. Paul's teaching in Romans 9, which Fr. Most simply dismisses. In fact, St. Thomas directs us to understand God's will by going to Scripture: "For such things as spring from God's will, and beyond the creature's due, can be made known to us only through being revealed in Sacred Scripture, in which the Divine Will is made known to us."[45] In Romans 9, God reveals that He hated Esau before he was "not yet born, nor had done any good or evil (that the purpose of God, according to election, might stand)" (v. 11).[46] God also reveals that "he hath mercy on whom he will; and whom he will, he hardeneth" (v. 18). Thus, Scripture reveals that God does not consider future demerits in decreeing reprobation. This is not only the plain meaning of Scripture, but also the position of both St. Augustine and St. Thomas. The burden is on their interlocutors to prove otherwise. It is not that Thomists have not proven their case; rather, Fr. Most *rejects the proof.*

Because Fr. Most rejects the traditional interpretation of Romans 9, he simply does not accept God's sovereignty in choosing whom He predestines and whom He reprobates. He says, "But if He picked them before consideration of demerits, He would have no reason for deserting this man rather than that

---

42. St. Thomas says that God's "willing things apart from Himself is not absolutely necessary. Yet it can be necessary by supposition, for supposing that He wills a thing, then He is unable not to will it, as his will cannot change." ST, Pt I, Q 19, Art 3.
43. ST, Pt I, Q 49, Art 2.
44. GPS, p. 54, cf. pp. 644-645.
45. ST, Pt III, Q 1, Art 3.
46. St. Thomas explains that God's "hatred" for individuals "is from the fact that God wills some greater good which would not exist without the privation of a lesser good. And so He is said to hate through this rather than love. For thus, in as much as He wills the good of justice or of the order of the universe which cannot be without the punishment or the corruption of some, he is said to hate those whose punishment He wills, or [whose] corruption He wills" (CG, 1.96).

man, for the order of the universe, as we have said, does not indicate which ones should be deserted. Nor do the desertion theologians suggest what rational basis God could have. Therefore, God would have to act without reason, blindly."[47] In Fr. Most's theology, man must find a "rational basis" for God's determinations or else God is acting "without reason." This is an incredible statement from such an astute theologian. St. Paul answers Fr. Most's objection in Romans 9:14: "Is there injustice with God? God forbid." While Fr. Most seeks a "reason" for God's decisions, St. Thomas says, "[W]hy He chooses some for glory, and reprobates others, *has no reason*, except the divine will."[48] Fr. Most's criticisms of the "desertion" theory actually reveal his desertion of St. Thomas on the question of reprobation.

The Catholic Church has always held that man is responsible for his condemnation, even though God decrees to permit it. For example, the regional Council of Arles condemned the idea that "the foreknowledge of God violently impels man to death, or that they who perish, perish by the will of God."[49] The Council of Orange II states: "We not only do not believe that some have been truly predestined to evil by divine power, but also with every execration we pronounce anathema upon those, if there are [any such], who wish to believe so great an evil."[50] The Council of Valence III also states: "Neither do we believe that anyone is condemned by a previous judgment on the part of God but by reason of his own iniquity;"[51] "But we do not only not believe the saying that 'some have been predestined to evil by divine power,' namely as if they could not be different, 'but even if there are those who wish to believe such malice, with all detestation,' as the Synod of Orange, 'we say anathema to them.'"[52]

In her canons on justification, the Council of Trent also declares: "If anyone shall say that it is not in the power of man to make his ways evil, but that God produces the evil as well as the good works, not only by permission, but also properly and of Himself, so that the betrayal of Judas is no less His own proper work than [is] the vocation of Paul: let him be anathema" (canon 6);[53] "If anyone shall say that the grace of justification is attained by those only who are predestined unto life, but that all others, who are called, are called indeed,

---

47. GPS, p. 63.
48. ST, Pt 1, Q 23, Art 5.
49. Denz., 160a.
50. Denz., 200.
51. Denz., 321.
52. Denz., 322.
53. Denz., 816.

but do not receive grace, as if they are by divine power predestined to evil: let him be anathema" (canon 17).[54] This is why St. Paul says, "For the wages of sin is death. But the grace of God, life everlasting, in Christ Jesus our Lord" (Rom. 6:23). Death, which is called "wages," is something that man can earn, while "the grace of God" is a gift that man cannot earn.

Thus, predestination causes grace and glory, but reprobation does not cause sin. Rather, reprobation is the cause of God's divine permission (to sin in this life) and His punishment of that sin (in this life and the next). God decrees to permit sin, and then punishes sin by abandoning man and withholding His grace from him. St. Thomas teaches, "Reprobation, however, is not the cause of what is in the present—namely, sin; but it is the cause of abandonment by God. It is the cause, however, of what is assigned in the future—namely, eternal punishment. But guilt proceeds from the free will of the person who is reprobated and deserted by grace. In this way the word of the prophet is true—namely, "Destruction is thy own, O Israel" (Osee 13:9).

This is why Thomists use the term "negative reprobation." God's withholding of grace is the *negation* of a good not due to man, and not the privation of a good due to him (which would be an evil).[55] Because God does not owe grace to any man, He does not offend justice by withholding it, so long as He deprives nobody of his due. As Scripture says, "[H]is justice remaineth for ever" (2 Cor. 9:9). Moreover, God does not withhold grace arbitrarily but withholds it as a punishment for sin. St. Thomas says that "God, of His own accord, withholds His grace from those in whom He finds an obstacle: so that the cause of grace being withheld is not only the man who raises an obstacle to grace; but God, Who, of His own accord, withholds His grace ... Blindness and hardheartedness, as regards the withholding of grace, are punishments."[56] The Council of Trent also says that God does not forsake man, unless He is first forsaken by man.[57]

Thus, in reprobation, God wills to permit sin before it occurs, and then He punishes sin after it occurs. The permission precedes the defect, and the defect precedes the punishment. As the Council of Valence teaches, "[O]f those who

---

54. Denz., 827.

55. This is why St. Thomas says, "Reprobation by God does not take anything away from the power of the person reprobated" (Pt I, Q 23, Art 3) and, "[T]he withholding of grace ... make[s] man no worse. It is because he is already worsened by sin that he incurs them, even as other punishments" (Pt I-II, Q 79, Art 3).

56. ST, Pt I-II, Q 79, Art 3.

57. See Denz., 804.

are to be lost, the evil which they have deserved precedes the just judgment of God."⁵⁸ God is responsible for granting permission, but man is responsible for his own damnation. This is a great mystery, for God could prevent a man from dying impenitent by granting him efficacious grace; as Job says, "I know that thou canst do all things" (42:2). But God does this only for His elect. God permits certain people to harden their hearts by rejecting grace, and God hardens their hearts as a punishment for sin by withholding His grace. As St. Paul says, "[W]hom he will, he hardeneth" (Rom. 9:18). This is also why the Book of Exodus reveals that *both* God and Pharao hardened Pharao's heart.

Scripture elsewhere teaches that God hardens man's heart. For example, in regard to obstinate sinners, St. Paul reveals how "God delivered them up to a reprobate sense" (Rom. 1:28) and how "God shall send them the operation of error, to believe lying" (2 Thess. 2:10). St. Paul in Romans also quotes the prophet Isaias when he says, "God hath given them the spirit of insensibility; eyes that they should not see; and ears that they should not hear" (11:8). St. John does likewise when he says, "He hath blinded their eyes, and hardened their heart, that they should not see with their eyes, nor understand with their heart, and be converted, and I should heal them."⁵⁹ These verses underscore that God is in control of the fate of the reprobate, even though He does not cause their falling away.⁶⁰

That God punishes sin after it occurs by withholding grace and hardening hearts does not mean that God changes or is determined by man's actions (recall that God is pure Act with no potentiality). God decrees the permission to sin before foreseen demerits, and wills the punishment of the sin as a consequence of His permission. As we saw in the councils of Quiersy (853) and Valence (855), God does not predestine man to sin but predestines His punishment of sin because He is just.⁶¹ As St. Thomas says, "[I]n willing justice He wills punishment."⁶²

Thus, God's will to give grace and His will to punish those who reject that grace imply no change in God's will, for St. Thomas teaches, "It is possible to

---

58. Denz., 322.
59. John 12:40; St. Paul and St. John are quoting from Isa. 6:9-10; 29:10. See Isa. 44:18; Matt. 11:25; 13:13-17; Luke 10:21-22; Acts 28:26-27; Rom. 11:7.
60. The early Church Fathers taught that God hardens man's heart as a punishment for sin, for example, Augustine (*Homilies on John*; *Against Julian*), John Chrysostom (*On Hebrews*), Jerome (*Dialogue Against the Pelagians*), and Cyril of Alexandria (*Commentary on the Psalms*).
61. Denz., 316, 322.
62. ST, Pt I, Q 19, Art 9.

58 THE MYSTERY OF PREDESTINATION

will a thing to be done now, and its contrary afterwards; and yet for the will to remain permanently the same."[63] In other words, God wills from all eternity the "who, what, when, where, and why" of both predestination and reprobation. For the reprobate, God eternally wills to give sufficient grace in His mercy (the thing to be done now) and to withdraw grace in His justice (the contrary afterwards), with His will remaining the same. This difference also reflects the antecedent and consequent wills of God.[64]

We must emphasize that God's motive for permitting sin and allowing final impenitence is not the desire to punish the sin per se. God doesn't permit man to reject His grace because of His love to chastise, for this would be unjust. Rather, as we have said, God permits sin in order to communicate His goodness to the greatest possible extent, and this necessarily includes the goodness of His justice. Father Garrigou-Lagrange, the popular Dominican Thomist, also says that God wills to permit and punish sin as a manifestation of His infinite justice and His right to be loved above all things.[65] This is the just desire of the Supreme Good.

Scripture Reveals God's Will to Save Sinners

With an understanding of God's antecedent and consequent wills, we don't get caught in the Protestant errors of Calvinism or Arminianism. When Scripture teaches that God wills all men to be saved, we don't have to interpret those texts (1 Tim. 2:4; 2 Pet. 3:9; John 3:16) solely in the exclusive sense like Calvinists, who hold that God wills only the elect to be saved. Neither do we have to interpret the text only in the inclusive sense like Arminians, who hold that God wills every single person to be saved but does not succeed in doing so. Rather, we can say that God antecedently wills the salvation of all men (Catholics and Arminians agree), but consequently wills the salvation of the elect (Catholics and Calvinists agree). In chapter 4, we will evaluate whether Christ's atonement was for all or for the elect only. For now, we will look at a few principal scriptural texts that address God's will to save sinners.

---

63. ST, Pt I, Q 19, Art 7.
64. St. Thomas notes that God's motive for withdrawing grace from the elect is directed medicinally to their spiritual welfare (He does it to humble the elect whom He eventually restores to grace in His mercy). For the reprobate, God's motive is punitive (He does it to punish these sinners in His justice). See ST, Pt I-II, Q 79, Art 4.
65. *Predestination*, pp. 207-208.

1 Timothy 2:4: God Wills All Men To Be Saved

In 1 Timothy 2:4 we find one of the clearest expressions of God's will to save man. Notwithstanding its perceived simplicity, however, there is great debate between Calvinists and Arminians over its true meaning. Calvinists interpret the passage to mean that God wills to save all *kinds* or *classes* of men, while Arminians say it applies to *all men* who ever lived. Let's examine verses 1-6 so that we can put the passage in its context. St. Paul says:

> I desire therefore, first of all, that supplications, prayers, intercessions, and thanksgivings be made for all men: For kings, and for all that are in high station: that we may lead a quiet and a peaceable life in all piety and chastity. For this is good and acceptable in the sight of God our Savior, Who will have all men to be saved, and to come to the knowledge of the truth. For there is one God, and one mediator of God and men, the man Christ Jesus: Who gave himself a redemption for all, a testimony in due times.

In verse 1, St. Paul asks for intercessory prayer and thanksgiving to be made for "all men." In verse 4, St. Paul says that God wills "all men" to be saved. The Greek for "all men" in both verses is *pas anthropos*. Thus, from a contextual standpoint, almost all exegetes conclude that the "all men" in verses 1 and 4 both refer to the same group of individuals. The question is whether "all" means every single person, or whether it refers to a specific group of people (the elect).

As we have mentioned, Calvinists contend that "all men" does not really mean all men absolutely, but rather all kinds of men. They so argue because St. Paul refers to "kings" and those in "high stations" (v. 2) right after he recommends prayer for "all men" (v. 1). Calvinists interpret this to mean that St. Paul is *defining* "all" as "classes" or "kinds" of men because he provides examples of such classes (kings and others in authority). Because Christians at this time were being persecuted by "kings" and men in "high stations," St. Paul is said to be urging Christians to pray for these "classes" of men as well.[66]

---

66. In denying the Arminian interpretation, Calvinist James White says that "Paul is not instructing Timothy to initiate never-ending prayer meetings where the Ephesian phone book would be opened and every single person ... would become the object of prayer" (*The Potter's Freedom*, p. 140). This is a silly argument because it implies that one cannot pray for all people cur-

In light of our understanding of the consequent will of God, the Calvinist offers a plausible interpretation. If God wills all men to be saved, but not all men are saved, it must be that God wills the salvation of kinds or classes of men vis-à-vis the total pool of all men. St. Thomas also believed in the plausibility of this interpretation, for he says, "[T]hey can be understood as applying to every class of individuals, not to every individual in each class; in which case they mean that God wills some men of every class and condition to be saved, males and females, Jews and Gentiles, great and small, but not all of every condition."[67] In other words, 1 Timothy 2:1-6 can certainly refer to the consequent or simple will of God to save His elect people.

However, St. Thomas, in referring to a commentary by St. John Damascene, also says those in the passage "are understood of the antecedent will of God; not of the consequent will."[68] This seems to be the better interpretation. St. Paul's prayer request for "kings" and those in "high stations" does not seem to be principally an effort to distinguish between classes of men but seems to include all men in prayer. Why? As we said, kings and rulers were persecuting Christians, and it would have been natural for Christians not to pray for such men. It seems more likely that St. Paul is simply teaching Christians to pray for our enemies as well as our friends and not to exclude them from our prayers. This teaching follows precisely the teaching of our Lord when He says, "Love your enemies: do good to them that hate you: and pray for them that persecute and calumniate you" (Matt. 5:44).

St. Paul's use of *pas anthropos* elsewhere in Scripture also indicates that 1 Timothy 2:4 is about the antecedent will of God.[69] For example, in Romans 5:12, St. Paul says, "[S]o death passed upon all men (*pas anthropos*), in whom

---

rently living without knowing each and every name. God is not limited by man's intention to offer prayers for all, and God can apply the prayers to all if He so desires.

67. ST, Pt I, Q 19, Art 6. In this article, St. Thomas also refers to St. Augustine's interpretation: "God wills all men to be saved that are saved, not because there is no man whom He does not wish saved, but because there is no man saved whose salvation He does not will" (*De praed. sanct.* 1:8; *Enchir.* 103).

68. Ibid.

69. It is true that "all" does not always mean "all" in Scripture. St. Paul uses "all" (*pas*) and "many" (*polus*) in different ways. For example, in Romans 5:15 and 19, the word "many" sometimes refers to all people ("many have died;" "many were made sinners") but can also refer to a select group of people ("many shall be made just"). In Colossians 3:11 and Galatians 3:28, "all" refers only to those in Christ. In these cases, *pas* and *polus* function as pronouns. However, when St. Paul uses *pas* (all) as an adjective to describe *anthropos* (men), the preponderant usage is "every single one" (see also Rom. 3:4; 1 Cor. 4:2; Gal. 5:3; Col. 1:28; 1 Tim. 4:10; Titus 2:11). Only rarely is the usage limited to kinds or classes (Rom. 5:19; 1 Cor. 7:7).

all have sinned." Because death has indeed passed to every human who ever lived (not just to the elect), St. Paul in this verse uses *pas anthropos* to refer to all men and not just the elect. In Titus 3:2, St. Paul says, "To speak evil of no man, not to be litigious, but gentle: shewing all mildness towards all men (*pas anthropos*)." Of course, because we are to show mildness to all men and not just to the elect shows that St. Paul is not using *pas anthropos* to distinguish between classes of men. Further, that St. Paul says we are to speak evil of "no man," and "no man" is the opposite of "all men" in the same verse, also shows that St. Paul uses *pas anthropos* in the inclusive sense and not in the restricted sense of Calvinism.[70]

This exegesis is consistent with the teachings of the Council of Valence. In interpreting 1 Timothy 2:4, the council stated in chapter 3: "Omnipotent God wishes *all men* without exception *to be saved* [1 Tim. 2:4] although not all will be saved. That certain ones are saved is the gift of the one who saves; that certain ones perish, however, is the deserved punishment of those who perish."[71] Thus, Valence sided with what St. Thomas would later explain to be the antecedent will of God: "God wills all men to be saved by His antecedent will, which is to will not simply but relatively; and not by His consequent will, which is to will simply."[72] With this teaching, the council also reiterates that salvation is the gratuitous gift of God, whereas damnation is the fault of man.

Finally, we note that St. Paul could have said that God wills all *kinds* of men to be saved, but he didn't. St. Paul knew that the word for "kinds" in Greek is *genos*. St. Paul uses *genos* to distinguish "kinds" of things elsewhere in Scripture. For example, in describing God's various gifts to man, St. Paul says that God grants "to another, diverse kinds (*genos*) of tongues" (1 Cor. 12:10). In the same letter, St. Paul also says that there are "so many kinds (*genos*) of tongues in this world" (14:10). The absence of the specific word for "kinds" (*genos*) in 1 Timothy 2:4, coupled with the exegetical and contextual analysis above, indicates that 1 Timothy 2:4 is about God's antecedent will to save all sinners and not His consequent will to save His elect.

---

70. In verse 6, St. Paul says that Christ "gave himself a redemption for all (*pas*)." The fact that this verse follows St. Paul's inclusive use of *pas anthropos* in regard to prayers (v. 1) and to God's will to save (v. 4) supports the conclusion that Christ's "redemption" was also for "all men" and not just the elect (more on this in chapter 4).

71. Denz., 318 (emphasis in original).

72. ST, Pt I, Q 23, Art 4.

2 Peter 3:9: God Does Not Will That Any Should Perish

This is another contentious verse between Calvinists and Arminians. In order to understand its context, it is necessary to quote from verse 3 through verse 9.

> Knowing this first, that in the last days there shall come deceitful scoffers, walking after their own lusts, [s]aying: Where is his promise or his coming? [F]or since the time that the fathers slept, all things continue as they were from the beginning of the creation. For this they are wilfully ignorant of, that the heavens were before, and the earth out of water, and through water, consisting by the word of God. Whereby the world that then was, being overflowed with water, perished. But the heavens and the earth which are now, by the same word are kept in store, reserved unto fire against the day of judgment and perdition of the ungodly men. But of this one thing be not ignorant, my beloved, that one day with the Lord is as a thousand years, and a thousand years as one day. The Lord delayeth not his promise, as some imagine, but dealeth patiently for your sake, not willing that any should perish, but that all should return to penance (2 Pet. 3:3-9).

As one can see, this passage is primarily about the Second Coming of Jesus Christ at the end of the world (eschatological) but also about God's will to save sinners (soteriological). St. Peter reveals that in the last days unbelievers will accuse believers of waiting in vain for Christ's return. They will ridicule Christians by saying, "Where is his promise or his coming?" (v. 4). They will point out that things haven't changed for many centuries and that they "continue as they were from the beginning of creation" (v. 4). Since they see no sign of Christ's return, and most of the world is in apostasy (see Luke 18:8), scoffers will proclaim that God has abandoned His people. St. Peter, however, reveals that the "Lord delayeth not his promise, as some imagine, but dealeth patiently for your sake, not willing that any should perish, but that all should return to penance" (v. 9).

As one may expect, Calvinists argue that St. Peter is referring only to the elect. They so conclude because St. Peter refers to the "scoffers" (v. 3) in the third person, while he speaks directly to his audience in the second person as "dearly beloved" (v. 1) and "my beloved" (v. 8). Thus, when in the next verse St. Peter says that the Lord "dealeth patiently for *your* sake" (v. 9), the Calvinist has good reason to believe that St. Peter is still speaking to the "beloved." To bolster their argument that St. Peter is addressing the elect, Calvinists also point out that St. Peter addresses his second epistle "to them that have obtained equal faith with us" (1:1). In fact, St. Peter addresses his first epistle to the "elect" (1:1), and he says that he is writing his second epistle to the same people (3:1).[73]

While 2 Peter 3:9 could be about God's consequent will to save His elect from perishing, it could also be about God's antecedent will to save all men. This is a reasonable conclusion, because St. Peter does not use the word "elect" in verse 9 (or anywhere in chapter 3). Rather, he uses the all-encompassing "any" (Greek, *tis*) and "all" (*pas*) to refer to those God wills to save. While the first part of verse 9 is arguably addressed to the beloved ("for your sake"), the Calvinist simply assumes that the rest of the verse also applies to the beloved and not to all men: "not willing that *any* (beloved only) should perish, but that *all* (beloved only) should return to penance." Just because St. Peter is addressing the "beloved" does not mean that God wishes unbelievers to perish. In fact, because St. Peter's audience is already "beloved" and "elect," it does not follow that God is dealing "patiently" for their sake and wishing that they "return to penance," for they are already converted to Christ (and Calvinists don't believe one can fall into grave sin after regeneration).

Calvinists respond by saying that God is exercising His patience for the *unbelieving* elect ("for your sake"). In terms of God's consequent will, this is true. God does indeed delay His coming until He gathers all of the elect into His fold. St. Luke records that "the Lord increased daily together such as should be saved" (Acts 2:47). He also writes, "And the Gentiles, hearing it, were glad, and glorified the word of the Lord: and as many as were ordained to life everlasting, believed" (Acts 13:48). Jesus asks, "And will God revenge his elect who cry to him day and night: and will he have patience in their regard?" (Luke 18:7). The answer, of course, is yes. In fact, Jesus says, "And unless those days had been shortened, no flesh should be saved: but for the sake of the elect those days shall be shortened" (Matt. 24:22).[74] St. Paul also says, "Therefore I endure all things for the sake of the elect, that they also may obtain the salvation, which is in Christ Jesus, with heavenly glory" (2 Tim. 2:10). God bears patiently with His elect to ensure their salvation.

---

73. St. Peter's identification of the elect as the "beloved" also underscores divine predilection.

74. See also Mark 13:20.

But the Calvinist's argument results in a bit of an equivocation. This is because St. Peter is addressing the *believing* elect, which the Calvinist admits. Remember, St. Peter says that they "have obtained equal faith" with the apostles (2 Pet. 1:1). In fact, the entire epistle is addressed to the believing elect. So when St. Peter says that God is dealing patiently "for *your* sake," the *your* must refer to this same believing elect. But since there is no need for the believing elect to "return to penance" to avoid damnation, the Calvinist must change the audience of the last half of verse nine to the *unbelieving* elect.

That is, the first half of the verse ("for your sake") refers to the believing elect, but the second half of the verse ("any" should perish; "all" return to penance) refers to the unbelieving elect. This is a tortured reading of the text. Since the Calvinist admits that the "any" and "all" refer to unbelievers, it is perfectly admissible to include "all men" in that category. The Calvinist has no basis to exclude the reprobate, especially when they are so quick to change the audience when it fits their theology. Such a conclusion would reflect God's antecedent will to save all men. We also note that St. Peter in 1 Peter 1:1 is writing to the churches in Asia Minor and says he is addressing the same audience in 2 Peter 3:1. All of these churches fell away from the faith as Our Lord prophesied in Apocalypse 2-3. This demonstrates that St. Peter's audience actually *included the reprobate*, which further supports an "antecedent will" interpretation. This also shows that those who "have obtained equal faith" with the apostles can fall away from the faith.

Mark Kielar, president of CrossTV and a popular and influential Baptist preacher, states in one of his television programs that the word for "any" (Greek, *tis*) in the phrase "not willing that *any* should perish" really means *some*. In the program, he shows that the online Strong Exhaustive Concordance defines *tis* as "a certain one" or "some." Kielar also points out that St. Peter's use of *tis* just twelve words earlier in the verse also means *some* when he says, "The Lord delayeth not his promise, as *some* imagine" (v. 9). Kielar's exegesis is deliberately one-sided. Although the Strong Concordance that Kielar uses does define *tis* as "certain" and "some," Kielar fails to mention that the same concordance also defines *tis* as "any man" and "any."[75] This means that "any should perish" could also really mean *any* (which is how Kielar's King James Version actually translates the verse!). In fact, Kielar's King James Version of Scripture uses *tis* 448

---

75. The Concordance, *inter alia*, provides the following usage: "Certain" (104 times), "some" (73 times), "any man" (55 times), and "any" (37 times). The Calvinist must accuse the King James Version translation of 2 Peter 3:9 (*tis* as "any") as the grossest of errors.

times with various shades of meaning, which demonstrates that the usage is not as definitive as Kielar argues to his television audience.

Kielar's contextual argument, that *tis* ("any") in the latter part of verse nine must mean "some" because *tis* ("some") in the former part of the verse means "some," is illogical. When St. Peter says "as some imagine," he is clearly referring to those who reject Christ. However, the "any should perish" group, according to Calvinists, refers to the elect. Kielar doesn't explain why the *tis* of the reprobate defines the *tis* of the elect. They are polar-opposite groups. Even if the Christ-rejecters were the unbelieving elect and not the reprobate, the subject matter relative to each group is different. The first *tis* (as "some" imagine) is being used to identify those who deny Christ's coming, while the second *tis* ("any" should perish) is being used to identify those God wills to save. There is no lexical or contextual relationship between the *tis* of group one and the *tis* of group two.

Of course, Kielar should know that the use of an adjective to describe two groups within a single verse doesn't mean that the adjective has the same meaning for both groups. For example, in Romans 5:18, St. Paul says "all men" are condemned by one (Adam), and "all men" are justified by one (Christ). The "all" of the condemned means *all*, while the "all" of the justified, ten words later, means *many*.[76] Finally, if Kielar insists that the "any" (in "any should perish") refers to the elect only, then his argument proves too much. That is, he must conclude that God does not want the reprobate "to return to penance," since they would be necessarily excluded from this injunction (v. 9). If that were true, then God positively wills (not just permits) the damnation of some, and this is repugnant to His infinite justice.

If the Calvinist wants a proper interpretation of 2 Peter 3:9, he should refer to the words of John Calvin himself. Unlike what today's Calvinists argue, Calvin says the following about 2 Peter 3:9:

> And as to the duration of the whole world, we must think exactly the same as of the life of every individual; for God by prolonging time to each, sustains him that he may repent. In the like manner he does not hasten the end of the world, *in order to give to all* time to repent. This is a

---

76. Kielar also argues that the *pas* in "all (*pas*) should return to penance" means *many*, which then defines the preceding *tis* ("any") as *many*. This is another example of reading one's theology into the text. As we have seen, *pas* often means *all* and not *many*, depending on the context (e.g., Romans 3:23: "For all (*pas*) have sinned, and do need the glory of God").

very necessary admonition, so that we may learn to employ time aright, as we shall otherwise suffer a just punishment for our idleness. "Not willing that any should perish." So wonderful is his love towards mankind, that he would have them *all to be saved*, and is of his own self prepared to bestow salvation *on the lost*. But the order is to be noticed, that God is ready to receive *all to repentance*, so that *none may perish*; for in these words the way and manner of obtaining salvation is pointed out. Every one of us, therefore, who is desirous of salvation, must learn to enter in by this way.[77]

JOHN 3:16: WHOEVER BELIEVES IN HIM MAY NOT PERISH BUT HAVE EVERLASTING LIFE

Most Christians know John 3:16; it is one of the most memorized passages in Scripture. Far fewer Christians know that there are competing interpretations of the verse. Arminians use this text to prove God's universal will to save all men, whereas Calvinists use it to prove God's will to save only His elect. Arminians also use this text to deny unconditional election; Calvinists, to prove unconditional election. Let's take a look at the verse in its native context. We begin at verse 14, which is toward the end of Jesus' discourse with Nicodemus, and finish at verse 19.

And as Moses lifted up the serpent in the desert, so must the Son of man be lifted up: That whosoever believeth in him, may not perish; but may have life everlasting. For God so loved the world, as to give his only begotten Son; that whosoever believeth in him, may not perish, but may have life everlasting. For God sent not his Son into the world, to judge the world, but that the world may be saved by him. He that believeth in him is not judged. But he that doth not believe, is already judged: because he believeth not in the name of the only begotten Son of God. And this is the judgment: because the light is come into the world, and men loved darkness rather than the light: for their works were evil.

As we see at the beginning of the passage, Jesus draws a parallel between His being lifted up on the Cross with Moses' lifting up the brass serpent in the

77. Calvin, *Commentary on 2 Peter 3:9* (emphasis added).

desert. As Moses "lifted up the serpent in the desert, so must the Son of man be lifted up" (v. 14). God instructed Moses to make the brass serpent to spare from physical death those who had been bitten by serpents. God said, "[W]hosoever being struck shall look on it, shall live" (Num. 21:8). Now, those who believe in Jesus and look upon Him raised on the Cross will be spared from spiritual death: "That whosoever believeth in him, may not perish; but may have life everlasting" (v. 15). Verse 15 begins with the *hina* conjunction ("That"), which means "in order that." This clause connects verses 14 and 15 and means that the purpose of Jesus being raised on the Cross is to save those who believe in Him.

Here is where it begins to get contentious. Translating the Koine Greek, verse 15 literally says "in order that every the one believing in him may be having life eternal."[78] Based on the original language, Arminians claim that this phrase demonstrates God's universal will to save all men. Catholics certainly agree insofar as this reflects God's antecedent will to save all, and not His consequent will to permit some to fall away. The Greek for "every one believing" is *pas ho pisteuo* (*pas*—every; *ho*—the; *pisteuo*—one believing). We have seen that *pas* often means every single one. Moreover, the Septuagint translation of "whosoever" in Numbers 21:8 is *anthropon pas,* which means "every man." This is essentially the same construction as the *pas anthropos* of 1 Timothy 2:4. Thus, Arminians have a good case for their interpretation.

Calvinists respond by correctly pointing out that Moses was dealing with God's chosen people of Israel, not every man who ever lived. Numbers 21:10 even refers to those in Numbers 21:8-9 as "the children of Israel." Even so, it is extremely likely that most of the carnal Israelites did look upon the serpent and were healed, while only a remnant of them were actually saved. Scripture indicates that most (if not all) of the Israelites were healed, for right after they regained their strength, they conquered kings Sehon and Og (Num. 21:21-35).

This being the case, Jesus' use of this parallel suggests that *more* people believe in Jesus during their lives *than are actually saved by Him* (just as more Israelites were cured by the serpent than were saved). The participial construction, "every the one believing" (*pas ho pisteuo*), supports this conclusion.[79] One must

---

78. The Greek transliteration is "*hina pas ho pisteuo en autos echo zoe aionios.*"

79. *Pas ho pisteuo* is a present active nominative participle that, as already stated, literally means "every the one believing." The article *ho* coupled with the participle *pisteuo* makes *pisteuo* function as a verbal noun. The "believing one" is someone who has abiding faith. But the construc-

have ongoing, abiding faith in Christ to "have life everlasting." This means that the "whosoever" in John 3:15 applies to all men—including the reprobate—and not to the elect only as Calvinists maintain (although, as we will see below, it does not mean that God loves everyone the same way).[80]

The next verse begins with "For God so loved the world" (v. 16). The word "For" (*gar*) is a transitive conjunction that in biblical Greek is used to explain the preceding context. That is, *gar* connects the objects ("whosoever believeth") of verse 15 with the action ("For God so loved") of verse 16. This means that people "believeth" in Christ *because God loves them*. As we have seen, God's love is the cause of goodness in things, including the gift of faith. Those who love God do so because God "first hath loved us" (1 John 4:19) and gives us the power to love Him. We also note that the verb "loved" (*agapao*) in verse 16 is in the aorist tense, which emphasizes that God has eternally decreed His love. This is the same tense verb God uses to describe His predilect love for the prenatal Jacob in Romans 9:13: "Jacob I have loved (*agapao*)." Thus, in verse 16, we see the principle of divine predilection: "For God so *loved* the world . . ."

We also note that the "so" in the phrase "For God *so* loved" is the adverb *houtos*, which precedes the conjunction *gar*.[81] The use of the adverb *houtos* makes the verb *agapao* more emphatic. It emphasizes the highest possible degree of God's love for man. As St. Thomas teaches, "Now, that the Son of God took to Himself flesh from the Virgin's womb was due to the *exceeding love* of God: wherefore it is said (John 3:16): God so loved the world as to give His only-begotten Son."[82] God manifested His exceeding love for man through the Cross of Christ: "Greater love than this no man hath, that a man lay down his life for his friends" (John 15:13). The adverb *houtos* reveals both the intense degree of God's love for man and the manner in which God expresses His love for man. Hence, the adverb is best translated as "thusly."

This means that the beginning of verse 16 literally reads, "For God thusly loved the world." The relationship between verses 15 and 16 underscores that God's exceeding love *precedes* election and predestination. Because He loves the

---

tion does not guarantee that the person will always be a believer. Of course, God causes His elect to persevere in faith. Nevertheless, nothing in the text limits the gift of faith to the elect.

80. The Council of Valence also concluded that John 3:16 refers to all men based on its interpretation of Numbers 21 (just as Moses raised the serpent to heal all the Israelites, Christ was raised on the Cross to save all men). See Denz., 323.

81. The transliteration of "For God so loved the world" is *houtos gar agapao ho theos ho kosmos*.

82. ST, Pt III, Q 32, Art 1 (emphasis added).

world, He "thusly" gives His only begotten Son to save the world. God decrees His love in eternity and implements His predestination plan in time. As St. Thomas teaches, "For His will, by which in loving He wishes good to someone, is the cause of that good possessed by some in preference to others. Thus it is clear that love precedes election in the order of reason, and election precedes predestination. When all the predestinate are objects of election and love."[83]

The object of God's "love" in John 3:16 is the "world." What does it mean that "God so loved the world?" It cannot mean that God loves everyone the same way, as many Arminians claim, for if that were true, then God would predestine everyone to heaven. We continually recall St. Thomas's teaching: "For since God's love is the cause of goodness in things . . . no one thing would be better than another, if God did not will greater good for one than for another."[84] The reason why the elect persevere unto salvation and the reprobate fall away from salvation is because God wills the elect a greater good. The elect are better than the reprobate because God makes them better and, hence, loves them more. St. Thomas is clear on this point when he says, "It must needs be, according to what has been said before, that God loves more the better things."[85]

But neither does John 3:16 mean that God doesn't love all men in some way, as certain Calvinists maintain. Such a view not only contradicts the plain meaning of the verse but also contradicts Wisdom 11:25, which says, "For God lovest all the things that are." God loves "the things that are" because all existing things are good, and God's love is the cause of all good. Thus, St. Thomas says, "To every existing thing, then, God wills some good. Hence, since to love anything is nothing else than to will good to that thing, it is manifest that God loves everything that exists."[86] As we will see in the next chapter, because God loves all men, He gives all men the grace to be saved: To the elect, efficacious grace, which ensures their salvation; to the reprobate, sufficient grace, which they reject to their own damnation.

St. John's use of the word "world" (Greek, *kosmos*) in John 3:16 must, therefore, be interpreted in its context. St. John uses *kosmos* 58 times in his gospel, and 21 times in his epistles and the Apocalypse, with many different mean-

83. ST, Pt I, Q 23, Art 4.
84. ST, Pt I, Q 20, Art 3.
85. ST, Pt I, Q 20, Art 4.
86. ST, Pt I, Q 20, Art 2.

ings. He uses it to describe believers,[87] unbelievers,[88] everyone,[89] the earth or earthly matters,[90] the general public,[91] or in hyperbole.[92] He even uses *kosmos* in seemingly contradictory ways within related passages. For example, in John 17:11, he records Jesus' reference to His chosen ones when He says, "[T]hese are in the world." But three verses later, in John 17:14, Jesus says, "[T]hey are not of the world" in reference to the same chosen ones. Many more examples could be provided, but the point is clear: St. John uses "world" in many different ways depending on the context.

So what is the meaning of "world" in John 3:16? We have learned that the "whosoever believeth in him" (*pas ho pisteuo*) of John 3:15 refers to all men and not the elect only. Literally, "every the one believing" must have an abiding faith to have life everlasting, and not all who believe in Christ are saved (just as not all the Israelites who looked on the serpent were saved).[93] God's love for the "world" in verse 16 must include the reprobate, because God's love is the cause of faith and because the reprobate can have faith before falling away. The "world" includes all men under the penalty of sin and death. This also means that the "whosoever believeth" in verse 16 has the same meaning as in verse 15.[94] This conclusion is consistent with St. Thomas's teaching that God loves all men because He wills them some good, but that He loves His elect more than the reprobate because He wills them a greater good. It is also consistent with the teaching of the Council of Valence: "Omnipotent God wishes *all men* without exception to be saved."

We also note that St. John uses "world" not only in verse 16, but also three times in verse 17 and one time in verse 19. Thus, St. John uses "world" five times in four verses. In verse 17, St. John says, "For God sent not his Son into the world, to judge the world, but that the world may be saved by him." In other

---

87. See John 1:9, 29; 3:16-17; 4:42; 6:33, 51; 8:12, 26; 9:5; 11:9; 12:46-47; 14:31; 17:6, 21, 23; 1 John 2:2; 4:9, 14; 5:4-5.

88. See John 7:7; 8:23; 9:39; 12:31; 14:17, 22, 30; 15:18-19; 16:8, 11, 20; 17:9, 14-16, 25; 1 John 3:1, 13; 5:19.

89. See John 1:10, 29; 3:16-17, 19; 4:42; 6:14, 33, 51; 8:12, 26; 11:9; 12:46-47; 14:22, 31; 17:21, 23; 1 John 2:2; 4:9, 14.

90. See John 1:10; 8:23; 9:5, 39; 10:36; 11:27; 12:25; 13:1; 14:19, 27; 15:19; 16:21, 28, 33; 17:5, 11-12; 17:16, 18, 24; 18:36-37; 1 John 2:15-17; 3:13, 17; 4:3-5, 17; 5:4-5; 2 John 1:7; Apoc. 11:15; 13:8; 17:8.

91. John 7:4; 8:26; 9:39; 17:13; 18:20.

92. John 12:19; 21:25.

93. We are going to demonstrate how regenerated sinners can fall away from the faith in chapter 5.

94. The identical Greek phrase *pas ho pisteuo* is used in both verses.

words, Christ came to save and not to condemn (that is, not to positively will damnation, only permit it). Because Christ will judge every single man in the "world," it also follows that Christ came into the "world" to save every single man in the "world," according to the antecedent will of God. Thus, in John 3:17, St. John seems to use "world" inclusively, as we concluded above. Further, in John 3:19, St. John says, "[T]he light is come into the world, and men loved darkness rather than the light." Because the reprobate, who are in the world, rejected the light that came into it, it also follows that "world" in John 3:19 includes the reprobate.

EZECHIEL 18:32 AND 33:11: GOD DOES NOT DESIRE THE DEATH OF THE WICKED

Let's finish this chapter by briefly turning to the Old Testament. In the book of the prophet Ezechiel, God also reveals his desire to save sinners from perishing. Making His will known in very plain language, in chapter 18 God says through the prophet: "For I desire not the death of him that dieth, saith the Lord God, return ye and live" (v. 32). In chapter 33, God similarly says: "As I live, saith the Lord God, I desire not the death of the wicked, but that the wicked turn from his way, and live. Turn ye, turn ye from your evil ways: and why will you die, O house of Israel?" (v. 11).[95]

These passages are clearly about God's will to save sinners. The Septuagint reveals that the language God uses in Ezechiel is similar to the principal New Testament passages that reveal His will and desire to save men. For example, the Greek word for God's willing (*thelo*) in Ezechiel 18:32 is the same word God uses in 1 Timothy 2:4 (*thelo*) to express His will that all men be saved. Also, the Greek word for God's desiring (*boulomai*) in Ezechiel 33:11 is the same word He uses in 2 Peter 3:9 (*boulomai*) to express His desire that no man perish.

As we have seen with other passages, the Calvinist interprets these passages in Ezechiel as applying only to the elect. As with 2 Peter 3:9, because God is urging their repentance, the passages must be about the unbelieving elect, but the elect nevertheless. To support this contention, the Calvinist correctly points out that God in these passages repeatedly refers to the "house of Israel."[96] Thus,

---

95. See also Ez. 3:20 and Wis. 1:13.
96. Ez. 18:6, 15, 25, 29-31; 33:7, 10-11, 20.

---

the Calvinist concludes that God's will to save men applies only to God's chosen people (similar to our analysis of Numbers 21). As we have stated before, this conclusion is true insofar as the passage is about God's consequent will. But again, nothing in these passages precludes them from being about God's antecedent will to save all men, and His gift of sufficient grace to all.

While God is speaking to the house of Israel, we know from other scriptures that He saves only a remnant of them. Thus, as with 2 Peter 3:9, Ezechiel's actual audience includes the reprobate as well.[97] The Calvinist will respond by saying that God requires a "general call" of repentance to all men according to His "perceptive" will because the elect are unknown. But Scripture never makes an *a priori* distinction between a "general" call and a "specific" call to sinners, nor does it distinguish the calls *a posteriori* based on results. Moreover, if God is not actually imploring the reprobate to repent and giving them the grace to do so, then His pleadings are lies and He positively wills their damnation. It would be as if God were taunting the reprobate for being unable to do something He never gave them the power to do.

It is true that God gives more to the elect than to the reprobate. No one thing would be better than another without being loved more by God.[98] While God loves all men, He has a special love for the elect and infallibly ensures their salvation. However, God does not command the reprobate to do the impossible. Although the call becomes efficacious for the elect and not for the reprobate because of God's eternal decree, this does not mean that God gave no grace to the reprobate to enable them to respond. Again, if that were true, God's pleadings to "[b]e converted, and do penance for all your iniquities" (Ez. 18:30) would be superfluous. We will explore this major distinction between Catholicism and Calvinism in greater detail in chapter 4.

God's revelations through Ezechiel pose a further anomaly for the Calvinist. We recall that Calvinists believe Ezechiel is pleading with the unbelieving elect. Calvinists also believe that once God regenerates the unbelieving elect, they become the believing elect and can never fall from salvation. If that were true, then God doesn't have the same audience in mind as the Calvinist. Look at what God says: "For when the just turneth himself away from his justice, and

---

97. This seems especially evident in the various passages where God threatens judgment and says, "I will requite their way upon their head" (9:10; see also 7:27; 18:30; 24:14; 33:20; 36:19).

98. Note how God says, "It is not for your sake that I will do this, O house of Israel, but for my holy name's sake" (Ez. 36:22; see also Ez. 36:32). This verse supports our position that God predestines based on divine election ("My sake") and not human merits ("not your sake").

committeth iniquity, he shall die therein" (18:26). God also says, "For when the just shall depart from his justice, and commit iniquities, he shall die in them" (33:18); and "all his justices shall be forgotten, and in his iniquity which he hath committed, in the same shall he die" (33:13). If God is addressing the elect, as the Calvinist claims, this clearly means the elect can fall away after regeneration and die in their sins. This of course is impossible, because God efficaciously wills the elect's salvation.

The Calvinist is forced to argue that the "just man" in Ezechiel 18 and 33 is unregenerate but still in the elect. The scriptures defeat such an argument. In these and other passages in Ezechiel, God uses the Greek verb *dikaioo*, which describes the salutary acts of a justified person, and the noun *dikaiosune*, which describes the person's state of justification.[99] These are the same words that St. Paul uses to describe the righteousness of justification throughout his epistle to the Romans.[100] For example, in Romans 4:3, St. Paul refers to Genesis 15:6 where it says, "Abraham believed God, and it was reputed to him unto justice (*dikaiosune*)." God uses this same word to describe the justified man in Ezechiel 18 and 33. There is simply no exegetical, grammatical, lexical, or contextual basis to argue that the "just man" in Ezechiel is not currently justified and saved. And yet God reveals that such a man can "turneth himself away from his justice, and commit iniquity" and be condemned.

If the justified man in Ezechiel 18 and 33 can lose his salvation, then God is not addressing the elect exclusively. He is addressing in these passages both the elect and the reprobate. This means that God's desire to save the sinner from death applies to all men and not just the elect. Thus, these passages can be interpreted to reflect God's antecedent will that not "any should perish, but that all should return to penance" (2 Pet. 3:9). This exegesis also demonstrates that one who is justified by regeneration can lose his justification, an idea that is inimical to Calvinist theology (more on this in chapter 5).

We also mention that God speaks through Ezechiel with a view toward the New Covenant. For example, God says, "And I will make a covenant of peace with them, it shall be an everlasting covenant with them."[101] They will enter the

---

99. See, for example, the Septuagint's translation of Ez. 18:24, 26; 33:13, 18 (*dikaiosune*) and Ez. 33:13 (*dikaio*).

100. Rom. 1:17; 2:13; 3:26; 5:7, 19; 7:12 (*dikaio*); Rom. 1:17; 3:5, 21-22, 25-26; 4:3, 5-6, 9, 11, 13, 22; 5:17, 21; 6:13, 19-20; 8:10; 9:28, 30-31; 10:3-6, 10; 14:17 (*dikaiosune*).

101. Ez. 37:26; see also Ez. 16:60, 62; 34:25; 37:19.

New Covenant through baptism,[102] their priests will offer sacrifice,[103] and they will be governed by one shepherd (34:23). The New Covenant, of course, would be established by the atoning death of Jesus Christ. On that day, "I will cover the sun with a cloud, and the moon shall not give her light. I will make all the lights of heaven to mourn over thee: and I will cause darkness upon thy land, saith the Lord God, when thy wounded shall fall in the midst of the land, saith the Lord God" (32:7-8). In light of God's will to save all men through the New Covenant, this is a great place to begin examining the distinction between sufficient and efficacious grace. We do so in the next two chapters.

---

102. Ez. 36:25; 36:33; 37:23; 39:29.
103. Ez. 37:26-27; 41:22; 42:13-14; 43:18; 44:16, 29; 46:13 (these verses reveal prototypes of the New Covenant sacrificial system).

3

God's Gift of Efficacious Grace

Now that we have an understanding of God's antecedent and consequent wills, we examine in detail the mystery of efficacious grace. Let's review what we have presented thus far. With sufficient grace, God gives man the *power* to perform the salutary act; with efficacious grace, God actually *causes* man to freely perform the act (although God doesn't coerce man; man remains free). With sufficient grace, man's power to perform the salutary act remains in potency and is never actualized (because God allows man to resist the grace). With efficacious grace, man's power to *resist* the grace is in potency and is never actualized (because God moves man to freely respond to the grace).[1] With the latter, the grace is intrinsically efficacious; with the former, it is inefficacious but truly sufficient. This means that God is the cause of all good and salvation, and man is responsible for all evil and damnation.

Because God grants grace according to the eternal decrees of His will, Thomists generally hold that the antecedent will is the principle of sufficient grace, and the consequent will is the principle of efficacious grace.[2] In His antecedent will, God wills all men to be saved and thus gives all men sufficient grace to that end (God considers each person absolutely). But in view of the greater good of the universe, He consequently wills to infallibly save His elect, and to permit the reprobate to be damned (God considers each person relative to the whole). It follows that the good that God antecedently wills, and the sufficient grace He grants to all men, are not efficacious, whereas His consequent

---

1. We recall that Molinism and Arminianism deny that grace is intrinsically efficacious, holding instead that it is extrinsically efficacious by virtue of man's cooperation. Such a concept renders God determined and not determining, which is incompatible with God who is pure Act.

2. See, for example, Garrigou-LaGrange, *Predestination*, pp. 74, 80. While this may be a helpful way to understand the distinction, God's consequent will determines both election and reprobation.

will and the related grace He eternally decrees for His elect are efficacious. Thus, St. Thomas says, "[I]t is clear that whatever God simply [consequently] wills takes place; although what He wills antecedently may not take place."[3]

Because God unconditionally elects man to salvation based on His decree and not foreseen merits, man does not determine the type of grace he receives. God has decreed the grace He would bestow upon man from all eternity. As St. Paul says, "Or what hast thou that thou hast not received?" (1 Cor. 4:7). St. Thomas comments on this verse: "Who is it that distinguisheth thee from the mass of those who are lost? This is more than thou canst do. Who is it that makes thee superior to another? Thou thyself canst not do this, and therefore why art thou proud of thyself?"[4] That one man receives sufficient grace, and another man efficacious grace, must be sought for in the will of God, not man. St. Thomas further explains:

> Hence the first cause of this diversity is to be sought on the part of God, Who dispenses His gifts of grace variously, in order that the beauty and perfection of the Church may result from these various degrees; even as He instituted various conditions of things, that the universe might be perfect.[5]

Just as God decrees man's end independently of anything in man, so He decrees the means to that end independently of anything in man. Thus, when Scripture says "God is not a respecter of persons" (Acts 10:34), it means there is nothing in man that determines his election, outside of what God willed to give him. God decrees His predestination plan in eternity, and implements the plan in time. God does this by granting man sufficient and efficacious graces.[6] In this way, God orders all men to their end for His greater glory and for the perfection of the universe.

Because God predestines the elect "according to the purpose of his will" (Eph. 1:5), St. Thomas explains efficacious grace in terms of the efficacy of the

---

3. ST, Pt I, Q 19, Art 6.

4. *Commentary on 1 Cor. 4:7*.

5. ST, Pt I-II, Q 112, Art 4.

6. As we have said, anyone (predestined or reprobated) who performs a salutary act does so by the power of efficacious grace. But the elect alone receive the efficacious grace of final perseverance.

divine will.[7] Put very simply, if God wills someone to receive grace efficaciously, that person will infallibly receive it. St. Thomas says, "Hence if God intends, while moving, that the one whose heart He moves should attain to grace, he will infallibly attain to it, according to John 6:45: Every one that hath heard the Father, and hath learned, cometh to Me."[8] St. Thomas also says, "Since, then, the will of God is the universal cause of all things, it is impossible that the divine will should not produce its effect."[9] This, of course, refers to God's consequent or simple will. St. Thomas echoes St. Augustine's famous teaching that "by God's good gifts whoever is liberated, is most certainly liberated."[10]

St. Thomas's teachings are consistent with the scriptures that reveal that nothing can resist God's will: "O Lord, Lord, almighty king, for all things are in thy power, and there is none that can resist thy will" (Esth. 13:9); "Thou art Lord of all, and there is none that can resist thy majesty (Esth. 13:11); "But our God is in heaven: he hath done all things whatsoever he would" (Ps. 113:11); "As the divisions of waters, so the heart of the king is in the hand of the Lord: whithersoever he will he shall turn it" (Prov. 21:1).

We also recall St. Paul's rhetorical questions in Romans 9: "Thou wilt say therefore to me: Why doth he then find fault? for who resisteth his will?" (v. 19); and also Joseph of the Old Testament: "Fear not: can we resist the will of God?" (Gen. 50:19); and David: "Thou art terrible, and who shall resist thee?" (Ps. 75:8); and Solomon: "who shall resist the strength of thy arm?" (Wis. 11:22); and, God Himself: "I will stir him up, like one that is cruel: for who can resist my countenance?" (Job 41:1). This means that when God wills a person to perform a salutary act (e.g., prayer, good works), He grants him the means (an efficacious grace) that infallibly produces the end (the act willed by God). If God wills to permit a person to resist His grace, He grants him a sufficient, and not an efficacious, grace.[11]

---

7. Fr. Most claims that St. Thomas never taught the distinction between sufficient and efficacious grace just because he didn't use those terms specifically in ST, Pt I-II, Q 111 where he divides grace into many categories. This is a misleading attempt to prove the erroneous view that there is only one kind of grace. First, St. Thomas does describe sufficient and efficacious graces in terms of their operating and cooperating effects (ST, Pt I-II, Q 111, Art 2) and in terms of God's antecedent and consequent wills (ST, Pt I, Q 19, Art 6). Second, St. Thomas *does* use the terminology "sufficient" and "efficacious" (or "effective") throughout his works to describe the effects of grace procured by Christ's Passion (see, for example, ST, Pt III, Q 79, Art 2; Pt I-II, Q 106, Art 2; CG, 4.55; *De veritate*, Q 29, Art 7; III *Sent*. d. 13, Q 2, Art 2; *Commentary on 1 Tim. 2:5*).

8. ST, Pt I-II, Q 112, Art 3.

9. ST, Pt I, Q 19, Art 6.

10. Ibid., citing *De Dono Persev.* xiv.

11. As we have seen, God wills to permit the elect to resist sufficient grace to spiritually heal

Moreover, God's efficacious will causes things to be done precisely the way He wants them done, as St. Thomas says: "From the very fact that nothing resists the divine will, it follows that not only those things happen that God wills to happen, but that they happen necessarily or contingently according to His will."[12] St. Thomas also says, "Since then the divine will is perfectly efficacious, it follows not only that things are done, which God wills to be done, but also that they are done in the way that He wills. Now God wills some things to be done necessarily, some things contingently, to the right ordering of things, for the building up of the universe."[13] In the mystery of God's providence, all things happen according to God's simple will. For the elect, who receive the efficacious grace of final perseverance, "all things work together unto good, to such as, according to his purpose, are called to be saints" (Rom. 8:28).

Many Protestants falsely believe that Catholics try to "earn" their salvation by good works. Such a view demonstrates a profound misunderstanding of efficacious grace and the power of God's will (not to mention Catholic teaching). Whenever we do anything beneficial to our salvation (faith, works, prayer), it is God's efficacious grace working in us to produce the result. While God requires both faith and works for salvation, He brings about our faith and works by His efficacious grace. St. Paul states this clearly when he says, "For it is God who worketh in you, both to will and to accomplish, according to his good will."[14] As we saw in Romans 9:21, because we are merely clay in the potter's hands, St. Paul says, "But we have this treasure in earthen vessels, that the excellency may be of the power of God, and not of us" (1 Cor. 4:7). Thus, St. Augustine rightly says that "God does not crown your merits as your merits, but as His gifts."[15] In quoting St. Augustine, the Catechism also says, "God brings to completion in us what he has begun, 'since he who completes his work by cooperating with our will began by working so that we might will it'" (CCC 2001).

Elsewhere in Scripture, St. Paul emphasizes the intrinsic efficacy of grace working within us. For example, St. Paul says, "Not that we are sufficient to think anything of ourselves, as of ourselves: but our sufficiency is from God"

---

them, and the reprobate to resist sufficient grace to spiritually blind them. ST, Pt I-II, Q 79, Art 4.

12. ST, Pt I, Q 19, Art 8.

13. Ibid.

14. Phil. 2:13. Notice that St. Paul says "according to his good will," and not according to foreseen merits or anything else in us.

15. *De gratia et libero arbitrio*, 6.15. Many such quotes from St. Augustine could be provided. See also CCC 2009.

(1 Cor. 3:5). He also says, "But by the grace of God, I am what I am; and his grace in me hath not been void, but I have labored more abundantly than all they: yet not I, but the grace of God with me" (1 Cor. 15:10). St. Paul is clear that God both begins and completes the salutary act for us by His grace: "Being confident of this very thing, that he, who hath begun a good work in you, will perfect it unto the day of Christ Jesus" (Phil. 1:6); for He "is able to do all things more abundantly than we desire or understand, according to the power that worketh in us" (Eph. 3:20). St. Paul also says, "Wherein also I labor, striving according to his working which he worketh in me in power" (Col. 1:29). When God so wills, man is "not able to resist the wisdom and the spirit" (Acts 6:10). Because "Christ liveth in me," St. Paul is able to say, "I cast not away the grace of God" (Gal. 2:20-21). Isaias also attributes our good works to God, not man: "Lord, thou wilt give us peace: for thou hast wrought all our works for us" (Isa. 26:12).

St. Paul reveals that God is able to direct a man to salvation if He so wills it: "The Lord hath delivered me from every evil work: and will preserve me unto his heavenly kingdom, to whom be glory for ever and ever. Amen;"[16] and, "To his own lord he standeth or falleth. And he shall stand: for God is able to make him stand" (Rom. 14:4). St. Jude similarly says, "Now to him who is able to preserve you without sin, and to present you spotless before the presence of his glory with exceeding joy, in the coming of our Lord Jesus Christ" (Jude 24). St. Peter also reveals that the elect "by the power of God, are kept by faith unto salvation, ready to be revealed in the last time" (1 Pet. 1:5). David also says, "For the Lord loveth judgment, and will not forsake his saints: they shall be preserved forever" (Ps. 36:28).

In the Book of Ezechiel, after revealing the promise of baptism (36:25), God tells us how His Spirit can change the heart of man and *cause* him to obey His commandments: "And I will give you a new heart, and put a new spirit within you: and I will take away the stony heart out of your flesh, and will give you a heart of flesh. And I will put my spirit in the midst of you: and I will cause you to walk in my commandments, and to keep my judgments, and do them" (36:26-27). The Lord also revealed to Moses: "The Lord thy God will circumcise they heart, and the heart of thy seed: that thou mayst love the Lord thy God with all thy heart and with all thy soul, that thou mayst live" (Deut.

---

16. 2 Tim. 4:18. God presumably gave St. Paul a revelation of his own election, perhaps when he was raptured into heaven (1 Cor. 12:1-6).

30:6). David also says, "Create a clean heart in me, O God: and renew a right spirit within my bowels" (Ps. 51:12). These and countless other scriptures reveal how the power of God's efficacious grace works in man to produce the result that God wills.

The particular councils of the Church reveal the intrinsic efficacy of certain grace and man's complete dependence on such grace. For example, canon 9 of the Council of Orange (529), entitled *The Assistance of God*, says, "It is a divine gift, both when we think rightly and when we restrain our feet from falsity and injustice; for as often as we do good, God operates in us and with us, that we may work."[17] In canon 16, the Council says, "Let no one glory in that which he seems to possess, as if he did not receive [it] . . . Whoever has, has from Him, but whoever denies that he has from Him, either does not truly possess, or that, which he possesses, is taken away from him [Matt. 25:29]."[18]

In canon 20, entitled *That Without God Man Can Do No Good*, the Council of Orange says, "God does many good things in man, which man does not do; indeed man can do no good that God does not expect that man do."[19] In canon 22, the same Council says, "No one has anything of his own except lying and sin. But if man has any truth and justice, it is from that fountain for which we ought to thirst in this desert, that bedewed by some drops of water from it, we may not falter on the way."[20] The Council of Sens (1140) condemned the idea that "free will is sufficient in itself for any good."[21] The Ecumenical Council of Trent also condemns the position that man can persevere "without a special help of God."[22]

THE WILL REMAINS FREE

While God works in man both to will and to accomplish His end, man remains free under the influence of efficacious grace. This is because man's will by nature is free, and God's grace works upon nature.[23] Thus, efficacious grace does not compel man's will, such as many Calvinists believe; but neither does its efficacy

17. Denz., 182; quoting St. Prosper.
18. Denz., 189; quoting St. Prosper.
19. Denz., 193; quoting St. Prosper.
20. Denz., 194, quoting St. Prosper.
21. Denz., 373; condemnation of the errors of Peter Abelard.
22. Denz., 832.
23. We will look at the Calvinist understanding of free will and man's "total depravity" later in the book. As we will see, while man's will is wounded by sin, it is free to perform natural good, and God's grace moves it to perform supernatural good.

depend on man's will, such as most Arminians believe. Rather, efficacious grace elicits the freedom of the will, so that man freely chooses the good and does not want to resist. As David says, "The Lord God hath opened my ear, and I do not resist" (Ps. 50:5). The Catechism also says, "the divine initiative in the work of grace precedes, prepares, *and elicits* the free response of man."[24] In other words, this grace perfects the will so that it chooses the good God created it to desire and possess. St. Thomas rightly describes the effect of efficacious grace on the will: "God moves the will immutably on account of the efficacy of the moving power which cannot fail; but on account of the nature of the will that is moved, which is indifferently disposed to various things, the will is not necessitated but *remains free*."[25]

St. Thomas also says, "God therefore, is the first cause, Who moves causes both natural and voluntary. And just as by moving natural causes He does not prevent their acts being natural, so by moving voluntary causes *He does not deprive their actions of being voluntary*: but rather is He the cause of this very thing in them; for He operates in each thing according to its own nature."[26] St. Thomas also says, "God changes the will without forcing it. But He can change the will from the fact that He Himself operates in the will as He does in nature."[27] He also says, "Only ... God can move the will as an agent without violence"[28] and, "Always ... does man choose this thing, according as God works in his will."[29]

In canon 4 on justification, the Council of Trent declares that man does not remain passive under the influence of justifying grace: "If anyone shall say that man's free will moved and aroused by God does not cooperate by assenting to God who rouses and calls, whereby it disposes and prepares itself to obtain the grace of justification; and that it cannot dissent, if it wishes, but that like something inanimate it does nothing at all and is merely in a passive state: let him be anathema."[30] In canon 23, the Council of Orange further says that when men serve the divine will, "*willingly* they do what they do, nevertheless, it is the will of Him by whom what they will is both prepared and ordered."[31]

24. CCC 2022 (emphasis added).
25. *De malo*, Q 6, Art 1 (emphasis added).
26. ST, Pt I, Q 83, Art 1 (emphasis added).
27. *De veritate*, 22:9.
28. CG, 3.88-89.
29. CG, 3.92.
30. Denz., 814.
31. Denz., 196; quoting St. Prosper (emphasis added).

St. Thomas divides efficacious grace into operating grace and cooperating grace, which are the two effects of the same efficacious grace. With operating grace, God moves man's mind to will the good. This interior movement of the will is entirely the work of God who is Prime Mover and First Agent of all being and action. Thus, St. Thomas says, "Hence in that effect in which our mind is moved and does not move, but in which God is the sole mover, the operation is attributed to God, and it is with reference to this that we speak of operating grace."[32] The Catechism also says that God "touches and directly moves the heart of man" (CCC 2002). Thus, all of our holy desires are caused by God's efficacious will and not our will, and solely because of His mercy and not our foreseen merits. As St. Thomas says, "[A]ll man's good is from God."[33] This is why St. Paul says, "So then it is not of him that willeth, nor of him that runneth, but of God that sheweth mercy" (Rom. 9:16).

With cooperating grace, God's operating movement causes man to freely choose the good that God wills for him. Because man is freely choosing the good, the operation can, in a sense, be attributable to man.[34] However, man is able to choose the good only because God continues to operate in his will, making him capable of performing the act. St. Thomas explains that "because God assists us in this act, both by strengthening our will interiorly so as to attain to the act, and by granting outwardly the capability of operating, it is with respect to this that we speak of cooperating grace."[35] Because the will remains free even though its movement is caused by God, St. Thomas says, "[T]he determination of the action and the end is placed in the power of free will; hence it retains its dominion over its act, though not in the same way as does the first agent."[36] As St. Paul says, God works within us, "For in him we live, and move, and are" (Acts 17:28).

Thus, God both moves man's will interiorly and makes man capable

---

32. ST, Pt I-II, Q 111, Art 2. Thomists uses the term "premotion" to describe the divine motion that moves secondary causes to act.

33. ST, Pt I-II, Q 114, Art 1.

34. We make this statement only to refute the claim that God's efficacious grace makes man an automaton or robot. It does not. Rather, efficacious grace causes man to freely desire and choose the good, which beings without free will are unable to do.

35. ST, Pt I, Q 111, Art 2.

36. 2 Sent. d.25, Q 1, Art 1, ad 3. We thus can properly understand St. Thomas's statement: "Now man is master of his actions through his reason and will" (ST, Pt I-II, Q 1, Art 1). Man is the master of his reason and will insofar as he freely chooses the good under the influence of cooperating (efficacious) grace, and freely rejects the good under the influence of operating (sufficient) grace.

outwardly of performing all salutary acts. This is why St. Paul says that God "worketh in you, both to *will* (operating grace) and to *accomplish* (cooperating grace), according to his good will" (Phil. 2:13). Salvation is the work of God, not man. As St. Thomas says, "Therefore, all movements of will and choice must be traced to the divine will: and not to any other cause, because God alone is the cause of our willing and choosing."[37] Thus, "[W]hatsoever good thing any man shall do, the same shall he receive from the Lord" (Eph. 6:8), for God "worketh all in all" (1 Cor. 12:6).

That man performs salutary acts freely is the reason why man can have merit before God. If man weren't free, St. Thomas says that "rewards and punishments would be in vain."[38] In Catholic theology, the word *merit* (or *reward*) means "deserving justly," and is the effect of efficacious grace. One deserves justly when he performs the work he was required to do, and this satisfies justice. However, because justice pertains to equality, and there is infinite inequality between God and man, man has no strict right to merit anything from God. Nevertheless, God rewards us on account of His gratuitous justice whenever we do His will. That is, God rewards us for doing what He gave us the power to do. This does not make God our debtor, for God lacks nothing. Rather, it gives God all the glory, for it is due to God that creatures carry out His will. St. Thomas says, "Hence we merit from God, not that by our works anything accrues to Him, but inasmuch as we work for His glory."[39]

While Thomists hold that God is the primary cause of our salutary acts and man is the subordinated secondary cause (and only because God applies man's will to act), Molina considered the primary and secondary causes as two partial and coordinated causes, like two men pulling a boat.[40] In this view, God does not move the secondary cause to act; rather, the two causes act simultaneously, and require the concurrence of each other to produce the effect. Thus, the total effect (the salutary act) is said to come from both God and man, without one being primary in causality over the other.

In light of the teachings of Scripture as explained by Church councils and St. Thomas, the Molinist position appears incorrect. If the divine motion

---

37. CG, 3.91, in *Predestination*, p. 284.
38. ST, Pt I, Q 83, Art 1.
39. ST, Pt I, Q 114, Art 1. The Catechism also says, "Man's merit, moreover, is due to God, for his good actions proceed in Christ, from the predispositions and assistance given by the Holy Spirit" (CCC 2008).
40. See, *Predestination*, p. 245.

happens simultaneously with the human action, then God is no longer the Prime Mover and the First Agent with respect to secondary causes. This would mean that something would move from potency to act while escaping God's universal causality and divine decree, which is impossible. Further, if the divine motion requires the concurrence of the human motion, then God who is pure Act is determined and not determining, which is also impossible. Finally, if God as the primary cause does not apply the will to act as a secondary cause, then some good (the human action) does not come from the Source of all good. The greater would come from the lesser. This, again, is impossible. St. Thomas properly explains the chain of causality:

> Again it is to be observed that where there are several agents in order, the second always acts in virtue of the first: for the first agent moves the second to act. And thus all agents act in virtue of God Himself: and therefore He is the cause of action in every agent.[41]

Because God is the cause of action in every agent, even man's free will determination to do good comes from God. We have seen that this determination comes entirely from God as first cause (operating grace), and from us as secondary cause (cooperating grace). St. Thomas is clear on this point: "Now there is no distinction between what flows from free will, and what is of predestination; as there is no distinction between what flows from a secondary cause and from a first cause."[42] Thus, God willed efficaciously that Mary would freely utter her fiat to become the Mother of God, and that Jesus would freely offer His life on the Cross for the forgiveness of sins. These divine actions were freely decreed and determined by God in eternity as first cause, and freely chosen by Mary and Jesus as secondary causes.[43] Both acts were free *because God efficaciously willed both acts to be performed freely*. Many other examples, of course, could be provided.

Because the will remains free and is not coerced by efficacious grace, the will truly has the power to resist the grace. Yet as we have said, this power is never actualized but remains in potency. This is why Scripture reveals that the elect have the *power* to fall away, although they do not fall away. For example,

---

41. ST, Pt I, Q 105, Art 5.
42. ST, Pt I, Q 23, Art 5.
43. The inspiration of Sacred Scripture also comes to mind. The sacred authors remained free even though they were writing under the direction and dictation of the Holy Ghost.

Jesus says, "For there shall arise false Christs and false prophets, and shall show great signs and wonders, insomuch as to deceive (if possible) the elect" (Matt. 24:24).[44] In his second letter to Timothy, St. Paul says that he "endures all things for the sake of the elect, that they also may obtain the salvation" (2 Tim. 2:10). In reference to this same elect, St. Paul then says, "If we deny him, he will also deny us. If we believe not, he continueth faithful, he can not deny himself" (v. 12). St. Paul reveals that the elect have the power to deny God, but they do not because God in His mercy prevents them from doing so. As David says, "[M]y God, his mercy shall prevent me" (Ps. 58:11).

Although Scripture is clear that God grants man grace that he resists, this refers to sufficient grace and not efficacious grace. Thus, it is incorrect to say that man's resistance of sufficient grace deprives him of efficacious grace. God wills to permit man to resist sufficient grace independently of His will to grant him efficacious grace. If God wills to grant man efficacious grace, He will grant it to him. As St. Thomas teaches, "[I]f God intends, while moving, that the one whose heart He moves should attain to grace, he will infallibly attain to it."[45] Man never determines God or the grace He gives man. Further, if resisting sufficient grace would deprive man of efficacious grace, then no one would receive efficacious grace. Why? *Because all men resist sufficient grace by sinning.* If one sins, one has resisted sufficient grace. If no one receives efficacious grace, then no one goes to heaven, for man cannot attain heaven unless God grants him the efficacious grace of final perseverance.

Molinists often argue that God deprives man of efficacious grace when he resists sufficient grace (as if man's cooperation or non-resistance, and not God's will, determined the efficacy of the grace). They often refer to the following statement by the Council of Trent (note that this statement was not part of the council's dogmatic canons): "For God, unless men be wanting in His grace, as He has begun a good work, so will He perfect it, working 'to will and to accomplish.'"[46] Trent's teaching does not say that man is deprived of efficacious grace if he resists sufficient grace. In fact, Trent's statement does not refer to man's will or conduct at all. It simply says that God perfects His work in man unless man lacks grace. God does not perfect the work He begins in man with

---

44. See also Mark 13:22. Jesus also threatens to blot the elect's names out of the "book of life" (Apoc. 3:5; 22:19), where the "book of life" refers to those predestined to glory (see ST, Pt I, Q 24, Art 1-3). This means the elect have the potency to fall away, but God preserves them in grace to the end.

45. ST, Pt I-II, Q 112, Art 3.

46. Denz., 806.

sufficient grace because man "is wanting," that is, he fails His grace by resisting it. Thus, Trent reiterates the truth that man can do no supernatural good without God's grace.

In his classic book *Predestination*, Dominican Thomist Fr. Reginald Garrigou-Lagrange appears to make this Molinist argument. Although he accurately presents the Thomistic principles on sufficient and efficacious grace, he seems to fall into the trappings of Molinism when he attempts to apply them. For example, Fr. Garrigou-Lagrange rightly says, "Grace is a gratuitous gift and God grants sufficient grace to all those who have the obligation to keep His commandments."[47] But in the next sentence, he says, "If they resist it, they merit thus to be deprived of the efficacious help which was virtually offered to them in the preceding grace."[48]

In this statement, Fr. Garrigou-Lagrange seems to say that man (his cooperation or resistance) determines God (His granting or denial of efficacious grace). Although Fr. Garrigou-Lagrange espouses the Thomist position, this particular view violates many principles of Thomism, including God as Prime Mover and divine predilection. From a Thomist perspective, "efficacious help" is determined by God's eternal decrees and not man's actions. Moreover, "efficacious help" cannot fail if it is truly efficacious. Finally, a Thomist would not say God "virtually" offers efficacious grace to man. As St. Thomas teaches, if God intends man to attain to grace, man will infallibly attain to it because of God's efficacious will.

In support of his opinion, Fr. Garrigou-Lagrange refers to St. Augustine, who says that if efficacious grace is granted to one, it is because of God's mercy; if it is refused to a certain other, it is because of His justice.[49] Although this statement is true, it does not mean that God refuses efficacious grace because of man's sin. As we have seen, Scripture says just the opposite. In Romans 9, God reveals that He has mercy on some, and exacts justice upon others, according to the purpose of His will, and not man's will. As with Jacob and Esau, God makes these determinations before we are born, and before we have done any good or evil, so that the purpose of His election might stand (see Rom. 9:11).

---

47. *Predestination*, p. 181.

48. Ibid., p. 181-182. Fr. Garrigou-Lagrange also says, "God's withdrawal of efficacious grace is a punishment" (p. 209). But efficacious grace automatically applies man's will to act, and so it is odd to speak about the "withdrawal" of efficacious grace. Further, while God does withhold grace as a punishment for sin, God alone (and not man's sin) determines the type of grace He gives man.

49. Ibid., p. 182.

This is why St. Paul says, "So then it is not of him that willeth, nor of him that runneth, but of God that sheweth mercy" (v. 16).

Fr. Garrigou-Lagrange further says that "nobody is deprived of an efficacious grace that is necessary for salvation except through his own fault" and that God refuses "efficacious grace on account of this sin."[50] It is also fair to hold these conclusions as a-Thomistic, if not erroneous, because God gives the elect the efficacious grace of final perseverance *even though they have sinned throughout their lives*. This truth demonstrates that human action (sin) is not dispositive in determining whether God grants efficacious grace.[51] Rather, God's eternal decrees determine the type of grace that He grants man. While God withholds grace out of justice, He grants efficacious grace out of His mercy. *Both* the with-holding *and* the granting of grace must be sought for in the eternal decrees of God, and *not* in the will of man.

Fr. Garrigou-Lagrange seems to confuse the distinction between sufficient and efficacious grace when he says, "[S]ufficient grace virtually contains the ef-ficacious grace that is offered to us in it, as the flower contains the fruit . . . This efficacious grace is thus within our power, though certainly not something that can be produced by us, but as a gift that would be granted to us if our will did not resist sufficient grace . . . Thus it is true to say that man is deprived of effica-cious grace because he resisted sufficient grace."[52] Like his other statements, Fr. Garrigou-Lagrange effectively says that man can convert sufficient grace into efficacious grace by his own will. St. Thomas never taught such a principle. Rather, St. Thomas teaches that "all movements of will and choice must be traced to the divine will: and not to any other cause, because God alone is the cause of our willing and choosing."[53]

Hence, efficacious grace does not depend upon man's power, but upon God's will, who "sheweth mercy." If man could make grace efficacious by his coopera-tion or non-resistance, then the good of cooperation or non-resistance would be attributable to man and not to God. God, the author of all good, would no longer produce all the good in man. Something good would escape God's divine causality, and God's efficacious will would depend upon man's will. Such a theology would necessarily hold that one man could be better than another

50. Ibid., p. 208.
51. It is correct to say that man is deprived of sufficient grace through his own fault, but not so with efficacious grace. That is because with sufficient grace, God wills to permit man to resist it, while with efficacious grace God wills man to receive it infallibly.
52. Pp. 331-333.
53. CG, 3.91.

without being loved more or helped more by God. Such a theology would also mean that man could boast in his good works and not in God. Man would be operating independently of God's eternal decrees and God would be determined, not determining. These propositions, from a Thomistic perspective, are absurd.[54]

A "MOST" UNUSUAL ALTERNATIVE

In his book, *Grace, Predestination and the Salvific Will of God*, Fr. William Most introduces a brand new theory about efficacious grace: that the *absence of a decision not to resist* makes grace efficacious.[55] Fr. Most's non-resistance theory makes the efficacy of grace conditioned upon something in man while at the same time claiming that man's non-resistance is not a salutary act. Fr. Most says, "St. Paul excluded from man's unaided power only the ability of performing or initiating any positive salutary good without grace. He did not say that man could not control whether or not he would resist grace."[56]

Thus, Fr. Most makes a distinction between a positive decision not to resist grace (which he admits is a salutary act caused by grace) and a negative, *non-decision* concerning the grace, which he claims is a non-salutary act that *also* renders grace efficacious. Notwithstanding his claims to the contrary, Fr. Most's novel theory falls into the trap of giving man—and not grace—credit for the salutary act. Thus, Fr. Most's interpretation runs afoul of St. Paul's teaching in 1 Cor. 4:7 (the Thomist interpretation of which Fr. Most rejects). Even though all good comes from God, Fr. Most's theory makes man the principal determiner of his salvation. Because he says "in this negative way he can control whether or not he attains salvation," Fr. Most declares that man is not dependent upon God for everything. Although Fr. Most claims his non-resistance theory is the proper interpretation of St. Thomas, as we will see, neither St. Thomas nor the

---

54. If one takes Fr. Garrigou-Lagrange's apparent conclusions to their logical end (that man determines grace's efficacy), one would have to conclude that man determines God's election, and not vice-versa.

55. Fr. Most's theory differs from that of Fr. Garrigou-Lagrange. Fr. Garrigou-Lagrange appears to hold that a positive decision not to resist the grace results in an efficacious grace, whereas Fr. Most holds that the absence of a decision (a "negative," non-decision) also results in an efficacious grace. Note that Fr. Most does acknowledge St. Thomas's teaching that man can respond to operating grace by his free will (a positive decision). Thus, Fr. Most's non-resistance scenario is posited as an alternative way in which grace is rendered efficacious (the absence of an evil decision).

56. GPS, p. 142.

Church has ever taught such a principle. This may be why the subtitle to Fr. Most's book is *New Answers to Old Questions*.[57]

Fr. Most describes his schema as follows:

> God first makes a decision to send to man a grace by which He wills to move a man to a specified effect.[58] Grace makes the beginning, for, as the Council of Orange says, it is not we who begin. Grace makes the beginning by presenting good to our intellect, causing it to perceive the good, and moving our will to an initial complacency in this good ... Next, a man can resist or not-resist grace. If he merely does nothing against these effects, he does not resist. He does not even make a decision: I will not resist.[59] On condition of this non-resistance, grace moves him to the positive consent, but in such a way that man becomes active too, for he is not like something passive ... Even though God begins the process and begins it with the purpose of moving a man to a specified thing, yet the first decisive step comes from man, for by his resistance or lack of resistance man really controls an outcome, an outcome which is not predetermined by God in advance of this negative determination by man.[60]

Fr. Most even goes on to say, "God does not move to positive consent until the condition of non-resistance is verified in man."[61] There are many problems with this schema from a Thomist perspective.

---

57. Fr. Most admits the novelty of his position and yet proclaims: "Is it not presumptuous for an ordinary man to think he can see the solution that was obscure or unknown to the great Saints and Doctors of the Church? The answer is: No" (p. 629). Likewise, this author does not believe it is presumptuous for a lay attorney—professionally trained to examine the written word—to humbly expose the errors of an esteemed theologian and to side with the greatest saints and doctors of the Church.

58. Thomists could stop here: God wills man to cooperate with grace, or to permit man to resist the grace. If God "wills to move a man to a specified effect," then man will be so moved.

59. Fr. Most says, "The absence of resistance of which we speak is not a positive decision or act of the will made under the form of *explicitly* making a decision to abstain from sin" (GPS, p. 6, ft 7, emphasis added). Note that such qualifying language indicates that a position is imprecise. If the decision is not explicit, does Fr. Most mean it is implicit?

60. GPS, p. 159.

61. GPS, p. 167. We cannot imagine a theory more violative of Thomism. By attributing the "decisive step" and the "outcome" to man, Fr. Most in this one sentence denies the Thomistic principles of universal causality, eternal decrees, predilection, election, and pure Act, and makes salvation ultimately the work of man. We don't believe it is too harsh to say that Fr. Most's theory is Arminian, if not Pelagian.

We first note that St. Thomas expressly disagrees with Fr. Most. St. Thomas says, "We must say that the very fact that a man does not place an obstacle proceeds from grace."[62] St. Thomas teaches that man's non-resistance is the work of grace in man, not a condition of "non-being" in man. If it is the work of grace, then God willed the non-resistance from the very beginning, because nothing escapes God's universal causality. As St. Thomas says, "Since then, all particular causes are included under the universal cause, it could not be that any effect should take place outside the range of that universal cause."[63] St. Thomas also says, "We must hold that the will of God is the cause of things."[64] Knowing these principles, Fr. Most admits that the non-resistance is "produced by grace" and that "doing nothing is sustained by grace inasmuch as grace attracts us, and maintains the two effects in our minds and wills by its own power, without any contribution from us."[65] Fr. Most also says "such an absence of resistance is merely *doing nothing*—a doing nothing that is sustained by grace itself."[66]

But these admissions are fatal to Fr. Most's theory. Because the will of God is the cause of all things[67] and God alone is the cause of grace,[68] God wills the non-resistance in man. This means "the first decisive step" does not come from man as Fr. Most argues, but from God.[69] If this weren't true, then man has something that he didn't receive from God, and man could boast in his works. Yet St. Paul says that we are saved by grace, "and that not of yourselves, for it is the gift of God: not of works, that no man may glory" (Eph. 2:8-9) and that nothing "distinguisheth thee" one from another except by God's will and intention (1 Cor. 4:7). For example, if God is not willing the non-resistance in John, but He is willing Peter to make a positive decision not to resist, then He is giving Peter more help than John, and yet the grace is efficacious for both of them.[70]

62. Cap XII. Lect. III 689, cited in GPS, p. 197.

63. ST, Pt I, Q 22, Art 2. In confirming the Council of Orange, Pope Boniface II says, "[I]t clearly appears that the faith by which we believe in Christ, just as all blessings, comes to each man from the gift of supernatural grace, not from the power of human nature." The "power of human nature" can be equated to the condition of non-resistance that is the "decisive step" in Fr. Most's theory.

64. ST, Pt I, Q 19, Art 4.

65. GPS, p. 140.

66. GPS, p. 141.

67. See ST, Pt I, Q 19, Art 4.

68. See ST, Pt I-II, Q 112, Art 1.

69. We fail to understand how non-resistance is "produced by grace" and yet the "first decisive step" of non-resistance comes from man.

70. Fr. Most admits that "it is not more glorious to use greater power so as to produce a lesser

This means John can boast in his works and claim he is intrinsically better than Peter, even though Scripture says that John's good comes from God and not from himself (and both Peter and John come from "the slime of the earth").[71] St. Thomas says, "Wherefore it cannot be said that anything begun in us can be the reason of the effect of predestination."[72] But, according to Fr. Most, non-resistance is a condition that "begun in us" (the "first decisive step") and therefore it cannot be the reason for the graces of the predestinate. Fr. Most contradicts the teaching of St. Thomas by claiming that God "positively predestines as soon as He sees that *there is not* a present condition which would require their rejection."[73] But God did not predestine Christ because there wasn't a "present condition" in Him that would have prevented His predestination. Because "Christ's predestination is the exemplar of ours"[74] (Christ who was not predestined because of non-resistance but due to God's eternal decree), Fr. Most's theory is false.

We also do not see how Fr. Most can argue that non-resistance is "non-being" because non-resistance is a condition of being (that is, the condition of man who is being). It is thus erroneous, from a metaphysical perspective, to label non-resistance in man as non-being. Rather, non-resistance in man is resistance in potency, and potency exists in being, not non-being. This is true because man has the power to resist, as Fr. Most admits. According to the spiritual axiom *agere sequitur esse* (action follows being), man, as being, either acts to cooperate with the grace (caused by God's will in the case of efficacious grace) or acts to resist the grace (caused by man's will in the case of sufficient grace).

If the resistance is not actualized, it is because God efficaciously willed to move man to freely cooperate with the grace. As Scripture says, "And how could any thing endure, if thou wouldst not? or be preserved, if not called by thee" (Wis. 11:26). Although Fr. Most says that grace is made efficacious "on condition of this non-resistance," non-being has no such influence because non-being doesn't exist. Grace operates in man on account of his being, not his non-being. As Fr. Most admits, non-resistance is an "ontological zero."[75] Grace

---

result" (GPS, p. 165), but he doesn't see the same problem with a lesser power producing the same result as a greater power.

71. See Gen. 2:7.
72. ST, Pt I, Q 23, Art 5.
73. GPS, p. 399 (emphasis in original).
74. ST, Pt III, Q 24, Art 3.
75. GPS, p. 469. Fr. Most contradicts himself when he says that "causality is not required for non-beings," and in the next sentence that "God wills that these non-beings be the condi-

also operates efficaciously in man on account of good (that is, the good that God moves man to freely choose), and not on account of evil (Fr. Most admits that "non-being" is "evil").[76]

We thus maintain that non-resistance comes from man's positive decision not to resist, *which is caused by efficacious grace* (and not from man's "non-decision" to "do nothing"). Because action follows being, and grace acts upon the will, man positively responds to that action with his own action (a positive decision to cooperate or resist). As Fr. Most describes this first stage of the process: "[G]race initiates the process by presenting a good to our mind, which God wishes us to perform, and by moving our will to take pleasure in that good."[77] Because the grace begins to move man's mind from potency to act, man will either resist the grace (in which case the grace will have been merely sufficient and has an operating effect), or will be moved to cooperate with it (in which case the grace will have been efficacious and has a cooperating effect). Man will respond to the positive movement of grace with a positive movement of his own, not a non-movement from a non-decision to do nothing.[78] Fr. Most admits the same when he acknowledges that man "perceives" the grace that causes the mind to see good and then calls non-resistance a "positive consent."[79]

When describing operating and cooperating grace, St. Thomas never says that the grace's efficacy is conditioned upon man's power to omit resistance or his non-decision to do nothing. Rather, St. Thomas says that man responds to the interior grace *by an exterior act of his will*. St. Thomas explains: "First, there is the interior act of the will, and with regard to this act the will is a thing moved, and God is the mover ... But there is another, exterior act; and since

---

tions according to which He will or will not move man" (GPS, p. 188). If God's will is the cause of all things and He wills non-beings to be conditions, then causality is required for non-beings (although we question how non-being can be a condition willed by God if non-being doesn't exist. How can nothing bring about something outside of God's causality?). St. Thomas confirms that non-being comes forth into being "from His knowledge according to His plan" (*De veritate*, 2.8.c).

76. GPS, p. 490.

77. GPS, p. 140.

78. Such a "non-resistance" theory is reminiscent of the heresy of quietism, where man's mind is wholly inactive (at least in this "first stage") and does not think or will on its own account, but remains passive while God acts within it. It also flirts with the condemnation of the Council of Trent, which declared that man does *not* remain passive under the influence of grace (even though in Fr. Most's theory man *does* remain passive—in a state of "do nothing"—under the influence of this first stage of grace).

79. GPS, p. 459. Fr. Most's statement negates his own claim that non-resistance is *not* a "positive, salutary act."

it is commanded by the will ... the operation of this act is attributed to the will."[80] St. Thomas further says, "God does not justify us without ourselves, because whilst we are being justified we consent to God's justification (*justitiae*) by a movement of our free will."[81]

Whereas St. Thomas says that man responds to the operating grace by a movement of his free will, Fr. Most says that man's will may not be involved at all. Under the influence of operating grace, in the non-resistance scenario, Fr. Most says that "the will does not move itself at all, in the first part of the process" and that "the will does not make a decision" for or against the operating grace.

Fr. Most sees his theory in St. Paul's exhortation to the Corinthians: "And we helping do exhort you, that you receive not the grace of God in vain" (1 Cor. 6:1). In light of St. Paul's statement, Fr. Most says, "Scripture also plainly supposes that still another negative thing is in our power, namely: when grace is offered, we can at least *merely do nothing*, or not resist grace."[82] However, St. Paul is urging the Corinthians to *respond* to God's grace, not to make a non-decision to do nothing. The word for "receive" (*dechomai*) in 1 Corinthians 6:1 is an aorist tense verb in the middle voice, which implies an act of the will (to receive, take, approve, get, etc.). St. Paul uses the word five other times in the same letter, and it always refers to a positive decision to act, not a negative free condition not to act.[83]

In support of his theory, Fr. Most also refers to Trent's canon 4 on justification: "If anyone shall say that man's free will moved and aroused by God does not cooperate by assenting to God who rouses and calls, whereby it disposes and prepares itself to obtain the grace of justification, and that it cannot dissent, if it wishes, but that like something inanimate it does nothing at all and is merely in a passive state: let him be anathema."[84] Because Trent says that man's will can dissent "if it wishes," Fr. Most concludes that man's ability not to dissent is the equivalent of a non-decision not to resist. In other words, a decision not to dissent is really the absence of an evil decision to dissent. Actually, Trent's canon only hurts Fr. Most's position.

First, Trent is talking about man's free will. The canon says that man's *free*

---

80. ST, Pt I-II, Q 111, Art 2.
81. Ibid.
82. GPS, p. 139 (emphasis in original).
83. See 1 Cor. 7:15; 8:4, 17; 11:4, 16. See also 1 Cor. 2:14; Gal. 4:14; Eph. 6:17; Phil. 4:18; Col. 4:10; 1 Thess. 1:6; 2:13; 2 Thess. 2:10; Heb. 11:31.
84. Denz., 814.

will can dissent if it "wishes"—a clear reference to an act of the will. Trent says nothing about a "non-wishing" of resistance which, according to Fr. Most, is *not* a movement of the will at all. Secondly, the canon provides only two alternative responses to grace: *cooperation* or *dissent* (both of which are acts of the will). Man can "cooperate by assenting to God who rouses and calls" (in the case of efficacious grace) or can "dissent if it wishes" (in the case of sufficient grace). Trent never mentions a third alternative whereby "the will does not move itself at all" resulting in "non-resistance." Thirdly, the canon seems to anathematize Fr. Most's theory. In the non-resistance scenario, Fr. Most claims that the will "does nothing." However, Trent condemns the view that the will "does nothing at all and is merely in a passive state" at the moment where non-resistance would occur. As St. Thomas teaches, the will does not remain inactive, but moves either to cooperate or dissent, depending on the nature of the grace.

Fr. Most also refers to St. Thomas's teaching that "this is in the power of free will [namely] to impede or not to impede the reception of divine grace ... but they only are deprived of grace who set up an impediment to grace in themselves."[85] But again, in Fr. Most's non-resistance scenario, not impeding grace does *not* come from "the power of free will;" it is a condition in man that exists independently of his free will. Like Trent, St. Thomas says that it is in the power of *man's will* to impede (dissent) or not to impede (cooperate). St. Thomas does not say that it is not in the power of free will, but rather a condition in man, not to impede the reception of grace. Neither St. Thomas nor any Church council ever introduced such an alternative where the efficacy of grace is conditioned upon a non-decision in man to do nothing.

When St. Thomas says that it "is in the power of free will to impede or not to impede" grace, he is simply teaching that man's power to impede grace is in potency. If the grace is efficacious, the power remains in potency. If the grace is sufficient, the potency is actualized. This must be true if the salutary act comes from God and the defect of sin comes from man. St. Thomas does not say that man *actually* impedes grace by his own free will when God efficaciously wills him to receive it. Man does have the power to resist efficacious grace, but he does not actually resist it. The corollary follows: If man actually resists a certain grace, then the grace did not produce the non-resistance (since not placing an obstacle to grace "proceeds from grace"). Because not placing an obstacle is a work of grace, if man does place an obstacle, God did not give him the grace of non-resistance. By concluding that man can impede or not impede *any* grace, Fr. Most confuses potency with act. What man has the *power* to do and what he *actually does* are two different things.

Because St. Thomas says, "[B]ut they only are deprived of grace who set up an impediment to grace," Fr. Most concludes: "St. Thomas makes it entirely clear that the distinction between those who are saved and those who are not saved depends on the two conditions, namely, to impede or not to impede grace."[86] Yet Fr. Most's conclusion is erroneous, because St. Thomas's statement is addressing only the impediment side of the equation, not the salvation side. St. Thomas does not say that "man is saved because he doesn't impede grace." Such a statement would make salvation the work of man, not God. Rather, St. Thomas simply says that those who are deprived of grace have set up an obstacle to the grace. This happens in the case of sufficient grace, whereby God permits man to place the obstacle, and not efficacious grace, which removes the obstacle. Thus, with this teaching, St. Thomas is explaining the reason for reprobation, not salvation.

To further argue that man's condition of non-resistance determines the efficacy of grace, Fr. Most refers to St. Thomas's statement: "God wills the non-occurrence of moral faults in His antecedent will, but not in His consequent will except in the case of those whom He knows do not will to commit moral fault: because the consequent will takes in [consideration] the condition of the creature."[87] Yet the condition to which St. Thomas refers is not the unwilled non-resistance of the creature but the creature's positive will not to commit a moral fault. So St. Thomas does not say what Fr. Most claims he says. Furthermore, God considers this good condition in the creature inasmuch as He created it and rewards him for it. Similarly, God considers the bad condition in the creature inasmuch as He permitted it and punishes him for it. Thus, God considers the condition of the creature, not because the creature is good, but because God wills the creature good and moves him to do good (or permits him to do evil).

Fr. Most also refers to St. Thomas's statement: "[W]e must say that although the divine will is not impeded or changed by anything else, yet according to the order of wisdom, it directs itself to a thing according to the condition of that

---

86. GPS, p. 198. Again, Fr. Most confuses potency with act. Man may have the power to impede or not to impede, but that does not mean that he actually does impede or does not impede.
87. I Sent. d. 46, Q 1, Art 4.

thing; and thus something from our part is attributed to the divine will."[88] As with St. Thomas's previous teaching, God's will directs itself according to man's condition inasmuch as He has created the condition (if it is good) or permitted the condition (if it is bad). In the case of efficacious grace, God's will directs itself to the good condition in us because, after He has moved us, He assists us "both by strengthening our will interiorly so as to attain to the act, and by granting outwardly the capability of operating."[89] Yet because we are freely choosing the good under the influence of this grace, "something from our part is attributed to the divine will."

In another similar statement, St. Thomas says, "God, so far as He is concerned, communicates Himself to all in accordance with their capacity hence, the fact that anything falls away from participation in His goodness comes from the fact that there is found in it some impediment to the divine participation."[90] Again, St. Thomas says nothing about negative decisions or ontological zeros. God communicates Himself in accordance with man's capacity because God's eternal decrees *have determined* man's capacity. As we will further see in the next chapter, God gives all men the capacity to cooperate with grace. However, God wills to permit some to fail in their capacity and others to realize their capacity, according to His plan of predestination.[91]

Because Fr. Most wishes to claim that the efficacy of grace is primarily determined by man's non-resistance, he claims that efficacious grace, which infallibly moves man to act, happens only in extraordinary circumstances. He says, *"[I]t is clear that infrustrable movements are extraordinary."*[92] However, St. Thomas teaches that such graces are extraordinary only in the case of hardened sinners, but not in the case of most people. St. Thomas says, "Although he who

---

88. *De veritate*, 23.2 ad 4. Based on this statement, Fr. Most asks, "But if God *freely wills* to await our *absence of resistance*, who could prove that He would be incapable of doing this if He so wills?" (GPS, p. 206, emphasis in original). However, if God would will to wait for a condition in man in order to determine the efficacy of grace, He would be passive until the condition materialized. God cannot will what is contrary to His nature.

89. ST, Pt I-II, Q 111, Art 2.

90. *De malo*, 3.1 ad 9.

91. To advance his theory, Fr. Most also uses the human father analogy. He says, "[A] human father simply would not be permitted to omit loving and caring for his small children precisely and formally because of the absence of a positive condition which he would demand from his child." This argument undermines Fr. Most's theory as well. A father does not look for "non-resistance" in his child before willing him good. He wills the child good independently of anything in the child.

92. GPS, p. 162; cf. p. 163 (emphasis in original). Of course, efficacious grace is "frustrable" insofar as man has the power (potency) to resist it.

sins places an impediment to grace, and, so far as the order of things calls for, should not receive grace: nevertheless, since God can work beyond the order that is built into things, as He does when He gives sight to a blind man or raises a dead man, sometimes God, out of the abundance of His goodness, forestalls by His help even those who place the impediment to grace, and turns them from evil and converts them to good."[93]

By comparing the sinner to a "blind man" or a "dead man," St. Thomas is not referring to the average sinner, but to a hardened sinner who has habitually resisted grace. For this type of sinner, God must "work beyond the order that is built into things" and remove his resistance through a miraculous grace. This does not mean that all efficacious graces are miraculous. In fact, contrary to the teaching of Fr. Most, St. Thomas says that "the justification of the ungodly is *not* miraculous, because the soul is naturally capable of grace; since from its having been made to the likeness of God, it is fit to receive God by grace."[94] This demonstrates that God chooses, according to His plan of election, who He will save in His mercy, and who He will punish in His justice, irrespective of anything in man.

Thus, St. Thomas does not teach that average sinners don't also receive efficacious grace, or that these graces are limited to extraordinary providence. St. Thomas simply teaches that "if God intends, while moving, that the one whose heart He moves should attain to grace, he will infallibly attain to it."[95] In this article, St. Thomas is speaking of the average, "whoever" sinner. The article is even entitled, "Whether Grace is Necessarily Given to *Whoever* Prepares Himself for It, or to *Whoever* Does What He Can?"[96] St. Thomas's teaching immediately follows St. Augustine's statement that "*whoever* is liberated, is most certainly liberated" (emphasis added), and immediately precedes the quote from John 6:45: "*Every one* that hath heard of the Father, and hath learned, cometh to me" (emphasis added). Thus, God infallibly moves by efficacious graces, not just blinded sinners but "whoever" He wills, for "he hath mercy on whom he will" (Rom. 9:18).

---

93. CG, 3.161.
94. ST, Pt I-II, Q 113, Art 10 (emphasis added).
95. ST, Pt I-II, Q 112, Art 3. Fr. Most acknowledges the truth of St. Thomas's statement, but responds by saying that it does "not prove that God is completely incapable of moving a man to consent in any other way" (GPS, p. 184). But the issue is not what God is capable of doing, but what Fr. Most is capable of proving.
96. ST, Pt I-II, Q 112, Art 3 (emphasis added).

Because God's will is the cause of all good, any salutary act we perform must be attributable to this efficacious and infallible will, whether it is saying a prayer, doing a good work, or even thinking of God. As St. Thomas teaches, man cannot wish or do any good without grace, nor even know any truth without being moved by grace.[97] This means that God grants efficacious graces all the time. As we will further examine, Jesus says, "No man can come to me, except the Father, who hath sent me, draw him" (John 6:44). Anyone who comes to Christ is being drawn by God's efficacious grace. This means that God does not limit such graces to extraordinary circumstances; in fact, millions of men come to Christ every single day. This also means that God gives efficacious grace to both the elect and the reprobate (because many of the reprobate come to Christ but do not remain with Him).

In summary, then, Fr. Most incorrectly believes there is only one kind of grace, which man can either impede or not impede, and not two kinds of graces (sufficient and efficacious). Of course, if there is only one kind of grace, then salvation is ultimately determined by man, not God.

EFFICACIOUS GRACE AND CALVINISM

Like Thomists, Calvinists believe in the intrinsic efficacy of grace. Further, like Thomists (and all Catholics), Calvinists correctly believe that man cannot do or wish any spiritual good without God's grace. Unlike Thomists, who believe that efficacious grace applies man's free will to act, Calvinists believe that God's efficacious grace operates completely independently of man's will. In fact, because Calvinists view man as a spiritual corpse, they generally deny that man *has* a free will. Rather, they believe that fallen man is totally corrupt, rotten to the core, and in complete bondage to the devil prior to being saved. Calvinists call man's fallen condition "Total Depravity" (one of the "Five Points" of Calvinism). Because God's grace operates independently of fallen man's depraved will, Calvinists also say that God's grace is never resisted but always efficacious. Calvinists call this grace "Irresistible Grace," another of Calvinism's Five Points.[98]

---

97. ST, Pt I-II, Q 109, Art 1 and 2.

98. From a Thomistic perspective, to maintain the T-U-L-I-P acronym, we would replace Calvinism's "Total Depravity" with "Total Dependence" (man is totally dependent upon God but maintains a free will). We would also replace Calvinism's "Irresistible Grace" with "Intrinsically Efficacious Grace" (grace is not irresistible but causes man's will to choose freely by its intrinsic efficacy).

TOTAL DEPRAVITY AND SLAVERY TO SIN

The doctrine of "total depravity" was the principal idea that led Luther to ignite the Protestant revolt. Luther stated that "the flesh cannot think, say, or do anything except what is diabolical and opposed to God."[99] In his commentary on the Galatians, Luther also says that "everything you think, speak, or do is opposed to God."[100] Consequently, Luther said that "free will is a fiction, a name without substance."[101] In response to these heresies, the Council of Trent (1545) declared: "If anyone shall say that after the sin of Adam man's free will was lost and destroyed, or that it is a thing in name only, indeed a title without a reality, a fiction, moreover, brought into the Church by Satan: let him be anathema."[102]

Calvin adopted Luther's view of man's complete depravity and viewed unregenerate man as one who thinks and does only evil. Calvin taught this throughout his *Institutes of the Christian Religion*. For example, he says, "For our nature is not only utterly devoid of goodness, but so prolific in all kinds of evil, that it can never be idle."[103] The Canons of Dort, which are official statements of Calvinist theology, state, "Therefore, all people are conceived in sin and are born children of wrath, unfit for any saving good, inclined to evil, dead in their sins, and slaves to sin."[104] The London Baptist Confession also says that man "is dead in sin and altogether opposed to that which is good."[105]

Today's Calvinists have a variety of views on the extent of man's depravity. Calvinists not only disagree with each other on the question but even contradict themselves. For example, in his book *The Potter's Freedom*, Calvinist James White says, "Scripture tells us that man does *not* understand and does *not* seek after God,"[106] and he repudiates the Arminian position that "the unregenerate man *can*, to some extent, know, understand . . . spiritual things."[107] However, in the same chapter, White says, "Calvinists surely *do* believe that unsaved people

99. *Luther's Works*, p. 125.

100. *Luther's Works*, p. 126.

101. *Assertio omnium articulorum* (1520), written in response to Pope Leo X's excommunication. Luther further explained his denial of man's free will in his work *De Servo Arbitrio* (1525), which is often translated as "Bondage of the Will" or "On the Enslaved Will."

102. Denz., 815.

103. Institutes of the Christian Religion, Book 2, Chapter 1, Section 8.

104. Canons of Dort, III and IV, Article 3.

105. S.M. Houghton, *A Faith to Confess: The Baptist Confession of Faith of 1689*, Chapter 9, Sec. 3.

106. *The Potter's Freedom*, pp. 82-83 (emphasis in original; Chapter 3, "The Inabilities of Man").

107. Ibid., p. 111 (emphasis in original; Chapter 4, "The Will of Man").

can and *do* understand the truth of the Gospel"[108] and that "unregenerate man is fully capable of understanding the facts of the gospel."[109] Which one is it? Do spiritually dead men understand the gospel or not?

The Church has always defended the free will of man, and long before Luther and Calvin's time. For example, the Council of Arles (475) condemns the idea that "after the fall of the first man the free choice of the will was totally destroyed" and proclaims that "the human will was not destroyed but enfeebled and weakened."[110] The Council of Orange (529) says that "through the sin of the first man free will was so changed and so weakened that afterwards no one could either love God as he ought, or believe in God, or perform what is good on account of God, unless the grace of divine mercy reached him first."[111] The council also says, "Freedom of the will weakened in the first man cannot be repaired except through the grace of baptism."[112] The Council of Quiersy (853) states, "The freedom of will which we lost in the first man, we have received back through Christ our Lord; and we have free will for good, preceded and aided by grace, and we have free will for evil, abandoned by grace. Moreover, because freed by grace and by grace healed from corruption, we have free will."[113] The Council of Valence (855) describes our free will as "weakened through sin in our first parents, but reintegrated and healed through the grace of our Lord Jesus for His faithful."[114]

If God did not give man a free will, then His many injunctions to choose good and reject evil would be nonsensical. For example, the Lord said to His people through Moses: "I call heaven and earth to witness this day, that I have set before you life and death, blessing and cursing. Choose therefore life, that both thou and thy seed may live" (Deut. 30:19). The Preacher also says, "Before man is life and death, good and evil, that which he shall choose shall be given him" (Ecclus. 15:18). God commands His people that they "shall keep my Sabbaths, and shall choose the things that please me, and shall hold fast my covenant" (Isa. 56:4). These and many other like commands presuppose that man has a free will to choose good and avoid evil through God's grace.

---

108. Ibid., p. 118, footnote 20 (emphasis in original; Chapter 4).

109. Ibid., p. 101 (Chapter 4).

110. Denz., 160a. This heresy was first proposed by a priest from Gaul named Lucidus. The Church recorded Lucidus's retraction in the cited condemnation.

111. Denz., 199.

112. Denz., 186.

113. Denz., 317.

114. Denz., 325.

St. Thomas affirms the teachings of Scripture and the Church, that man has a free will.[115] St. Thomas teaches that man's free will exists because he is a rational creature. Even though his nature has been wounded by sin, he still acts from judgment through his reasoning abilities. St. Thomas says, "[B]ecause this judgment, in the case of some particular act, is not from a natural instinct, but from some act of comparison in the reason, therefore he acts from free judgment and retains the power of being inclined to various things ... And forasmuch as man is rational is it necessary that man have a free will."[116] As Scripture teaches, "God made man from the beginning, and left him in the hand of his own counsel" (Ecclus. 15:14). If man weren't left to his own counsel, then everything happens of necessity—including sin—and this makes God the author of evil.

To prove man's total depravity, Calvinists refer to Jesus' statement to the Jews, "[W]hosoever committeth sin, is the servant of sin" (John 8:34). Jesus is clear that those who commit sin are slaves to sin. However, Calvinists errone-ously equate slavery to sin with total depravity, which means the absence of free will. Calvinist James White says, "Slavery is antithetical to free will."[117] This is incorrect. Why? Because regenerated man continues to sin, as Calvinists would admit. Even St. Paul continued to sin after his conversion, as he says, "[T]he evil which I will not, that I do" (Rom. 7:19). If regenerated man continues to sin (which he does), that would mean he is still a slave and not regenerated, accord-ing to the Calvinist argument. But this is not true (Calvinists say St. Paul was regenerated and no longer a slave to sin). This means that Jesus' use of servitude to sin refers not to an ontological depravity but to the act of sin itself. St. Peter confirms the same when he says, "For by whom a man is overcome, of the same also he is the slave" (2 Pet. 2:19).

In fact, St. Peter is referring to those who have already been freed from sins through Jesus Christ and who have become "again entangled in them and over-come" (v. 20).[118] St. Peter is revealing the truth that regenerated man can fall

---

115. The early Church Fathers taught that man has free will. See, for example, Irenaeus (*Against Heresies*); Clement of Alexandria (*The Rich Man*); Gregory of Nyssa (*The Great Catechism*); John Chrysostom (*Homilies on Genesis; On John; On Romans; On Ephesians; On Hebrews*); Jerome (*Against Jovian; Commentaries on Jonas*); Augustine (*Letters; Sermons; Questions to Simplician; Debate with Felix; Forgiveness of Sins; The Spirit and the Letter; Homilies on John; Homilies on the Epistle of John; Grace and Original Sin; Against the Pelagians; Admonition and Grace*); and John Damascene (*The Source of Knowledge*).

116. ST, Pt I, Q 83, Art 1.

117. *The Potter's Freedom*, p. 87.

118. Recall that Calvinists claim St. Peter is writing only to the elect. Even if that were true,

back into sin by resisting God's sufficient grace, and by an act of his free will. This is also the context of Jesus' statement in John 8:34. Jesus was speaking "to those Jews, who believed him" (v. 31). Jesus tells them, "If you continue in my word, you shall be my disciples indeed. And you shall know the truth, and the truth shall make you free" (vv. 31-32). It is obvious that those who "committeth sin" and become "again entangled" in sin are not lacking a free will. Rather, they have the ability both to believe in God (God moving them to believe) and to resist His grace (God permitting them to resist).

Calvinists also refer to many verses from St. Paul. For example, in his letter to the Romans, St. Paul says, "There is not any man just. There is none that understandeth, there is none that seeketh after God. All have turned out of the way; they are become unprofitable together: there is none that doth good, there is not so much as one" (vv. 10-12). St. Paul's teaching simply affirms that man can do nothing spiritually without God's grace (the Catholic position). St. Paul does not say that God's grace cannot apply man's will to choose freely because of some kind of pervasive depravity. Such a view actually limits the power of God's grace. Further, St. Paul is quoting from Psalm 13, which begins with the statement: "The fool hath said in his heart: There is no God" (v. 1). Hence, St. Paul's indictment in Romans 3 primarily relates to those who deny God's existence, which St. Paul elsewhere in the letter says is contrary to reason (Rom. 1:18-21).

Calvinists also point to Romans 8:6-7: "For the wisdom of the flesh is death; but the wisdom of the spirit is life and peace. Because the wisdom of the flesh is an enemy to God, for it is not subject to the law of God, neither can it be." Again, St. Paul is teaching that carnal man is not capable of doing anything spiritually good outside of God's grace (Catholics agree). Fallen man needs God's efficacious grace to move him to act. But note that St. Paul is addressing Christians: "Therefore, *brethren*, we are debtors, not to the flesh, to live according to the flesh. For if you live according to the flesh, you shall die: but if by the Spirit you mortify the deeds of the flesh, you shall live" (vv. 12-13). That St. Paul is warning "saved" Christians not to live according to the flesh means that God's grace is not always irresistible, as Calvinists maintain. Rather, God also provides sufficient grace after "regeneration," which man resists by turning back to the flesh.

---

2 Pet. 2:20 would demonstrate that the elect have the ability to fall back into sin and final impenitence, as Thomists maintain (although God prevents them from doing so through efficacious grace).

St. Paul also writes to the Corinthians: "But the sensual man perceiveth not these things that are of the spirit of God; for it is foolishness to him, and he cannot understand, because it is spiritually examined" (1 Cor. 2:14). Of course, because spiritual things surpass man's nature, he cannot attain to them without the supernatural help of God. In fact, as we will further see below, St. Thomas teaches that even in the state of integrity man "needs the help of God as First Mover, to do or wish any good whatsoever."[119] From a Thomist perspective, the Calvinist argument for man's inability without God's grace is a straw man. Moreover, Scripture never says that man is so depraved that he does not choose freely under the influence of God's grace. As St. Thomas teaches, God's grace does not cause man's choosing to be involuntary, just as His moving natural causes does not cause them to be unnatural.

Calvinists also refer to St. Paul's descriptions of man as "dead" in sin. For example, St. Paul tells the Ephesians, "[Y]ou were dead in your offenses, and sins, [w]herein in time past you walked according to the course of this world, according to the prince of the power of this air, of the spirit that now worketh on the children of unbelief . . . and were by nature children of wrath" (2:1-3). Two verses later, St. Paul again says, "Even when we were dead in sins, [God] hath quickened us together in Christ (by whose grace you are saved)" (2:5). He similarly tells the Colossians, "[Y]ou were dead in your sins, and the uncircumcision of your flesh; he hath quickened together with him, forgiving you all offenses" (2:13). St. Paul uses "dead" as a metaphor to describe those who are outside God's grace, which is the source of spiritual "life."

IRRESISTIBLE GRACE AND THE LAZARUS EXAMPLE

Whereas St. Paul in these verses is describing the *spiritual* death of fallen man, Calvinists view fallen man in the same light as the *physical* death of Lazarus in John 11. Because Jesus raised the physically dead Lazarus from the dead without "asking him permission," Calvinists argue that God raises spiritually dead men to new life independently of any action on their part. That is, because Lazarus was physically raised to new life without regard to his free will, fallen man is spiritually raised to new life without regard to his free will. In using the Lazarus example, the Calvinist has a very noble goal: He wants to demonstrate the complete sovereignty and mercy of God in saving sinful man. However,

---

119. ST, Pt I-II, Q 109, Art 2.

using the Lazarus analogy to explain spiritual regeneration is a faulty herme-
neutic for a number of reasons.

First, from a Thomist perspective, using the Lazarus example to emphasize
God's sovereign grace and mercy is unnecessary. As we have stated, Thomists
agree that God grants His grace completely independently of anything in man,
and that man can do nothing spiritually beneficial without the grace of God.[120]
We remember the verse: "So then it is not of him that willeth, nor of him that
runneth, but of God that sheweth mercy" (Rom. 9:16). Man cannot even know
truth unless His intellect is moved by God.[121] Although the Calvinist seeks
to give all the glory to God in saving the sinner, the Thomist position in fact
gives God more glory. This is because in Calvinism God bypasses man's will,
whereas in Thomism God *applies* man's free will to act. God is so powerful that
He moves man to freely choose what He wills Him to choose. God does not
ignore the nature He gave man when He saves him but rather uses it in His
divine operation. In Catholic theology, God's grace is more powerful than in
Calvinism.

Secondly, it is illogical to analogize the physical resurrection of Lazarus with
the spiritual resurrection of fallen man. There are obvious differences between
physical and spiritual death and resurrection. A spiritually dead man is still a
rational creature, whereas a physically dead man is not, for he no longer has use
of his intellective or appetitive powers. This fact makes the Calvinist analogy
completely inappropriate. According to Calvinists, a spiritually dead man can
understand the gospel message; however, a physically dead man cannot understand anything. Also, according to Calvinists, a spiritually dead man is active in
doing evil; however, a physically dead man is not active at all.

Further, in his (pre-Parousia) resurrected state, Lazarus was both a sinner
and in a state of grace. However, at the General Judgment, when all the dead
will be raised, it will be one or the other. The elect will be perfected in grace and
the reprobate will be completely without grace. There is simply no exegetical
or hermeneutical basis to use Lazarus as an example of spiritual resurrection.
Rather, if one wants to use the physical body as an analogy to describe fallen
man, it is more accurate to call him injured—yes, even seriously injured—but
not dead (which is how the Catholic Church has always described fallen man).
This is because fallen man still has natural abilities to know God and truth and

---

120. The other major difference between these two schools concerns *when* man is regenerated
by God (more on this later).
121. ST, Pt I-II, Q 109, Art 1 and 2.

to reason as a rational creature. In his tomb, Lazarus was not a rational creature; he was a dead one.

In fact, the primary focus of John 11 is the physical, not spiritual, resurrection of Lazarus and all men. When Jesus tells Martha that her brother "shall rise again" (v. 23), Martha responds by saying, "I know that he shall rise again, in the resurrection on the last day" (v. 24). The phrase "last day" (Greek, *eschatos hemera*) is used only six other times, all of which occur in the same Gospel of John.[122] In each usage, the phrase refers to the physical resurrection of man at the end of the world. As Jesus will be the one who raises dead men to life on the "last day," He responds to Martha by saying, "I am the resurrection and the life: he that believeth in me, although he be dead, shall live" (v. 25). Jesus then physically raised Lazarus from the dead, which foreshadows the physical resurrection of all men at the end of time (v. 44). There is nothing in this account that suggests it is even remotely about a spiritual resurrection based on faith in Jesus Christ.

The story of the Prodigal Son in Luke 15 best describes a "spiritual resurrection," because it provides an example of a living person who falls from grace and then rises to grace again (Calvinists don't use this parable to explain grace and free will because it defeats their theology). In this well-known parable, the younger son asks his father for his share of the inheritance before his father dies, and then he squanders it on an evil lifestyle. When he becomes impoverished, he realizes how foolish he was and returns to his father, begging for forgiveness. When his father sees him returning in the distance, he runs out to meet his son to embrace and kiss him. And the son says to the father, "Father, I have sinned against heaven, and before thee, I am not now worthy to be called thy son" (v. 21).

The father replies by ordering his servants to clothe his son with the best robe and to put a ring on his hand and shoes on his feet. The father also orders the servants to kill the fatted calf for a feast, "Because this my son was *dead*, and is come to life again: was lost, and is found" (v. 24). When the elder brother discovers how his younger brother is being treated, he, who was always faithful to the father, refuses to celebrate his brother's return. But the father pleads with the elder brother by explaining his younger brother's "spiritual resurrection" in the same words he used with the servants: "But it was fit that we should make merry and be glad, for this thy brother was *dead* and is come to life again; he was lost, and is found" (v. 32).

---

122. John 6:39-40, 44, 55; 11:24; 12:48.

In two separate verses, the father describes the younger son's former spiritual condition as "dead" (verses 24 and 32). The word for "dead" in these verses (Greek, *nekros*) is the same word St. Paul uses in Ephesians 2:1, 5 and in Colossians 2:13 to describe those who are "dead" in sin.[123] Surely, St. Paul knew of the parable of the Prodigal Son through apostolic Tradition. Thus, Luke 15 provides us with a sound interpretation of the meaning of being "dead" in sin, namely, that fallen man is not a spiritual corpse, but is able to know and do the Father's will by God's grace.

Calvinists may be tempted to argue that the Prodigal Son proves their case: that the sinful lifestyle of the younger son shows he was totally depraved, and his complete turnaround was a product of God's gift of irresistible grace. But although the son's conversion was certainly the result of God's efficacious grace, the father's description of his son's condition strikes a critical blow to Calvinist theology. The father says that the Prodigal Son "is come to life *again*" (vv. 24, 32). Clearly, the father is referring to the son's spiritual condition. The Greek verb for "come to life again" is *anazao*, which literally means "revived." It is used only two other times in the New Testament in the context of "resurrection," and both times to describe a resurrection from a previous state of grace.[124] Thus, being "revived" (*anazao*) describes *only those who once had the life of grace, and not those who never had it.*

This is why Calvinists don't use the term "revived" or "restored" when referring to the spiritual resurrection of a sinner (even though they unwittingly do when they refer to the Prodigal Son parable). In Calvinism, fallen man never had spiritual life to begin with. He is "dead in sin" until he is born again in Christ. Prior to being born again, he is totally depraved and at enmity with God. Further, Calvinists maintain that once man is born again, his grace of conversion is irresistible and he can never fall away from grace (more on this erroneous view in the last chapter on God's gift of perseverance).

The parable of the Prodigal Son refutes these positions. The Prodigal Son's being "revived" to life presupposes that he was in a state of grace before falling.

---

123. In Romans 6:11, St. Paul also says, "So do you also reckon, that you are dead (*nekros*) to sin, but alive unto God, in Christ Jesus our Lord." This is another example where St. Paul uses "dead" in a spiritual and metaphorical sense. The Romans weren't literally unable to commit sin even though St. Paul says they were "dead to sin." In the same vein, fallen man isn't literally unable to know and respond to God even though he is "dead in sin."

124. See Rom. 14:9 (Christ's resurrection from grace to glory) and Apoc. 20:5 (the elect's resurrection from grace to glory).

Indeed, the Prodigal Son's life with his father prior to acquiring the inheritance represents his life of grace with God the Father before falling from grace through sin. Further, the son's returning to his father in repentance represents his restoration to grace by the Father's efficacious will. In short, the parable reveals the dynamic relationship between God's grace and human free will, namely, that man can reject sufficient grace and fall away from God, and then can return to God through efficacious grace.

PREVENIENT GRACE AND REGENERATION

The story of Lazarus also brings up the issues of prevenient grace and regeneration. Calvinists and most other Protestants use the term "regeneration" to describe the moment one is "born again" in Christ and experiences a "spiritual resurrection." That is, when one is regenerated he is saved in Christ. Most Protestants say this happens when one "accepts Jesus as personal Lord and Savior." For the Calvinist, as we have explained, when one is born again one transitions from total depravity to salvation through an irresistible grace. Because man is totally depraved, he can be moved only by an irresistible grace, which bypasses his corrupted will and regenerates him on the spot.

Because of man's "total depravity," Calvinists do not believe that man receives any graces that *precede* regeneration and dispose him to salvation. These graces, which the Church calls *prevenient* (or "actual") graces, are those that come before salvation, and which move man to good and prepare him for rebirth in Christ. Rather, Calvinists take an "all or nothing" view of regenerating grace.[125] Man goes from being totally depraved to being saved at once, without first being moved by preceding graces. In the Calvinist system, just as grace cannot be resisted, grace cannot precede regeneration.[126]

First, we note that regeneration occurs not when one "accepts Christ as Savior," *but when one is baptized into Christ.* Briefly, when Nicodemus asks Jesus how a man can be "born again," Jesus says, "Amen, amen I say to thee, unless a man be born again of water and the Holy Ghost, he cannot enter into the

---

125. Many Calvinists also believe in what they call "common grace," which restrains man from being more evil than he is (more on this later).

126. Calvinists disagree on whether faith precedes or follows regeneration. Strict Calvinists believe that faith follows regeneration, while Arminians believe that faith precedes regeneration. In Catholic theology, the theological virtue of faith is given *at the same time* as regeneration—in baptism—when God infuses faith, hope, and charity into the soul (Rom. 5:1-5; CCC 1266; 1991).

kingdom of God" (John 3:5). Previous to this passage, St. John connects "water" and "Spirit" to baptism (see John 1:31-33). Immediately following the passage, St. John explains that the disciples went into Judea and baptized (see John 3:23; 4:1-2). This is why the early Church Fathers were unanimous in their interpretation of John 3:5 as referring to baptism.[127]

Further, in his letter to Titus, St. Paul uses the word "regeneration" to describe baptism: "Not by the works of justice, which we have done, but according to his mercy, he saved us, by the laver of *regeneration*, and renovation of the Holy Ghost" (3:5). The "laver of regeneration" literally means the "bath of rebirth" or being "born again of water," and the "Holy Ghost" is, of course, the Spirit.[128] Baptism regenerates the sinner and infuses his soul with faith, hope and charity (see Rom. 5:1-5). This is why St. Peter says that "baptism . . . now saveth you" (1 Pet. 3:21). In reference to baptism, St. Paul also says, "[Y]ou are washed, but you are sanctified, but you are justified in the name of our Lord Jesus Christ, and the Spirit of our God" (1 Cor. 6:11).

Secondly, while Calvinists are correct to say that man is not saved until he is regenerated (although they err on what regeneration is), they are wrong to deny the existence of prevenient grace. Most Calvinists reject prevenient grace because they confuse the Arminian understanding of prevenient grace with the Catholic understanding. Arminians view prevenient grace in a similar way that Thomists view sufficient grace—grace that gives man the power to act but which he may resist (in the Thomist school, man *does* resist sufficient grace). The Arminian understanding of prevenient grace is *not* the same as the Catholic doctrine.

In Catholicism, prevenient grace efficaciously leads the person to salvation

---

127. The following Fathers interpreted being "born again" (John 3:5) as referring to water baptism: Justin Martyr (*First Apology*); Theophilus of Antioch (*To Autolycus*); Irenaeus (*Fragment*); Tertullian (*On Baptism*); Hippolytus (*Discourse on the Holy Theophany*); Clement (*Recognitions of Clement*); Pseudo-Clementines (*Homily*); Origen (*Commentary on Romans*); Cyprian (*To Stephen*); Lactantius (*Divine Institutes*); Hilary of Poitiers (*Trinity*); Athanasius (*Discourse Against the Arians*); Ephraim (*Hymns for the Feast of the Epiphany*); Basil (*On the Spirit*); John Chrysostom (*On the Priesthood*); Gregory of Nazianzen (*Oration on Holy Baptism*); Ambrose (*Concerning Repentance; and On the Mysteries*); Gregory of Nyssa (*On the Baptism of Christ*); Jerome (*To Oceanus; Against the Pelagians*); Augustine (*To Boniface; On Forgiveness of Sin and Baptism; City of God; On the Soul and Its Origin*); Fulgentius (*On Faith*); and John of Damascus (*Orthodox Faith*).

128. The word "laver" or "bath" (Greek, *loutron*) is used only one other time in the New Testament, in Ephesians 5:26, where Christ cleanses the Church "by the laver of water in the word of life." The word for "water" (*hudor*) is used in both John 3:5 and Ephesians 5:26, and the word for "Spirit" (*pneuma*) is used in both John 3:5 and Titus 3:5.

(regeneration).[129] For example, prevenient grace moves a person to listen to a sermon about Christ, which then leads the person to baptism (regeneration). Thus, prevenient grace is an efficacious grace that precedes regeneration. Prevenient grace produces a temporal effect willed by God (listening to a sermon), which precedes a subsequent effect (baptism). St. Thomas further says, "And hence grace, inasmuch as it causes the first effect in us, is called prevenient with respect to the second, and inasmuch as it causes the second, it is called subsequent with respect to the first effect."[130] In fact, the irresistible grace of Calvinism is also a prevenient grace with respect to heavenly glory, because it *precedes* salvation and leads a person to it.

Calvinists deny that efficacious grace can precede regeneration. Calvinists view efficacious grace (in their words, "irresistible grace") *only as regenerating grace.* In Calvinism, if grace doesn't regenerate, then it is not efficacious; and if it is not efficacious, it's not grace at all; and if man doesn't have grace, then he remains totally depraved and can do nothing spiritually beneficial for himself or pleasing to God. This all-or-nothing view is a fundamental error. The Calvinist is hard-pressed to deny the role that prevenient grace played in his own conversion. When one asks a Calvinist how he came to Christ, he might say that he began reading the Bible or attending a church. When you ask him when he was "saved," he invariably provides you with some date *after* his Bible studies or church attendance (sometimes long after).

Clearly, the Calvinist would agree that these spiritual activities leading to his regeneration were good and pleasing to God. He wouldn't say that reading Scripture is an evil activity. But since he was totally depraved (unregenerate) during this time, how could he do anything that pleased God? How could he be moved to read Scripture or attend church outside of God's grace and favor? We again refer to St. Paul's question, "[W]hat hast thou that thou hast not received?" (1 Cor. 4:7), and to Jesus' admonition, "[F]or without me you can do nothing" (John 15:5). If the Calvinist admits that he was moved by an initial efficacious but non-regenerating grace (which he must have been),[131] then he must also admit that Calvinism's notions of total depravity and irresistible

---

129. In some cases, God may send man a prevenient grace that is sufficient only (in which case God willed to permit man to resist the grace through his own choice).

130. ST, Pt I-II, Q 111, Art 3. This means that prevenient or actual graces are God's interventions either "at the beginning of conversion or in the course of the work of sanctification" (CCC 2000).

131. God grants non-Catholics efficacious graces for the ultimate purpose of bringing them into the Catholic Church.

grace are erroneous. Man can please God and do spiritual good *before* he is regenerated because of the intrinsic efficacy of prevenient grace. Scripture also supports the Catholic position.

Let's go back to the parable of the Prodigal Son. The son represents a sinner who rejected sufficient grace (by leaving the Father) and who repented of his sin through efficacious grace (by returning to the Father). After the son falls from grace and realizes he has done evil, he says, "I will arise, and will go to my father, and say to him: Father, I have sinned against heaven, and before thee" (Luke 15:18). At this point, the son is still estranged from his father (represented by his being in a foreign land). He also speaks in the future tense about asking for his father's forgiveness.[132] He has not yet asked his father for forgiveness and thus remains in a state of sin. Even when he approaches his father's house, he is said to be "a great way off" (v. 20). It is only when the father embraces him and he confesses his sins that the father says, "[T]his my son was dead, and is come to life again" (v. 24). This means that God efficaciously moved the son by prevenient grace prior to his regeneration (or rather, prior to his restoration, since the parable symbolizes that the son was living in the father's grace before he sinned).

The conversion of St. Paul is an outstanding real-life example of prevenient grace. Calvinists love to use St. Paul's experience on the Damascus road to demonstrate God's irresistible grace. When Christ revealed Himself to St. Paul on his way to Damascus, Calvinists claim that He converted St. Paul on the spot.[133] They say that St. Paul was immediately regenerated by an irresistible grace, and irrespective of his free will. To further support immediate regeneration, Calvinists point out that Jesus' Damascus road revelation to St. Paul included explaining to him his mission: "To open their eyes, that they may be converted from darkness to light, and from the power of Satan to God, that they may receive forgiveness of sins, and a lot among the saints, by the faith that is in me" (Acts 26:18). By all accounts, the Calvinist argues, St. Paul is regenerated and his sins are forgiven on the Damascus road.

Scripture, however, tells a different story. After St. Paul's companions bring him to Damascus, where he doesn't eat or drink for three days, St. Paul is greeted by Ananias who tells him, "Rise up, and be baptized, and *wash away thy sins*, invoking his name" (Acts 22:16); " . . . and rising up, he was baptized"

---

132. The verb "I will rise" (*poreuomai*) is in the future tense, middle voice.
133. See Acts 9:3-8; 22:6-11; 26:12-18.

(Acts 9:18). But wait a minute. According to Calvinism, St. Paul's sins were *already* washed away several days earlier (on the road to Damascus) when he was regenerated by the irresistible grace of Christ's revelation. Yet here Scripture reveals that St. Paul's sins were washed away in baptism days later (in the city of Damascus). What does this mean for the Calvinist?

It means that his theology is wrong. If St. Paul was really regenerated by an irresistible grace on the Damascus road, then the Calvinist must admit that it didn't wash away his sins because Ananias declared that St. Paul was still in his sins (the Calvinist, of course, would admit no such thing). If St. Paul were actually regenerated and his sins forgiven in baptism, then the Calvinist must admit that St. Paul received an efficacious but non-regenerating grace—that is, a *prevenient* grace—on the Damascus road that led to his salvation days later. The Calvinist must also admit that water baptism is the "laver of regeneration" that St. Paul reveals in Titus 3:5. In other words, the Calvinist must abandon his Calvinism and embrace the Catholic position.

We also recall that St. Paul refers to baptism as being "washed, sanctified, and justified" in Jesus Christ (see 1 Cor. 6:11). The Greek word for "washed" (*apolouo*) is used only one other time in the New Testament: in Acts 22:16 when Ananias tells St. Paul to be baptized and "wash away thy sins." It is no wonder that St. Paul uses *apolouo* (wash) in 1 Corinthians 6:11; he heard Ananias use the same word at his own baptism. This usage connects 1 Corinthians 6:11 and Acts 22:16, and demonstrates that baptism is the act of regeneration because it sanctifies and justifies man by washing away his sin.

The story of the Ethiopian eunuch in the Acts of the Apostles provides another clear example of the workings of prevenient grace. In chapter 8, we learn that the eunuch came to Jerusalem seeking God. Although we don't know much about the eunuch, it is safe to conclude that he did not have any relationship with or even know the true God. In other words, he was totally depraved. Having been a eunuch (castrating boys was practiced in the ancient Near East) meant that he would have been forbidden from entering into the Mosaic Covenant (see Deut. 23:1). He also was not a Christian. Nevertheless, because in his chariot he was reading Sacred Scripture (from the prophet Isaias), God was efficaciously moving him by prevenient grace to salvation in Christ *before his regeneration*.

When Philip discovered that the eunuch was reading Isaias, he asked him: "Thinkest thou that thou understandest what thou readest?" (v. 30). The eunuch responded, "And how can I, unless some man shew me? And he desired Philip that he would come up and sit with him" (v. 31). After the eunuch showed Philip what he was reading, he asked Philip, "I beseech thee, of whom doth the prophet speak this? Of himself, or of some other man?" (v. 34). Philip explained to the eunuch that Isaias was speaking about Jesus Christ. Thereafter, after they went on their way, the eunuch sees water and desires baptism: "See, here is water: what doth hinder me from being baptized? (v. 36). Philip responded, "If thou believest with all thy heart, thou mayest" (v. 37). The eunuch answered, "I believe that Jesus Christ is the Son of God . . . and they went down into the water, both Philip and the eunuch: and he baptized him" (v. 37-38).

The story of the Ethiopian is another clear-cut example of someone whom God efficaciously moves by a prevenient grace before He regenerates him. God first moves the eunuch to come to Jerusalem to find God; God then moves him to read Scripture; thereafter God moves him to ask Philip for an interpretation of Scripture; [134] He then moves him to desire baptism, and then to confess his faith in Jesus Christ. Finally, God regenerates the eunuch in baptism and he goes on his way rejoicing (v. 39). Was the eunuch totally depraved before his confession of faith in Christ? Was he fixated only on evil before his baptism? Was he totally opposed to good as he read Scripture and sought God? No, he wasn't, due to the prevenient grace of God.

We emphasize that the good acts that one does prior to baptism do not save the person; they only dispose the person to salvation. Moreover, the acts are the product of God's efficacious grace, which moves man's will to freely perform them. The point is that God's prevenient grace is intrinsically efficacious *but it precedes regeneration.* Under the influence of prevenient grace, God moves man to salvation by good deeds (reading Scripture; seeking truth) even though he is still under God's condemnation. St. Paul acknowledges the same when he says, "Not by the *works of justice,* which we have done, but according to his mercy, he saved us, by the laver of regeneration" (Titus 3:5).

In fact, St. Paul says that man is capable of incredible things under God's prevenient grace. These include speaking in tongues, prophesying, knowing all divine mysteries, having faith that can move mountains, giving away all one's goods to the poor, and even giving one's body over to be burned! (see 1 Cor. 13:1-3). These are certainly not actions of one who is totally depraved and intoxicated by evil. Nevertheless, St. Paul says that if one does all these good

---

134. Philip was ordained with apostolic authority in Acts 6:6 and therefore had the authority to interpret the scriptures for the eunuch.

deeds, and doesn't have the theological virtue of charity, "it profiteth me nothing" (v. 3). God gives us charity in the laver of baptism, when "the charity of God is poured forth in our hearts, by the Holy Ghost, who is given to us" (Rom. 5:5). Thus, while Calvinists are correct to say that God's regenerating grace is always efficacious, they err when they deny the efficacy of prevenient grace, which precedes regeneration.

Calvinists and other Reformed theologians deny the truth of prevenient grace because of their erroneous understanding of Adam's Fall. Because they view grace only as irresistible, Calvinists say that God didn't infuse Adam with any grace before the Fall (otherwise, he wouldn't have sinned). Rather, God gave Adam free will and let him utilize it according to his own natural powers (Luther and Calvin falsely believed that Adam was the only man who ever had free will).[135] Once Adam sinned, Calvinists say that Adam lost free will and became totally depraved and incapable of coming back to God without irresistible grace.

However, the Church teaches that God infused Adam with sufficient grace to resist temptation and to perform his duties with charity. St. Thomas says that "neither in the state of perfect nature, nor in the state of corrupt nature can man fulfill the commandments of the law without grace."[136] God, however, willed to permit Adam to reject His grace and to sin. Once Adam sinned, his soul lost its state of sanctifying grace, but he was still able to respond to God through prevenient grace. When God called upon Adam after his sin, Adam responded and still feared God (see Gen. 3:9-10). Adam also obeyed God's commandment to be fruitful and multiply by knowing his wife Eve.[137] Like the Prodigal Son, God moved Adam to repentance and obedience through prevenient, efficacious graces prior to regenerating his soul with infused grace.

MORE FROM THE CHURCH AND ST. THOMAS ON FREE WILL AND GRACE

Hence, prevenient grace is not a "Pelagian" idea, as many Calvinists contend. The Church is clear that man cannot exercise his free will for the good without

---

135. Those Calvinists who believe that Adam had free will before the Fall are called infralapsarians. Some Calvinists do not believe that Adam had free will but rather that God predestined Adam to sin. They are called supralapsarians.

136. ST, Pt I-II, Q 109, Art 4. Ironically, the Church views Adam as *more* dependent upon God and His grace than the Reformed view does!

137. See, for example, Gen. 1:28; 2:24; 4:1, 17, 25.

the aid of grace, a truth that was rejected by Pelagius (d. 420). Pelagius believed that man could move himself toward God by an act of his will without the prompting of grace, and that grace is needed only to assist the will. In other words, man takes the first step in his salvation.[138] Guided by the teachings of St. Augustine, the Council of Carthage (418) responded to the Pelagian heresy stating: "It has likewise been decided that whoever says that the grace of justification is given to us for this reason: that what we are ordered to do through free will, we may be able to accomplish more easily through grace, just as if, even if grace were not given, we could nevertheless fulfill the divine commands without it, though not indeed easily, let him be anathema."[139]

Semi-Pelagianism was a subtler form of Pelganiasm introduced by Faustus of Riez (d. 490). Semi-Pelagians held that man initiated his salvation by his free will and that God provided equal grace to everyone (denying divine predilection). In response to this heresy, the Council of Orange issued her canons on grace and predestination. Canon 4 says, "If anyone contends that in order that we may be cleansed from sin, God waits for our good will, but does not acknowledge that even the wish to be purged is produced in us through the infusion and operation of the Holy Spirit, he opposes the Holy Spirit Himself, who says through Solomon: Good will is prepared by the Lord" [Prov. 8:35].[140]

Canon 6 says, "If anyone asserts that without the grace of God mercy is divinely given to us when we believe, will, desire, try, labor, pray, watch, study, seek, ask, urge, but does not confess that through the infusion and the inspiration of the Holy Spirit in us, it is brought about that we believe, wish, or are able to do all these things as we ought, and does not join either to human humility or obedience the help of grace, not agree that it is the gift of His grace that we are obedient and humble, opposes the Apostle who says: 'What have you, that you have not received?' [1 Cor. 4:7]; and: 'By the grace of God I am that, which I am'" [1 Cor. 15:10; cf. St. Augustine and St. Prosper of Aquitaine].[141]

Canon 7 says:

If anyone affirms that without the illumination and the inspiration of the Holy Spirit, who gives to all sweetness in consenting to and believing

---

138. Pelagius had other heretical ideas, such as his denial of original sin, that physical death was not from sin but a necessity of nature, and that Christ does not bring us new life but rather sets an example for us of a good life.

139. Denz., 105.

140. Denz., 177.

141. Denz., 179.

in the truth, through the strength of nature he can think anything good which pertains to the salvation of eternal life, as he should, or choose, or consent to salvation, that is to the evangelical proclamation, he is deceived by a heretical spirit, not understanding the voice of God speaking in the Gospel: "Without me you can do nothing" [John 15:5]; and that of the Apostle: Not that we are fit to think everything by ourselves as of ourselves, but our sufficiency is from God [1 Cor. 3:5; cf. St. Augustine]."[142]

We also have seen that the Council of Sens (1140) condemned the idea that free will is sufficient in itself for any good.[143]

The Council of Trent specifically teaches about the efficacy of prevenient grace, which leads to baptism:

Now they are disposed to that justice [can. 7 and 9] when, aroused and assisted by divine grace, receiving faith "by hearing" [Rom. 10:17], they are freely moved toward God ... and when knowing that they are sinners, turning themselves away from the fear of divine justice, by which they are profitably aroused [can. 8], to a consideration of the mercy of God, they are raised to hope, trusting that God will be merciful to them for the sake of Christ, and they begin to love him as the source of all justice and therefore moved against sins by a certain hatred and detestation [can. 9], that is, by that repentance, which must be performed before baptism [Acts 2:38]; and finally when they resolve to receive baptism, to begin a new life and to keep the commandments of God.[144]

The Council of Trent also reiterated the Church's long-standing teachings on the necessity of grace to perform salutary acts. In its first canon on justification, the council says, "If anyone shall say that man can be justified before God by his own works which are done either by his own natural powers ... without divine grace through Christ Jesus: let him be anathema."[145] Also, in canon 3, the council says, "If anyone shall say that without the anticipatory inspiration

---

142. Denz., 180. See also CCC 406.
143. Denz., 373. The council condemned the views of Peter Abelard (d. 1142) who believed that man's free will acted independently of grace.
144. Denz., 798.
145. Denz., 811.

of the Holy Spirit and without His assistance man can believe, hope, and love or be repentant, as he ought, so that the grace of justification may be conferred upon him: let him be anathema."[146]

St. Thomas beautifully explains the Church's teachings on the necessity of grace in his *Summa*. As we have previously indicated, St. Thomas is clear that man cannot know any truth without God's assistance. God as Prime Mover must move man's intellect to its proper object, which is truth. This is the case not only for supernatural knowledge but for natural knowledge as well. St. Thomas says, "Hence we must say that for the knowledge of *any truth what-soever* man needs Divine help, that the intellect may be moved by God to its act."[147] Even though man has free will to exercise his deliberate reason, his deliberations are based on a series of previous deliberations. That being the case, St. Thomas says "[S]ince it cannot go on to infinity, we must come at length to this, that man's free will is moved by an extrinsic principle, which is above the human mind, to wit by God."[148]

St. Thomas is also clear that fallen man cannot do or wish any spiritual good without God's grace. This was the case for Adam and Eve even before the Fall. As we said at the beginning of the book, because attaining supernatural life is beyond man's natural abilities, he must be directed to that end by God (which is predestination). St. Thomas explains, "And thus in the state of perfect nature man needs a gratuitous strength superadded to natural strength for one reason, viz., in order to do and wish supernatural good; but for two reasons, in the state of corrupt nature, viz., in order to be healed, and furthermore in order to carry out works of supernatural value, which are meritorious. Beyond this, in both states man needs the Divine help, that he may be moved to act well."[149] Moreover, even if God continues to give a certain man efficacious graces, St. Thomas teaches that God must preserve him in that state of grace: "for every creature needs to be preserved in the good received from Him . . . since man will need the Divine help even in the state of glory."[150]

In fact, St. Thomas teaches that man needs God's grace even to prepare himself to receive grace. This is because God is Prime Mover and it is by His motion that creatures seek the good. St. Thomas explains the preparation to receive

---

146. Denz., 813.
147. ST, Pt I-II, Q 109, Art 1 (emphasis added).
148. ST, Pt I-II, Q 109, Art 2.
149. Ibid.
150. ST, Pt I-II, Q 109, Art 9.

grace as follows: "Now to prepare oneself for grace is, as it were, to be turned to God; just as, whoever has his eyes turned away from the light of the sun, prepares himself to receive the sun's light, by turning his eyes towards the sun. Hence it is clear that man cannot prepare himself to receive the light of grace except by the gratuitous help of God moving him inwardly."[151] St. Thomas also says, "Hence even a man who already possesses grace needs a further assistance of grace in order to live righteously."[152]

While St. Thomas says that man turns to God by his own free will, he explains that "free-will can only be turned to God, when God turns it, according to Jeremias 31:18: 'Convert me and I shall be converted, for Thou art the Lord, my God'; and Lamentations 5:21: 'Convert us, O Lord, to Thee, and we shall be converted.'"[153] St. Thomas also refers to John 6:44: "No man can come to me, except the Father, who hath sent me, draw him," and then explains: "But if man could prepare himself, he would not need to be drawn by another. Hence man cannot prepare himself without the help of grace."[154] Based on Scripture and the teachings of the Church, St. Thomas is clear that man cannot do anything spiritually without being moved by God's intrinsically efficacious grace.

---

151. ST, Pt I-II, Q 109, Art 6. See also CCC 2001.
152. ST, Pt I-II, Q 109, Art 9.
153. ST, Pt I-II, Q 109, Art 6. The Council of Trent uses St. Thomas's analysis in chapter 5 of its decree on justification (*On the Necessity of Preparation for Justification of Adults, and Whence it Proceeds*), Denz., 797.
154. Ibid. We provide an exegesis of the relevant passages in John 6 in the next chapter.

4

God's Gift of Sufficient Grace

Having looked in detail at efficacious grace, we now turn to the mystery of sufficient grace. Like efficacious grace, sufficient grace gives man the power to do God's will, for God never commands the impossible. However, unlike efficacious grace, the power of sufficient grace remains in potency and is not actualized, because man resists it. This is a great mystery, for God could have willed to grant an efficacious grace to break man's resistance. Instead, God willed to permit man to freely resist the grace, and from all eternity. Nevertheless, even though efficacious grace is required to break resistance, *sufficient grace empowers man not to resist in the first place*. This means that the defect is always attributable to man, not God. This is because God ordains all things to Himself, and it is impossible that He should be the cause of the departure from the order of His own divine ordination. We are again reminded of the prophet's statement: "Destruction is thy own, O Israel" (Osee 13:9).

Let's provide a basic illustration of potency and act in the context of sufficiency. If I am sitting on my couch, my power to stand is in potency. This means I truly have the ability to stand, not just a theoretical ability. If the phone rings, I have the power to stand up (move from potency to act) and answer the phone. If I choose to remain sitting, my power to stand remains in potency. If I later discover that my wife was calling me due to an emergency, I will not be able to blame my wife for my refusal to stand up (actualize my potency) and answer the phone. I can only blame myself. Moreover, if my wife warned me earlier in the day that she would call if she had an emergency, I will be guilty of not responding to her call. Similarly, if God grants me sufficient grace to perform a salutary act, I can only blame myself for resisting the grace, especially when God has warned me in advance about doing His will.

As we have seen, St. Thomas teaches that an operating and a cooperating grace are the same grace. Critics of Thomism say this is proof that there is only one kind of grace (not two different graces) whose efficacy is determined by man's cooperation or non-resistance. These critics misread St. Thomas. One reconciles St. Thomas's description of one grace with two effects and his teaching that there are two different graces (sufficient and efficacious) by understanding that efficacious grace has both effects, whereas sufficient grace has only one. We recall that St. Thomas defines operating grace as the grace that presents man's will with a good and moves his will toward that good. If this grace is not efficacious, then man freely resists it. If this grace is efficacious, then man freely cooperates with it. This is why St. Paul in Philippians 2:13 says that God works in man both to will (operating grace) and to accomplish (co-operating grace). God wills the grace to be either sufficient or efficacious *from the very beginning of the operation.*

Hence, a sufficient grace has an operating effect only (empowering the will to act), whereas an efficacious grace has both an operating and a cooperating effect (applying the will to act). Sufficient grace remains an interior impulse, whereas an efficacious grace produces an exterior act. Again, the mystery is that with sufficient grace, man *is truly able* to cooperate with the grace to perform the salutary act, but freely chooses not to, and God permits him to resist. With efficacious grace, man is able to resist the grace but does not, because the grace causes him to freely choose the good. In both cases, man is completely free, but in the former, the resistance (which is an evil) comes from man, while in the latter, the cooperation (which is a good) comes from God. St. Thomas clearly teaches that God chooses to communicate grace either sufficiently or efficaciously when he says, "[T]he merit of Christ, as far as its sufficiency is concerned, is the same towards all, but not as far as efficacy is concerned. This happens partly as a result of free will, partly from divine choice, by which to some the effect of the merits of Christ is mercifully conferred, but from others it is withheld by just judgment."[1]

Notwithstanding God's choice of election, God gives *all* men the gift of sufficient grace. St. Thomas says, "For God so far as He is concerned, is ready to

---

1. *De veritate*, 29.7. When St. Thomas says "partly as a result of free will," he is referring to man's cooperation with efficacious grace and resistance of sufficient grace. When he says "partly from divine choice," he is referring to God's will to "mercifully confer" efficacious grace to some and withhold it from others "by just judgment." St. Thomas's teaching demands this distinction because God gives all men grace but not all men are saved.

give grace to all 'for He wills all men to be saved.'"[2] Just as God in His mercy gives man a human nature, in His justice He gives man the power to obey the laws of nature. This is why St. Thomas says, "Thus also God exercises justice, when He gives to each thing what is due to it by its nature and condition."[3] St. Thomas also says, "It is also due to a created thing that it should possess what is ordered to it."[4] This means that God gives all men the ability to obey the moral laws, which are ordered to man and his happiness.

In the Acts of the Apostles, St. Paul says, "And hath made of one, all mankind, to dwell upon the whole face of the earth, determining appointed times, and the limits of their habitation. That they should seek God, if happily they may feel after him or find him, although he be not far from every one of us" (Acts 17:26-27). God made "all mankind" so that man could "find him," not so that man would be *unable* to "find him." As the Catechism teaches, "The desire for God is written in the human heart, because man is created by God and for God; and God never ceases to draw man to himself" (CCC 27). God gives all men sufficient grace to seek and find Him, which makes salvation a possibility for all.

Even though God wills to permit man to resist sufficient grace for the greater good of the universe, this does not mean the grace is "insufficient" for salvation. This truth is probably the most profound mystery presented in this book. Sufficient grace *is truly sufficient for salvation.* As we said, God truly gives all men the power to obey His commandments through the grace of the New Covenant. St. Thomas explains, "And this is why the New Law is not said to work wrath: because as far as it is concerned it gives man *sufficient help* to avoid sin."[5] If God did not give man the power to do His will, then man would not be accountable for his sin. Neither would God punish man for his sin, or reward him for his virtue. As we have seen St. Thomas say, if man did not have the power to respond to God, then "counsels, exhortations, commands, prohibitions, rewards, and punishments would be in vain."[6] Thus, even though God allows man to resist sufficient grace, the grace is absolutely sufficient to obey God's laws.

In fact, because God's justice is founded upon His infinite mercy, St. Thomas

2. CG, 3.159.
3. ST, Pt I, Q 21, Art 1. St. Thomas calls this "distributive justice," whereby a ruler gives to each what his rank deserves.
4. ST, Pt I, Q 21, Art 1.
5. ST, Pt I-II, Q 106, Art 2 (emphasis added).
6. ST, Pt I, Q 83, Art 1.

teaches that God gives all men much more than strict justice demands. He says, "For this reason does God out of the abundance of His goodness bestow upon creatures what is due to them more bountifully than is proportionate to their deserts: since less would suffice for preserving the order of justice than what the divine goodness confers; because between creatures and God's goodness there can be no proportion."[7] This means that God's gift of sufficient grace is *more* than sufficient to save man's soul. Man has no one to blame but himself for refusing it.

Notwithstanding St. Thomas's teaching on the sufficiency of God's grace, Fr. Most says that sufficient grace is really insufficient, based on a metaphysical argument. He says, "These graces give the ability to do good, but do not give the application. For the application, efficacious grace is required. Without the application, a good act is metaphysically impossible. The application is given to those who do not resist sufficient grace. But efficacious grace is required not to resist."[8] Thus, in Thomistic terminology, Fr. Most identifies the metaphysical issue as follows: Sufficient grace gives man the potency to do good, but efficacious grace is required to move him from potency to act. Therefore, sufficient grace is insufficient to move him to act. This is what Fr. Most calls the "vicious circle."[9]

Here Fr. Most imagines there is an inconsistency or incompatibility between St. Thomas's metaphysics and divine revelation, even though no such contradiction exists. Rather, the Thomist understanding of grace flows from both the metaphysical truth (known by reason) and the theological truth (revealed by Scripture) that all good comes from God and all evil comes from man.

Moreover, Fr. Most does not follow the metaphysics of St. Thomas. As we have seen, St. Thomas does not teach the principle that man's non-resistance (potency) is the "first decisive step" to his action (act). This is a gross deviation from St. Thomas's metaphysical principles, which hold that God is the cause of all being and action. Pope St. Pius X also warns theologians that "if they deviated so much as a step, in metaphysics especially, from Aquinas, they

---

7. ST, Pt I, Q 21, Art 4. In the same article, St. Thomas even says that God's mercy is seen in the damnation of the reprobate insofar as their punishments are "short of what is deserved."
8. GPS, p. 14. Throughout his book, Fr. Most says that it is "metaphysically impossible" for sufficient grace to apply man to act.
9. Note that Fr. Most criticizes Thomists for "trying to deduce the whole solution from metaphysics" (GPS, p. 2; see also p. 55) but then tries to rebut the Thomist position using a metaphysical argument himself, all the while rejecting St. Thomas's *theological* interpretation of Romans 9.

exposed themselves to grave risk."[10] Pope Pius XI also says, "The metaphysical philosophy of St. Thomas, although exposed to this day to the bitter onslaughts of prejudiced critics, yet still retains, like gold which no acid can dissolve, its full force and splendor unimpaired."[11] Pope Pius XI even says that "the Church has adopted his [St. Thomas's] philosophy for her own."[12]

Regarding Fr. Most's argument, it is true that some older Thomists (but not St. Thomas himself) held sufficient grace to be insufficient to apply man to act, based on the metaphysical principle that God must cause man to act. Nevertheless, we maintain that although sufficient grace is less powerful than efficacious grace, *it is still sufficient to apply man's will to act.* It is still in man's created power to work with this grace. God gives man everything he needs to obey His laws. Sufficient grace does not lack the application. Rather, man prevents the application.[13] As St. Thomas teaches, "The power of the divine incarnation is indeed sufficient for the salvation of all. The fact that some are not saved thereby comes from their indisposition, because they are unwilling to receive the fruit of the incarnation within themselves."[14]

St. Thomas also says, "Now this lacking of grace comes about as a result of two things: both because [the man] himself does not will to receive [it], and because God does not infuse it into him, or does not will to infuse it into him. But the sequence of these two is such that the second does not happen except on condition that the first has happened . . . It is clear, then, that the absolutely first cause of this lack [of grace] is on the part of the man who lacks the grace; but on the part of God there is no cause of this lack, except on condition of that which is the cause on the part of man."[15]

In contending for the insufficiency of sufficient grace, Fr. Most refers to St. Thomas's comparison: "Whatever applies the power of acting to acting is said to be the cause of that action: for an artisan applying the power of a natural

---

10. Pope St. Pius X, *Doctoris Angelici* (1914).

11. Pope Pius XI, *Studiorem Ducem* (1923).

12. Ibid.

13. Because Fr. Most believes that sufficient grace is insufficient for salvation, he claims that "God cannot, within the Thomistic system, simultaneously reprobate any man and still say He wills the salvation of that same man" (GPS, p. 162). This is why Fr. Most says that "in the system of the older Thomists, God becomes the author of sin" (GPS, p. 196). This, of course, is not true. St. Thomas answers Fr. Most's dilemma by saying that God antecedently wills the salvation of the man (when considered in isolation) but consequently wills to permit his damnation (in view of the greater good). Thus, contrary to Fr. Most's contention, St. Thomas teaches that both reprobation and God's universal salvific will can coexist.

14. CG, 4.55.

15. I Sent. d. 40, Q 4, Art 2.

thing to some action is said to be the cause of that action, just as a cook [is said to be] the cause of cooking which is [done] through fire."[16] Based on this statement, Fr. Most concludes that "just as the fire never can or will cook anything unless the fire is applied to the food, similarly a man even with sufficient grace never will act unless God applies the will of man to act."[17]

Thus, Fr. Most's understanding of sufficient grace attributes the defect to God, not man. This understanding, of course, is incompatible with St. Thomas's teaching. As we have seen, God orders all things to Himself, and so He cannot be the cause of man's failure to act. Using St. Thomas's comparison, the cook (God) can be prevênted from applying the fire (grace) to the food (man) because of a defect in the food (for example, the food is spoiled). This doesn't mean the cook willed the food to spoil; he only allowed it to spoil. Similarly, God's sufficient grace is prevented from applying man's will to act because of the defect in man (he resists). God did not will man's resistance; He only allowed him to resist.

In the deepest recesses of the mystery, it seems that if man would only cooperate with sufficient grace, it would have an efficacious effect.[18] If this were not the case, *man would not be culpable for resisting.* Even though man needs an efficacious grace to apply his will to act, sufficient grace is sufficient for this purpose if he would only cooperate with it. While this seems like a contradiction, we resist the temptation to abandon the principles and simply resign ourselves to the mystery.[19] Moreover, because we can comprehend the truths of sufficient and efficacious grace in isolation, the mystery lies only in their reconciliation but not in the truth of their independent existences. Fr. Most acknowledges the truth of our approach when he describes the conclusion of the good theologian: "Now we are in theology, in lofty divine matters. It is not strange if mysteries appear. Therefore, even though I cannot see how to reconcile two lines, yet I must hold both truths."[20]

---

16. CG, 3.67.

17. GPS, pp. 427-428.

18. If this were true, man's non-resistance would be attributable to the sufficient grace, thereby preserving the principles of God's universal causality and predilection. Recall also that Fr. Most, in support of his non-resistance theory, cites St. Thomas's teaching: "[I]t is in the power of free will to impede or not to impede the reception of divine grace" (CG, 3.159). If Fr. Most believes that man truly has the power not to impede divine grace (which Fr. Most does), then he cannot at the same time argue that it is metaphysically impossible for man not to impede sufficient grace.

19. In theology, this is called a paradox, not a contradiction. Our finite intellects cannot comprehend the many paradoxes of the Christian faith.

20. GPS, p. 3.

Let's penetrate the mystery another way. As we have seen, according to St. Thomas's principle of God's consequent will, when God gives man sufficient grace, He wills to permit him to resist the grace. As St. Thomas says, God does not will man to sin, nor does He will man not to sin; rather, He wills to permit man to sin, and this for a greater good. However, because God wills only the *permission* to reject the grace, *God must also will to allow man to cooperate with the grace.* If God is neither willing the acceptance nor willing the rejection of the grace (only willing the permission), then God is willing to give man a choice. This means the grace must truly give man everything he needs to act.

This does not mean God is passive during the operation, because the sufficient grace does begin to move man (presenting his mind with a good and moving him to it); but he impedes it. This also does not mean God is determined by man, because He decreed to permit man to resist the grace from all eternity. God does give less help with sufficient grace than with efficacious grace, but the help is sufficient to perform the salutary act and resist sin. *Less powerful does not necessarily mean insufficient.* A bicycle is less powerful than a car, but it is sufficient to take me to my neighbor's house next door. If these conclusions weren't true, then sufficient grace would indeed be insufficient and man would not be guilty for his sins. As St. Thomas says, "[F]or no one is charged with that which depends on another."[21]

Perhaps the best way to explain the truth of sufficient grace is to apply it to our own lives. Let's think back to the moments before we committed serious sins. We know that we had the grace to resist committing those sins. We know in our heart that we could have avoided giving in to those temptations. But we didn't. We know it is our fault, not God's fault. The people in hell will not be saying, "God, you only gave me graces that were metaphysically impossible for me to apply myself! It is your fault I am in hell!" As we said, the doctrines concerning sin and reprobation are more mysterious than those dealing with grace and salvation. We don't know how sufficient grace can be sufficient when an efficacious grace is required. But we do know that sin is *our fault* and not God's doing. Thus, we can have some comfort in letting the mystery be a mystery and putting our trust in the Lord.

We do not criticize Fr. Most for using metaphysics to address the issue, for metaphysics deals with truth and cannot be inconsistent with divine revelation. Yet, although Fr. Most raises a legitimate (but rebuttable) argument against

---

21. CG, 3.159.

sufficient grace, he also admits that man does resist grace and that all good (including non-resistance) comes from God. Fr. Most and all theologians would also admit that our understanding of metaphysical principles (and any branch of study) is limited by the fallible human intellect. Our finite minds cannot put all the pieces together, and we dare not say that God is determined by metaphysical conclusions. Although it may appear metaphysically impossible for man to cooperate with sufficient grace, nothing is impossible with God (see Luke 1:37). As we have shown, just because man resists sufficient grace does not mean that it is impossible for him not to resist. In other words, just as it is not impossible to resist sufficient grace, it is also not impossible to cooperate with sufficient grace. *And this conclusion violates no metaphysical principles.*

Scripture is clear that God gives grace to all men.[22] To Titus, St. Paul writes, "For the grace of God our Savior hath appeared to all men" (2:11). To the Ephesians, St. Paul says, "But to every one of us is given grace, according to the measure of the giving of Christ" (4:7). Because St. Paul opens his letter to the Ephesians with a dissertation on divine election, Calvinists argue that St. Paul in Ephesians 4:7 is referring only to the elect. However, in the next verse, St. Paul says that "he gave gifts to men," which is a quote from Psalm 67:19. This verse in the Psalms continues by saying, "Yea for those also that do not believe." Thus, St. Paul teaches very clearly that God gives grace to all men, *even to the reprobate.*

St. Peter also says, "As every man hath received grace, ministering the same one to another: as good stewards of the manifold grace of God" (1 Pet. 4:10). Like St. Paul, St. Peter does not teach that God gives grace only to His elect. St. Paul also reveals that this grace is sufficient for salutary acts. For example, St. Paul tells the Corinthians, "God is able to make all grace abound in you; that ye always, having all sufficiency in all things, may abound to every good work" (1 Cor. 9:8). Man is able to abound to every good work because God empowers him to do so. St. Paul also says, "[B]ut our sufficiency is from God" (1 Cor. 3:5). If our sufficiency comes from God, then we have no one to blame for sin but ourselves. Jesus also tells St. Paul, "My grace is sufficient for thee: for power is made perfect in infirmity" (1 Cor. 12:9). Even though St. Paul continued to

---

22. The early Church Fathers also taught that God gives all men sufficient grace for salvation. See, for example: Clement (*Letter to the Corinthians*); Arnobius (*Against the Pagans*); John Chrysostom (*On John*); Ambrose (*On Psalms*); Augustine (*Psalms; Genesis Defended; Nature and Grace; Corrections; Predestination of the Saints*); and, Prosper of Aquitaine (*The Call of All Nations*).

commit sin throughout his life (see Rom. 7:15-25), he had sufficient grace to resist those sins.

Jesus' parable of the laborers in the vineyard (Matt. 20:1-16) illustrates the truth that God gives sufficient help to all men . In the parable, the householder agreed to give all the laborers a penny for a day's work. Some worked from the very beginning of the day, while others were invited to work much later in the day, but all were paid "what shall be just" (v. 4). At the end of the day, the householder paid each laborer a penny. But those who worked the longest and bore most of the day's heat murmured against the householder saying, "[T]hou hast made them equal to us" (v. 12). And the householder responded, "Friend, I do thee no wrong: didst thou not agree with me for a penny? Take what is thine, and go thy way: I will also give to this last even as to thee. Or, is it not lawful for me to do what I will?" (vv. 13-15).

The point of the parable is that in God's gratuitous justice, *everyone* is given the grace to receive his eternal reward; but in His mercy, some are given more grace than others. Thus, Jesus finishes the parable by communicating the truth of divine election: "For many are called, but few chosen" (v. 16).

Just as Scripture reveals that God gives all men grace and no one resists God's will, Scripture also reveals that man is able to resist God's grace (proving the distinction between sufficient and efficacious grace). For example, St. Paul tells the Corinthians, "And we helping do exhort you, that you receive not the grace of God in vain" (1 Cor. 6:1). We cannot receive grace "in vain" if all grace is efficacious. St. Paul also warns Timothy about those who "resist the truth, men corrupted in mind, reprobate concerning the faith."[23] Men resist the truth that is intended for them, not for someone else. St. Paul also warns the Hebrews, "See that you refuse him not that speaketh" in reference to the grace of Christ's heavenly intercession (12:25). St. Stephen, the first martyr of the Church, declared to the council of the Jews: "You stiffnecked and uncircumcised in heart and ears, you always resist the Holy Ghost: as your fathers did, so do you also" (Acts 7:51). The Jews could not have resisted the Holy Ghost if He didn't intend to reach them. St. Paul and Barnabas also tell the Jews: "To you it behoved us first to speak the word of God: but because you reject it, and judge yourselves unworthy of eternal life, behold we turn to the Gentiles" (Acts 13:46). Jesus also tells the Jews, "And you will not come to me that you may have life" (John 5:40).

There are countless scriptures where God implores man to repent of his

---

23. 2 Tim. 2:25; see also 2 Tim. 3:8.

sins, choose good, and avoid evil. For example, we read in Ecclesiasticus: "Turn to the Lord, and forsake thy sins" (17:21); "Return to the Lord, and turn away from thy injustice, and greatly hate abomination" (17:23); "Go not after thy lusts, but turn away from thy own will" (18:30); "Turn away from sin and order thy hands aright, and cleanse thy heart from all offense" (38:10). David says, "Turn away from evil and do good: seek after peace and pursue it" (Ps. 33:15); and, "Be converted, O ye sons of men" (Ps. 89:3). God also says through the prophet Isaias: "Return as you had deeply revolted, O children of Israel" (31:6); "[R]eturn to me, for I have redeemed thee" (44:22); "[L]et him return to the Lord, and he will have mercy on him" (55:7); "[R]eturn for the sake of thy servants, the tribes of my inheritance" (63:17).

God says through the prophet Jeremias: "Return, O rebellious Israel, saith the Lord, and I will not turn away my face from you" (3:12); "Return, O ye revolting children, saith the Lord: for I am your husband" (3:14); "Return, you rebellious children, and I will heal your rebellions" (3:22); "If thou wilt return, O Israel, saith the Lord, return to me" (4:1); "[L]et every man of you return from his evil way, and make ye your ways and your doings good" (18:11); "Return ye, every one from his evil way, and from your wicked devices" (25:5); "Return ye every man from his wicked way, and make your ways good" (36:15). Osee also says, "Therefore turn thou to thy God: keep mercy and judgment, and hope in thy God always" (12:6); "Return, O Israel, to the Lord thy God: for thou hast fallen down by thy iniquity" (14:3).

Based on Scripture and Apostolic Tradition, the Catholic Church has consistently taught that God gives man all of the graces necessary to obey His commandments. For example, the Council of Arles says that "he who perished, could have been saved."[24] The Council of Trent teaches that "[w]hile God touches the heart of man through the illumination of the Holy Spirit . . . he can indeed reject it."[25] Trent also teaches that "no one should make use of that rash statement forbidden under an anathema by the Fathers, that the commandments of God are *impossible* to observe for a man who is justified . . . For God does not command impossibilities, but by commanding admonishes you both to do what you can do, and to pray for what you cannot do, and assists you that you may be able; 'whose commandments are not heavy' [1 John 5:3], 'whose yoke is sweet and whose burden is light'" [Matt. 11:30].[26]

24. Denz., 160a.
25. Denz., 797.
26. Denz., 804.

Under Pope Innocent (1644-1655), the Church condemned as heretical the following propositions of Jansenius: "Some of God's precepts are impossible to the just, who wish and strive to keep them, according to the present powers which they have; the grace, by which they are made possible, is also wanting;"[27] "In the state of fallen nature one never resists interior grace."[28] In the dogmatic Constitution *Unigenitus*, Pope Clement XI (1700-1721) also condemned the following propositions of Quesnel which denied sufficient, resistible grace: "Grace is the working of the omnipotent hand of God, which nothing can hinder or retard;"[29] "When God wishes to save a soul and touches it with the interior hand of His grace, no human will resists Him;"[30] "There are no attractions which do not yield to the attractions of grace, because nothing resists the Almighty."[31]

St. Thomas's teaching on sufficient grace, which gives us the power to act freely, and efficacious grace, which infallibly moves us to act freely, allows us to hold in balance the two truths that God gives all men the chance of salvation but only predestines His elect. St. Thomas's use of potency and act in light of these two types of graces helps us to reconcile, insofar as possible this side of heaven, God's sovereign election with human free will. It also mandates that we attribute divine election to God (through the cause of intrinsically efficacious grace) and reprobation to man (through the resistance of sufficient grace). No other system within either Catholicism or Protestantism results in such a harmony of these seemingly contradictory truths.

SUFFICIENT GRACE AND JOHN 6

Calvinists use Jesus' teaching in John 6 to deny the truth of sufficient grace and to demonstrate the truth of predestination and irresistible grace. Arminians, on the other hand, say that John 6 teaches God's sufficient grace is made efficacious by man's free will to believe. As with Romans 9, 1 Timothy 2:4, 2 Peter 3:9, and other texts, Calvinists and Arminians have fierce debates over

---

27. Denz., 1092.
28. Denz., 1093.
29. Denz., 1360.
30. Denz., 1363. This statement is heretical because it adheres to the Calvinist belief that all grace is irresistible and consequently denies that God provides even the reprobate sufficient grace for salvation. It also denies God's antecedent will to save all men.
31. Denz., 1366.

the meaning of Jesus' teaching on grace in John 6. Let's attempt to sort out these issues by examining the applicable texts. In so doing, it is very helpful to keep in mind St. Thomas's teaching on God's antecedent/consequent wills and the distinction between sufficient and efficacious grace.

In the first part of John 6 (v. 1-34), St. John establishes the unbelief of the Jews. This is an important fact to keep in mind as we proceed with our analysis. Jesus performs the miracle of the loaves and fishes for the multitude (v. 11) and then travels to Capharnaum (v. 17). When the multitude discovers that Jesus is gone, they search for Him. When the crowd finds Him, Jesus rebukes them for their carnal ways. They seek Him not for His divine miracles, but because He has filled their bellies (v. 26). Jesus tells them, "Labor not for the meat which perisheth, but for that which endureth unto life everlasting" (v. 27). After the Jews ask how they may do the works of God, Jesus tells them to "believe in him whom he hath sent" (v. 29).

After witnessing the miracle of the loaves and fishes, the hardened Jews have the nerve to ask Jesus, "What sign therefore does thou shew, that we may see, and may believe thee?" (v. 30). Then the Jews boast about how God miraculously gave their fathers manna in the desert to eat (v. 31). Jesus replies by saying, "Moses gave you not bread from heaven, but my Father giveth you the true bread from heaven" (v. 32). After the Jews ask for this bread, Jesus says, "I am the bread of life: he that cometh to me shall not hunger: and he that believeth in me shall never thirst" (v. 35). Then Jesus upbraids the Jews for their ongoing unbelief: "But I said unto you, that you also have seen me, and you believe not" (v. 36).

Having indicted the Jews for their unbelief, Jesus begins His teaching on the dynamic relationship between God and man in His work of salvation. He says:

All that the Father giveth to me shall come to me; and him that cometh to me, I will not cast out. Because I came down from heaven, not to do my own will, but the will of him that sent me. Now this is the will of the Father who sent me: that of all that he hath given me, I should lose nothing: but should raise it up again in the last day. And this is the will of my Father that sent me: that every one who seeth the Son, and believeth in him, may have life everlasting, and I will raise him up in the last day (vv. 37-40).

In the first half of verse 37, Jesus says, "[A]ll that the Father giveth to me shall come to me." It is clear that those who come to Jesus come only because the Father has given them to Jesus. The Father's giving precedes the person's coming. The person cannot come unless the Father gives him to Christ. In this one verse, Jesus reveals the divine causality of efficacious grace: the Father's giving is the primary cause, and the person's coming is the secondary cause. As St. Thomas says, "[T]he second always acts in virtue of the first: for the first agent moves the second to act. And thus all agents act in virtue of God Himself: and therefore He is the cause of action in every agent."[32]

The causes are not partial and coordinated, as Molina argued. Rather, the divine motion (the Father's giving) moves the secondary cause (the person's coming) to act. The determination of one who comes to Christ is entirely from God as first cause (operating grace) and from the one who comes as secondary cause (cooperating grace). This means the entire operation (the giving and the coming) is a work of grace. As St. Thomas says, "Now there is no distinction between what flows from free will, and what is of predestination; as there is no distinction between what flows from a secondary cause and from a first cause."[33]

What does it mean to "come to Jesus?" It means *to believe in Him*. This is because we do not come to Christ by the physical act of walking, but by the intellectual assent of faith. While the act of faith necessarily involves our free-will choosing, we have learned that God must move man's will to freely choose the good. This means the Father's giving results in the person's believing. The resulting faith is a gift from the Father, as St. Paul teaches: "For by grace you are saved through faith ... for it is a gift of God" (Eph. 2:8). St. Paul also says that we "believe according to the operation of the might of his power" (Eph. 1:19); and, "For unto you it is given for Christ ... to believe in him" (Phil. 1:29). Jesus also says, "This is the work of God, that you believe in him whom he hath sent" (John 6:29). This is why St. Thomas says, "All that the Father gives me shall come to me, i.e., *those who believe in me*, whom the Father makes adhere to me by his gift."[34]

Although verse 37 does not reveal how the Father chooses those He gives

---

32. ST, Pt I, Q 105, Art 5.
33. ST, Pt I, Q 23, Art 5.
34. *Commentary on St. John's Gospel* (emphasis added). Notice that Jesus first says, "All that the Father giveth to me," but then says "him that cometh..." Jesus switches from "all" to "him" to emphasize the personal nature of the faith that is required to have a relationship with Him.

to Christ, we have seen that God's decisions are not determined by man's will or works, for "it is not of him that willeth, nor of him that runneth, but of God that sheweth mercy" (Rom. 9:16). Thus, the Father's giving is not dependent upon the person's willingness to come or his foreseen response to the Father's giving.[35] Instead, the Father's giving is inspired solely by His love and mercy. No one thing would be better than another unless God loved it more. Although God loves all men, He loves and gives more to those who come to Christ, for God is the source of all goodness, including the good of our free-will actions.

Although verse 37 speaks of the causal relationship between God's giving and man's coming (believing), Calvinists often make too much out of the verse. For example, Calvinist James White says, "And since *all* of those so given *infallibly* come, we have here both unconditional election as well as irresistible grace, and that in the space of nine words!"[36] Although Thomists believe in unconditional election and infallibly efficacious grace, proper exegesis requires one to assert only what the verse asserts, and not any more. With that in mind, the verse does not mention either election or grace—terms that White and other Calvinists automatically read into the verse.

Of course, from a Thomist perspective, the verse certainly *can* be about divine election. In fact, St. Thomas says that one of the ways to understand the verse is in the context of predestination. St. Thomas says, "In one way, those who come to him are those who have been given to him by the Father through eternal predestination. Of these he says: the one who comes to me, predestined by the Father, I will not cast out: 'God has not rejected his people, the people he chose'" (Rom. 11:2).[37] Thomists would even say that election is the preponderant meaning of the passage. However, the verse does not *have* to be about predestination as Calvinists maintain. Why?

Because the verse does not say the person who comes to Jesus *will stay with Jesus*. White says that the person "infallibly comes," but the verse doesn't say that the person "infallibly stays." In fact, the verb for "shall come" (Greek, *heko*) denotes ongoing as opposed to completed action, and ongoing actions

35. Protestant apologist Norman Geisler, who claims he is a Calvinist, provides an Arminian understanding of John 6:37 when he says, "[T]heir being drawn by God was conditioned on their faith. The context of their being 'drawn' (6:37) was 'he who believes' (6:35) or 'everyone who believes in him'" (6:40; cf. v. 47). *Chosen But Free*, p. 95. Of course, God's drawing of people to the Son is not conditioned upon anything (including faith, which is a gift from God). As we have seen, God is determining, not determined.

36. *The Potter's Freedom*, pp. 155-156 (emphasis in original).

37. *Commentary on St. John's Gospel.*

can cease in the future. In the second half of verse 37, Jesus says "[H]e that comes to me I will not cast out." But this speaks to what Christ will do (the divine action) and not what man will do (the human action). If Christ efficaciously wills the person to remain with Him, then he is predestined to heaven. However, if Christ wills to permit the person to fall away for a greater good, then he is among the reprobate.

Catholics agree with Calvinists that the elect have been given by the Father to Christ. However, does the Father give the efficacious grace of final perseverance to every single person He gives to Christ? Verse 37 doesn't say. In fact, the Father's giving (Greek, *didomi*), like the person's coming, is a substantive participle that denotes an ongoing action that doesn't necessarily have to continue in the future. That is, the Father could cease giving certain people to Christ whom He formerly gave to Him. Why would God do this? To punish them for their sins. As we have seen in the teachings of Scripture, the councils and St. Thomas, God withholds graces previously given to punish "those in whom He finds an obstacle."[38] In short, the Father could have willed to give the person the efficacious grace of coming to Christ, but a less powerful sufficient grace for remaining with Christ which the person resisted through sin.

Jesus says as much in the previous chapter. After He tells the Jews to search the scriptures that reveal that He is the Messiah, He says, "And you will not come to me that you may have life" (John 5:40). In this verse, Jesus puts the responsibility of "coming" to Him on the Jews. If the Jews weren't given sufficient grace to come to Jesus, then Jesus would be rebuking them for failing to do the impossible, which violates justice. In the same chapter, Jesus reveals that "they that have done good things, shall come forth unto the resurrection of life; but they that have done evil, unto the resurrection of judgment" (v. 29). If those who did evil were not given sufficient grace to do good, then, as St. Thomas says, "exhortations, commands, prohibitions, rewards, and punishments would be in vain."[39]

Clearly, God did not efficaciously will these Jews to freely come to Jesus. Rather, He gave them sufficient grace to come to Him. And that is the point. If "coming" to Jesus is not *always* efficaciously willed by God, then "remaining" with Him may not *always* be efficaciously willed either. Those who don't remain with Jesus are those who "believe for a while, and in time of temptation,

38. ST, Pt I-II, Q 79, Art 3.
39. ST, Pt I, Q 83, Art 1.

they fall away" (Luke 8:13). These are the ones whom God wills to permit to fail in their goodness for the greater good of the universe. Although Thomists would not view this to be the primary meaning of John 6:37, the verse does not deny the truth of sufficient grace as Calvinism does, or deny that those who come to Jesus may not stay with Him.

As we have seen, Scripture reveals that God often gives people sufficient grace to believe but does not always will it efficaciously. In St. John's gospel, Jesus repeatedly pleads with people to believe in Him to have eternal life, but not all responded.[40] St. Paul also continually exhorts people to believe in Christ.[41] St. Peter does the same[42] and so does St. John.[43] We also recall Jesus' famous invitation: "Come to me, all you that labor, and are burdened, and I will refresh you" (Matt. 11:29). In these and many other verses in Scripture, God puts on man the responsibility to believe. This is a great mystery, for God could efficaciously will everyone to have faith in Christ. Nevertheless, because sufficient grace gives one the power to believe, it is the person's responsibility for not believing in Christ. As St. Thomas says, "But those who do not come are responsible, because they create an obstacle to their own coming by turning away from salvation, the way to which is of itself open to all."[44]

In light of the reality of sufficient grace, St. Thomas provides an alternative interpretation of John 6:37: "In a second way, those who do go out are not cast out by Christ, rather, they cast themselves out, because through their unbelief and sins they abandon the sanctuary of an upright conscience. Thus we read: I will not cast out such; but they do cast themselves out: 'You are the burden, and I will cast you aside, says the Lord' (Jer. 23:33). It was in this way that the man who came to the wedding feast without wedding clothes was cast out (Matt. 22:13)."[45] In other words, St. Thomas sees the possibility that some who come to Christ will later cast themselves away from Christ. Thus, St. Thomas sees John 6:37 as revealing both sides of the mystery: Those who remain with Christ receive an efficacious grace of perseverance, and those who cast themselves away receive only a sufficient grace which they reject.

40. John 3:12, 18; 4:21, 48; 5:44, 46-47; 6:36, 65; 8:24, 45-46; 9:35; 10:25-26, 37-38; 11:15, 40, 42; 12:36, 44; 13:19; 14:1, 10-12, 29; 16:31; 17:20-21; 19:35.
41. Rom. 3:22; 4:11, 24; 10:9-10, 14; 11:30; 1 Cor. 1:21; 1 Cor. 4:13; Gal. 2:16; 3:22; Eph. 1:19; Phil. 1:29; 1Thess 4:13; 1 Tim. 1:16; 2 Tim. 2:13; Titus 3:8; Heb. 11:6.
42. 1 Pet. 1:8; 2:6-8; 4:17.
43. 1 John 3:23; 5:13.
44. *Commentary on St. John's Gospel.*
45. Ibid.

In verse 38, Jesus says that He came down from heaven "not to do my own will, but the will of him that sent me." In verse 39, He reveals that will: "Now this is the will of the Father who sent me: that of all that he hath given me, I should lose nothing; but should raise it up again in the last day." Further revealing the Father's will in verse 40, Jesus explains that those who are given by the Father and raised up by the Son are the ones who believe in the Son: "that every one who seeth the Son, and believeth in him, may have life everlasting, and I will raise him up in the last day." This string of verses flows naturally from verse 37: The Father gives a people to the Son, these people believe in the Son, and the Son raises them up on the last day.

Again, it is plausible to conclude that Jesus is referring to God's elect in these verses. But it is not a necessary conclusion. Although Calvinists maintain that those whom the Father gives to Christ are infallibly raised on the last day, verses 39 and 40 reveal only the Father's *will* that they be raised. If Jesus is referring to the Father's consequent will, then it is a certainty that those whom the Father gives are raised. However, if Jesus is revealing the Father's antecedent will (as He does in John 3:16, for example), then not all those whom the Father gives are raised. Only those who are predestined to eternal life will remain with Christ and be raised by Him. The verses simply do not say whether Christ is referring to the elect. He may be referring to those who "believe for a while" before God wills to permit them to "fall away" (Luke 8:13).

In fact, Jesus reveals that some of those whom the Father gives to Him *do fall away*. In John 17:12, in reference to Judas Iscariot, Jesus prays to the Father, "Those whom thou gavest me have I kept; and none of them is lost, but the son of perdition." The verb Jesus uses for "gavest" in John 17:12 (*didomi*) is the same that He uses for "hath given" in John 6:39 (*didomi*).[46] Since the Father gave Judas Iscariot to Jesus (just like He gave Him those in John 6:37 and 39), but Judas fell away, one can conclude that Jesus is revealing the antecedent will of the Father in John 6:38-40. Not all those given by the Father to Christ are among the elect. As St. Thomas concludes, of those given by the Father, "some will be lost, the wicked; but none of those given to Christ through eternal predestination will be among them."[47]

The Greek verb tenses in John 6:37 and 17:12 also provide some insights. In John 6:37, Jesus says, "I will not cast out" (*ekballo*). In John 17:12, He says,

46. Both are singular active verbs in the perfect tense.
47. *Commentary on St. John's Gospel.*

"I have kept" (*phulasso*). Both of these verbs are in the aorist tense, active voice. These characteristics speak to Christ's divine action of preserving His elect, which the Father decreed before time began. However, when Jesus says that none "is lost" (*apollumi*) but Judas, He uses an aorist tense, middle voice. This indicates that Judas was responsible for his own destruction, which the Father also permitted before time began.[48] This distinction underscores that the elect are saved by God's gratuitous mercy, and the reprobate are condemned through their own fault, according to God's eternal decrees. It also reveals that the group the Father gives to Christ includes both those preserved by efficacious grace as well as those who are given (and reject) sufficient grace.

After Jesus presents these teachings, the Jews murmur at Him (v. 41). After Jesus rebukes them for their murmuring (v. 43), He thus explains: "No man can come to me, except the Father, who hath sent me, draw him; and I will raise him up in the last day" (v. 44). This verse reveals two important points. First (and this should now be obvious to us), if one is to come to Christ, he must be drawn by the Father's efficacious grace; he cannot come to Christ by his own natural powers. Because obtaining eternal life with Christ surpasses our natural abilities, man must be directed (or predestined) to that end by God. As Scripture often says, "Convert us, O God: and show us thy face, and we shall be saved."[49]

Second, Jesus is revealing why the Jews don't believe in Him: *because the Father is no longer drawing them.* This is the primary purpose for Jesus' statement in John 6:44 (it is not to provide a dogmatic statement on grace and predestination, as many Calvinists contend). The Jews murmur at Jesus, Jesus rebukes them for their murmuring, and then Jesus explains *why* they were murmuring. As. St. Thomas says, "First, he checks their complaining; secondly, he tells why they were doing it (v. 44)."[50] The Jews were given sufficient grace to come to Jesus in John 5:40 but resisted. Now, Jesus reveals that they will be punished for their resistance. The Father will not give them to Jesus. God is going to withhold His grace from them in John 6:44 and hand them over to unbelief. As St. Thomas teaches, when God withholds His grace as a punishment for sin, "God is the cause of spiritual blindness, deafness of ear, and hardness of heart."[51]

48. As we noted, this distinction in voice is seen in Romans 9 between the "vessels of wrath, fitted for destruction" (v. 22) and the "vessels of mercy . . . prepared unto glory" (v. 23).
49. Ps. 79:4. See also Ps. 79:8, 20; 84:5; Lam. 5:21; Jer. 31:18.
50. *Commentary on St. John's Gospel.*
51. ST, Pt I-II, Q 79, Art 3.

Jesus drives home this point at the end of His sermon. After He presents His discourse on the Eucharist, the Jews "murmured" at Him once again (v. 62). Jesus responds by saying that "the spirit quickeneth" and "the flesh profiteth nothing" (v. 63). Jesus emphasizes that belief comes from the Spirit of God and not man's natural powers, which He also does elsewhere in Scripture.[52] Then, after Jesus says, "[T]here are some of you that believe not," He says: "Therefore did I say to you, that no man can come to me, unless it be given him by my Father" (v. 66). Jesus, once again, explains the reason for the Jews' unbelief: The Father is no longer drawing them. They had the power to come to Jesus in John 5:40, but no longer have the power in John 6:44 and 66. This is why Scripture says, "After this many of his disciples went back; and walked no more with him" (v. 67). The verse does not say that they merely "left," but that they "went back." This means these disciples had been empowered to believe (through sufficient grace), but "turned back" from this power (by resisting sufficient grace).[53]

Calvinists make a very common error when they conclude that *all* those the Father draws are infallibly raised up on the last day. In John 6:44, Jesus does *not* say that He raises all those who are drawn by the Father. He simply says that no one comes to Him unless he is drawn. There is a direct, causal relationship between drawing and coming, but there is not the same direct relationship between drawing and raising. That is, all who are drawn come, and all who come are drawn. But whereas all who are raised are drawn, not all who are drawn are raised. As we have seen, not all who come to Christ remain with Christ. Some are given and then are "lost" (John 17:12). Some "believe for a while" and then "fall away" (Luke 8:13). Such people are drawn *but not raised*. The Father antecedently wills to raise all those He draws, but consequently wills to permit some of them to fall away by their own choosing, for the greater good of the universe.

Calvinists deny the Thomist position because they view God's drawing grace exclusively as irresistible. In fact, Calvinists interpret the word for "draw" in John 6:44 (*helkuo*) as "drag" or "force." For example, Calvinist R.C. Sproul says, "Linguistically and lexicographically, the word means "to compel.""[54] Although

52. See John 1:13; 3:6; 8:15; Mark 14:38. St. Paul also uses the "Spirit versus flesh" paradigm in Rom. 8:5; 1 Cor. 2:12-15; 3:3; Gal. 5:7.

53. See also Jer. 8:5: "Why then is this people in Jerusalem turned away with a stubborn revolting? they have laid hold on lying, and have refused to return." These people were given grace but "turned away" from it. That is why the verse says that they "refused to return," that is, to the state of grace they formerly had.

54. *Chosen by God*, p. 69. Sproul takes his definition from the Kittle's *Theological Dictionary of the New Testament*. However, Sproul fails to mention that this same resource also defines *helkuo* as "a powerful impulse" expressing "the force of love" and that "the compulsion is not automatic"

Scripture does use *helkuo* in the sense of compelling or dragging,[55] it does not do so exclusively. In John 12:32, Jesus uses the same word when He says, "And I, if I be lifted up from the earth, will draw (*helkuo*) all things to myself." Jesus is not saying that He will "drag" or "compel" or "coerce" all things to Himself. Further, because all men do not come or remain with Jesus, His "drawing" in John 12:32 cannot refer only to an irresistible grace. The Calvinist interpretation not only denies the truth of sufficient grace, but also the proper effects of efficacious grace, which does not bypass man's free will through coercion but elicits its free-will response.

The Septuagint uses "draw" with many different shades of meaning.[56] For example, in Solomon's Canticle of Canticles, he says, "Draw me: we will run after thee to the odor of thy ointments . . . the righteous love thee" (1:3). God also says through the prophet Osee, "I will draw them with the cords of Adam, with the bands of love" (11:4). In these verses, God draws man by His "love" (predilection), and elicits man's love in return ("the righteous love thee"). Because love is an act of the will, God's drawing does not "compel" man to love Him, but moves man's will to freely love Him. This is why the God of the Catholic Church is more sovereign than the God of Calvinism. He is in complete control of His entire creation in light of, and even in spite of, man's free will.

Although God's drawing produces man's believing, Scripture does not eliminate man's free will in the drawing process. For example, the Apostle James says, "Draw nigh to God, and he will draw nigh to you" (4:8). God says through Malachias, "Return to me, and I will return to you" (3:7). Scripture also says, "The Lord is with you, because you have been with him. If you seek him, you shall find: but if you forsake him, he will forsake you" (2 Para. 15:2). Of course, man can only "draw nigh," "seek," and "return" to God by means of efficacious grace. But these verses also reveal that God empowers man with sufficient grace to come to Him, and that man is responsible for resisting the grace.

Because the universal drawing of "all things" in John 12:32 is problematic for Calvinists, they argue that "all" in this verse cannot mean "all" (just like they do with 1 Timothy 2:4). To convince us of this conclusion, they point out that Gentiles are seeking after Jesus in John 12:20. Because of this rather nonconsequential fact, Calvinists argue that the "all" in John 12:32 must mean "all

---

(p. 227).
   55. John 18:10; 21:6, 11; Acts 16:19; 21:30; Jas. 2:6.
   56. See, for example, Deut. 21:4; 2 Esd. 9:30; Job 20:28; Eccles. 1:5; 2:3; Isa. 10:15; Dan. 7:10.

kinds" of men out of the pool of Jews and Gentiles (similar to their "kinds" of men argument in 1 Timothy 2:4). Although Jesus' drawing is efficacious only for the elect, the Calvinist interpretation is eisegetical (which means reading one's own preconceived belief into a text). Jesus gives no indication that He will draw only certain people out of the total pool of Jews and Gentiles, for "both Jews, and Greeks . . . are all under sin" (Rom. 3:9). In fact, prior to verse 32, Jesus says, "If *any* man minister to me, him will my Father honor" (v. 26). As we have seen with 2 Pet. 3:9, "any" (Greek, *tis*) can mean every single one, which it does in verse 26. The Father will honor *every* man who ministers to Christ, not just some of them. This means that the object of Jesus' discourse in John 12 is not limited to the elect.

Jesus further indicates that He draws "all men" in the world. In verse 31, Jesus says, "Now is the judgment of the world: now shall the prince of this world be cast out." Clearly, God judges every single person in the "world," for the entire "world" is in sin. This means Jesus will draw "all men" of that same world to Himself. There is no exegetical basis to conclude that Jesus will draw only some men of the world, when all men of the world are in sin. The purpose of the drawing is to save sinners, and since every single man is a sinner, every man will be drawn in some way (efficaciously for the elect, and sufficiently for the reprobate). How God chooses those whom He efficaciously draws must be sought for in the divine will and goodness of God, for "he hath mercy on whom he will; and whom he will, he hardeneth" (Rom. 9:18). St. Thomas's commentary on John 6:44 follows precisely His teachings in the *Summa* on predestination:

> A general reason can be given why God does not draw all who are turned away from him, but certain ones, even though all are equally turned away. The reason is so that the order of divine justice may appear and shine forth in those who are not drawn, while the immensity of the divine mercy may appear and shine in those who are drawn. But as to why in particular he draws this person and does not draw that person, there is no reason except the pleasure of the divine will . . . So God, for the completion of the universe, draws certain ones in order that his mercy may appear in them; and other he does not draw in order that his justice may be shown in them. But that he draws these and does not draw those, depends on the pleasure of his will.[57]

---

57. *Commentary on St. John's Gospel.*

To give God all the glory, Calvinists often describe their theology of grace as *monergism*, and pejoratively label the Catholic view as *synergism*.[58] Of course, it all depends on how one defines the terms. If God's grace and human free will are viewed as two partial and coordinated causes that act simultaneously, as Molina held, then such a view is synergistic. However, if God's grace is *causing* the cooperation of the will, as Thomists maintain, then such a view can be called monergistic.

There is no true synergism where the primary cause moves the secondary cause to act. God is the First Cause of all action. Moreover, a man can cooperate with a power outside of himself and still remain determined (that is, he does not determine the outcome). St. Thomas answers the Calvinist charge of "synergism" when he says, "God does not justify us without ourselves, because while we are being justified we consent to God's justification by a movement of our free-will. Nevertheless this movement is not the cause of grace, but the effect; hence *the whole operation pertains to grace*."[59]

Nevertheless, although Calvinists despise the word "synergism" when discussing grace and man's will, Scripture actually uses the word to describe how God works with man. At the end of Mark's gospel, he says, "But they going forth preached everywhere: the Lord working withal, and confirming the word with signs that followed" (16:20). The Greek for "working withal" is *sunergeo*, which literally means "working together with"[60] In fact, from this word we get the English cognate *synergize*. St. Paul also uses this word when he says, "And we helping (*sunergeo*) do exhort you, that you receive not the grace of God in vain" (1 Cor. 6:1). St. Paul is helping the Corinthians receive the grace of God by cooperating with God as a minister of His grace. If the Holy Ghost uses a word (*sunergeo*) that can be properly understood as "synergize" when describing grace and free will, then Calvinists should have no problem with the word.

Sufficient Grace and Calvinism

As we have learned, Calvinism believes that God wills to regenerate man only through irresistible grace. If a person does not accept Christ, then in Calvinism

---

58. Because Molinism and Arminianism hold that God's grace is dependent upon the will of man, the theology of these two views can be rightfully described as synergistic.

59. ST, I-II, Q 111, Art 2 (emphasis added).

60. The subject and predicate phrase "they going forth" (*ekeinos de exerchomai*) is the only referent for the verb "working withal" (*sunergeo*), which definitively demonstrates that God was collaborating with the apostles in their preaching of the gospel.

God granted him no grace at all and left him in sin. However, if God commands that man repent but does not give man the *power* to repent, then Calvinism makes God a liar. Scripture teaches that "it is impossible for God to lie" (Heb. 6:18) and that God "lieth not" (Titus 1:2). If God is commanding man to do the impossible, then God is lying to man. God is also mocking man by threatening him with punishments that he cannot avoid. Although Calvinists accuse Catholics of having an anthropocentric religion, there is nothing more anthropocentric than the Calvinist view of God. It is a religion created by the mind and logic of sinful man.

The Calvinist will respond by saying God's pleadings to man for repentance are not lies because He doesn't intend the message for the reprobate. As we saw with 2 Peter 3:9, Calvinists interpret God's pleadings with man as exhortations to the unbelieving elect, not to all people. Because we don't know who is in the elect, the Calvinist argues, it is necessary to give a "general call" to all in order to get the "special call" to the elect. God's call for repentance is not intended for all men, but only for the predestinate. Moreover, even though God never gives the reprobate sufficient grace to respond to His call (remember, only the elect get "irresistible" grace), God still holds them responsible for their sins. For the Calvinist, the "general call" evidently gets God "off the hook" for such an injustice.

As we have said, Scripture never makes a distinction between a "general call" to all men and a "special call" to the elect. Calvinists create this distinction to make their theology work. Moreover, Scripture is clear that God's pleadings *are intended for those who refuse them*, and not for the unbelieving elect alone. This fact refutes the Calvinist position. For example, the people Jeremias begged to repent "have refused to receive correction" (5:3) and "have refused to return" (8:5). Why would God lament of their refusal to respond, if they were incapable of responding? Why would God express displeasure for their refusing correction, if He didn't empower them to repent?

In the Book of Proverbs, we read, "Because I called, and you refused: I stretched out my hand, and there was none that regarded. You have despised all my counsel, and have neglected my reprehensions" (1:24-25). Again, God's call is intended for those who refuse it, and not just for those who accept it. God says through Isaias, "I have spread forth my hands all the day to an unbelieving people, who walk in a way that is not good after their own thoughts" (65:2). God also says through Zacharias, "Turn ye from your evil ways, and from your wicked thoughts: but they did not give ear, neither did they hearken to me, saith the Lord" (1:4). It would be redundant to provide more verses. If

God doesn't provide sufficient grace to those with whom He pleads, then He is commanding them to do the impossible. This denigrates the absolute integrity and truthfulness of God.[61] As we have said, such continual pleadings to the reprobate would be no more than lies and mockeries—an unthinkable suggestion for our holy God.

Calvinists also deny sufficient grace by referring to those scriptures where God blinds and hardens man. Isaias reveals that God will "blind the heart of this people, and make their ears heavy, and shut their eyes: lest they see with their eyes, and hear with their ears, and understand with their heart, and be converted" (6:9). Jesus refers to Isaias's revelation when He says, "He hath blinded their eyes, and hardened their heart, that they should not see with their eyes, nor understand with their heart, and be converted."[62] St. Paul does the same when he says, "That which Israel sought, he hath not obtained: but the election hath obtained it; and the rest have been blinded" (Rom. 11:7). St. Paul also reveals, "With the ear you shall hear, and shall not understand; and seeing you shall see, and shall not perceive" (Acts 28:26).

Although man can do nothing spiritual without God's assistance, the Calvinist errs when he assumes that God never gave sufficient grace to those He blinds. The Calvinist simply assumes that these verses describe man's original, pre-regeneration state. In other words, the Calvinist argues that spiritual blindness always precedes regeneration. The Calvinist also assumes that God, contrary to His infinite justice, wills to leave man in this blindness without giving him any help. How such a position glorifies God, we don't know. Moreover, Scripture does not teach that God creates people in order to blind them, but blinds them *as a punishment for sin*. We just saw this truth with the Jews of John 6. We also saw this truth with Pharao in the Book of Exodus[63] and the sodomites in St. Paul's letter to the Romans (1:28). God does not will the destruction of the blind, as Calvinists maintain. Rather, He wills to permit them to resist His grace and to punish them by withholding His grace for this resistance.

Thus, St. Thomas teaches that both man and God are the cause of spiritual blindness: "One is the movement of the human mind in cleaving to evil, and

---

61. Incredibly, many Calvinists see no problem with claiming that God commands the impossible. For example, about the Jews in John's gospel, Dr. James White says, "Yes, they had been called upon to repent and believe. It does not follow, however, that 'they were able to do so'" *The Potter's Freedom*, p. 108.

62. John 12:40, citing Isa. 6:9.

63. Ex. 4:21; 7:3-4; 9:12; 10:1, 20, 27; 14:4, 8.

turning away from the Divine light; and as regards this, God is not the cause of spiritual blindness and hardness of heart, just as He is not the cause of sin. The other thing is the withdrawal of grace, the result of which is that the mind is not enlightened by God to see aright; and as regards this God is the cause of spiritual blindness and hardness of heart."[64] This is why St. John says, "But he that hateth his brother, is in darkness, and walketh in darkness, and knoweth not wither he goeth; because the darkness hath blinded his eyes" (1 John 2:11). He that hates his brother rejects the grace that God gave him to obey the Commandments. St. Thomas analogizes such resistance "to a house whose window-shutters are closed, although the sun is in no way the cause of the house being darkened, since it does not act of its own accord in failing to light up the interior of the house."[65]

On the other hand, St. Thomas explains that "God, of His own accord, withholds His grace from those in whom He finds an obstacle."[66] Unlike salutary acts, where God's grace precedes and produces the effect, man's defect always precedes God's punishment. Nevertheless, as we have learned, this does not mean God is determined by man's actions. God wills both the permission to sin and the punishment for sin from all eternity. As we saw in the councils of Quiersy and Valence, God does not predestine man's sin, but He does predestine man's punishments (including the withdrawal of grace and hardening of his heart). This is because both the permission to sin and the punishment for sin are part of God's eternal decree. As Scripture teaches, "Judgments are prepared for scorners: and striking hammers for the bodies of fools" (Prov. 19:29).

Jesus' admonition to the Jews also reveals the truth that man resists grace. Jesus laments: "Jerusalem, Jerusalem, thou that killest the prophets, and stonest them that are sent unto thee, how often would I have gathered together thy children, as the hen doth gather her chickens under her wings, and thou wouldest not? Behold, your house shall be left to you, desolate" (Matt. 23:37-38). Because this passage reveals that man can resist grace, Calvinists are forced to respond. They do so by arguing that Jesus was trying to gather the Jewish leaders' children, and not the leaders themselves. Since the Jewish leaders hindered the gospel message but were already among the reprobate, the Calvinist argues that they didn't resist sufficient grace.

This is another example of reading one's theology into a passage. First, who

---

64. ST, Pt I-II, Q 79, Art 3.
65. Ibid.
66. Ibid.

says Jesus wasn't trying to gather the Jewish leaders as well? After all, Jesus preached the gospel to Nicodemus, who was a Jewish leader (John 3:1-15). In order to prevent his theology from unraveling (by admitting that the Jewish leaders rejected sufficient grace), the Calvinist must say that Jesus wasn't seeking to save the Jewish leaders. Furthermore, what stopped Jesus from gathering the children, anyway? Couldn't Jesus have regenerated the children in spite of their leaders' resistance? For the Calvinist to argue that the "reprobate" Jewish leaders hindered the children from receiving the grace of the gospel is a tacit admission that man's will (here, the will of the Jewish leaders) can thwart God's sufficient grace.

Calvinist John Gill unwittingly admits the same. In his analysis of the passage, Gill first says, "The opposition and resistance to the will of Christ, were not made by the people, but by their governors."[67] But then he says that there "is no proof of men's resisting the operations of the Spirit and grace of God, but of obstructions and discouragements thrown in the way of attendance on the external ministry of the word."[68] This mouthful makes little sense. First, Gill admits that the leaders did resist the will of Christ, because Christ willed to gather the children but the Jewish leaders prevented Him from doing so. Secondly, if the will of Christ is an "operation of the Spirit and grace of God" (which it is), then Gill contradicts himself by saying that there is no proof of men resisting that operation (Gill just admitted that the Jewish leaders did resist it). Thirdly, how there is any distinction between "resisting the operations" of the Holy Ghost and throwing "obstructions and discouragements" in His way, Gill doesn't explain.

The Calvinist's denial of sufficient grace not only distorts the truth of God's justice but also denigrates the truth of His infinite mercy. This is the most glaring error in Calvinism's denial of sufficient grace. Although in every work of God is found both mercy and justice, God's justice *presupposes* His mercy. This means that God *first* grants sufficient grace (out of His mercy) *before* He punishes (out of His justice) for resisting the grace. As Scripture says, "All the ways of the Lord are mercy and truth" (Psalm 24:10). St. Thomas explains, "Now the work of divine justice always presupposes the work of mercy; and is founded thereon. For nothing is due to creatures, except for something pre-existing in them, or foreknown. Again, if this is due to a creature, it must

67. John Gill, *The Cause of God and Truth*, p. 29.
68. Ibid.

be due on account of something that precedes. And since we cannot go on to infinity, we must come to something that depends only on the goodness of the divine will—which is the ultimate end ... So in every work of God, viewed as its primary source, there appears mercy."[69]

Moreover, if God deprives the reprobate of the sufficient grace to be saved, then He predestines them to hell and positively wills evil. Why? Because evil is a privation of good, and God is the greatest good. If God wills to deprive the reprobate of the greatest good (Himself), then God wills evil per se more than the good (the punishment) that is derived from the reprobate's evil. This is absurd. St. Thomas explains,

> No[,] the evil that accompanies one good, is the privation of another good. Never therefore would evil be sought after, not even accidentally, unless the good that accompanies the evil were more desired than the good of which the evil is the privation. Now God wills no good more than He wills His own goodness; yet He wills one good more than another. Hence He in no way wills the evil of sin, which is the privation of the right order towards the divine good. The evil of natural defect, or of punishment, He does will, by willing the good to which such evils are attached.[70]

The Church is also clear that God does not will evil or predestine man to hell. The Council of Orange says, "We not only do not believe that some have been truly predestined to evil by divine power, but also with every execration we pronounce anathema upon those, if there are [any such], who wish to believe so great an evil."[71] The Council of Valence reiterated Orange's condemnation.[72] Valence also says, "Certainly neither (do we believe) that the foreknowledge of God has placed a necessity on any wicked man, so that he cannot be different" and that "God foreknew their malice, because it is from them, but that He did not predestine it, because it is not from Him."[73]

The Council of Trent further says, "If anyone shall say that it is not in the power of man to make his ways evil, but that God produces the evil as well as

69. ST, Pt I, Q 21, Art 4.
70. ST, Pt I, Q 19, Art 9.
71. Denz., 200.
72. Denz., 321.
73. Denz., 321-322.

the good works, not only by permission, but also properly and of Himself, so that the betrayal of Judas is no less His own proper work than the vocation of Paul: let him be anathema."[74] Trent also says, "If anyone shall say that the grace of justification is attained by those only who are predestined to life, but that all others, who are called, are called indeed, but do not receive grace, as if they are by divine power predestined to evil: let him be anathema."[75]

Thus, God's gift of sufficient grace to the reprobate is a crucial difference between Calvinism and Catholicism. Catholics believe that God permits the damnation, but does not will it. The permission to do something means that one has the power not to do it. If I give my child the permission to ride her bicycle, she has the power not to ride it. Similarly, if God gives a person the permission to sin, that means the person has the power not to sin. But the person can have the power not to sin only if God gives him the grace not to sin. And for God to give a person grace means that Christ won the grace for that person. In other words, Christ died for that person. This means that Christ died for all men, which is the teaching of Scripture and the Catholic Church. Let's look at this issue in greater detail.

General Versus Limited Atonement

Calvinists deny the truth of sufficient grace because of an erroneous understanding of Christ's atonement. Calvinists view the atonement as a legal transaction whereby Christ pays the full penalty for man's sin by offering Himself as a substitute victim. Two conclusions flow from this premise. First, because Christ makes a full payment for sin, those who benefit from the payment are eternally secure. Christ has died in their place and has made full satisfaction for their sins. Secondly, because not all people go to heaven, Christ must have died only for the elect. Calvinists call this view "Limited Atonement" (one of the Five Points of Calvinism).[76] In Calvinism, Christ did not die for the reprobate, because God would not require a second payment from them (in hell) if Christ already satisfied the payment (on the Cross). Thus, based on the doctrine of limited atonement, the Calvinist concludes that the elect receive irresistible grace, and the reprobate receive no grace.

---

74. Denz., 816.

75. Denz., 827.

76. Ironically, Calvinists vehemently debate whether John Calvin actually believed in "Limited Atonement." In many of his writings, Calvin states that Christ atoned for the sins of all men.

Although there is a coherent, logical consistency in the Calvinist's conclusions (which is why many people fall for the error), the premise is wrong: Christ's atonement is *not* a legal transaction whereby He pays the penalty for the sins. In fact, Christ could not have legally satisfied the Father's justice against sin because He was under no legal obligation to do so. Although Scripture does refer to Christ as "purchasing" our redemption and the Passion as its "price," it uses such terms metaphorically.[77] As St. Thomas says, "Now Christ made satisfaction, not by giving money or anything of the sort, but by bestowing what was of greatest price—Himself—for us. And therefore Christ's Passion is called our redemption."[78] Jesus' atonement is rightfully described as the price of our redemption, but it does not connote a legal exchange like the payment of money for goods or services.[79]

Rather, Christ's atonement is a personal propitiation of the Father's wrath against sin.[80] Propitiation is the means by which God's anger toward sin is appeased and His honor restored through sacrifice. St. Thomas explains, "A sacrifice properly so called is something done for that honor which is properly due to God, in order to appease Him."[81] St. Thomas also says, "Now it is the proper effect of sacrifice to appease God: just as man likewise overlooks an offense committed against him on account of some pleasing act of homage shown him ... And in like fashion Christ's voluntary suffering was such a good act that, because of its being found in human nature, God was appeased for every offense of the human race with regard to those who are made one with the crucified Christ."[82] The Catechism of Trent also says that the Passion of Christ "was a sacrifice most acceptable to God, for when offered by His Son on the altar of the cross, it entirely appeased the wrath and indignation of the Father."[83] This is why St. John says, "And he is the propitiation for our sins: and not for ours only, but also for those of the whole world" (1 John 2:2).

Propitiation is principally a part of personal relationships and not legal ones. If I steal money from a stranger, the stranger will seek a legal remedy. He will

---

77. See, for example, Acts 20:28; 1 Cor. 6:20; 7:23; 2 Pet. 2:1; Apoc. 5:9; 14:3-4.

78. ST, Pt III, Q 48, Art 4.

79. Moreover, if God made Christ a substitute victim in place of the elect, then Christ would have to suffer a substitute penalty. This means that Christ in His human nature would have to suffer for all eternity.

80. For more on the propitiatory nature of Christ's sacrifice, see my book *The Biblical Basis for the Eucharist*, pp. 24-41.

81. ST, Pt III, Q 48, Art 3.

82. ST, Pt III, Q 49, Art 4.

83. *Catechism of the Council of Trent*, p. 60.

not care how much I apologize or try to appease him in other ways. He will only want his money back. That is because I don't have a personal relationship with the stranger. However, if I steal from my parents, they won't care as much about the money. They will be personally offended. Even if I return the money to them, they will continue to be hurt by my actions. It will not be about the money, but about my having harmed our relationship. Whereas the stranger will desire legal payment, my parents will desire to be appeased. They will desire some sort of sacrifice from me to prove my love for them, and to restore their honor and justice. A heart-felt apology in charity will mean far more to them than a return of the money. In a word, they will want to be propitiated for my sin.

In the same way, Jesus Christ did not satisfy the Father's justice with an impersonal legal payment for our sins, but with a personal sacrifice that appeased the Father's wrath and acknowledged His honor. In His voluntary offering for sin, it was Christ's charity, and not legality, that satisfied God's justice. Jesus says, "Therefore doth the Father love me: because I lay down my life, that I may take it again" (John 10:17). St. John also says, "In this is charity: not as though we had loved God, but because he hath first loved us, and sent his Son to be a propitiation for our sins" (1 John 4:10). Christ's sacrifice propitiated the Father because it pleased Him more than He hated man's sins. As a result, God offers man grace out of His gracious benevolence and not legal obligation. As St. Paul says, in the New Covenant "you are not under the law, but under grace" (Rom. 6:14).

Calvinists also see Christ as a substitute victim because Isaias says that "he hath borne our infirmities" and "hath borne the sins of many."[84] St. Peter also says, "Who his own self bore our sins in his body on the tree" (1 Pet. 2:24). If Christ literally bore the reprobate's sins and their penalty on the Cross, then He is a substitute and God would not require those same sins to be punished again in hell. This is precisely why Calvinists argue that Christ didn't die for the reprobate. However, the Greek word for "bore" (*anaphero*) in 1 Peter 2:24 is used five other times in the New Testament in the context of sacrifice, and it never connotes a transfer of sin to the victim or the sacrificer.[85] The word simply refers to a sacrificial offering for sin, but not a transfer or infusion of

---

84. Isa. 53:4 and 53:12. See also Isa. 53:11.
85. See Heb. 7:27; 9:28; 13:15; Jas 2:21; 1 Pet. 2:5. Scripture never says that our sins were infused into or imputed to Christ. Rather, Scripture teaches that Christ made an offering for those sins (1 Cor. 5:7; Eph. 5:2; Heb. 7:27; 9:28; 10:12).

sin.[86] Jesus didn't literally bear our sins in his body, but offered God a sacrifice to appease His anger *against* those sins.

Moreover, it is heretical to say that Christ was infused with our sins, because the Son of God could never assume anything evil or sinful. As St. Paul says, "Or what fellowship hath light with darkness? And what concord hath Christ with Belial?" (1 Cor. 6:14-15). The same applies to other like scriptures. For example, St. Paul says, "Christ hath redeemed us from the curse of the law, being made a curse for us: for it is written: Cursed is every one that hangeth on a tree" (Gal. 3:13). St. Paul also says, "Him, who knew no sin, he hath made sin for us, that we might be made the justice of God in him" (1 Cor. 5:21). Because Christ is God who is the Light of the world, He does not literally become sin, or accursed, for there is no communion between light and darkness. Instead, Christ removes the curse of sin through His propitiatory sacrifice, efficaciously for the elect, but sufficiently for all.

When St. Paul in Galatians 3:13 and in 1 Corinthians 5:21 says that Christ became a curse and sin "for" us, the preposition "for" is the Greek *huper*. It is used in other verses dealing with the atonement. For example, St. Paul says, "Husbands, love your wives, as Christ also loved the church, and delivered himself up for (*huper*) it" (Eph. 5:25). St. Paul also says, "He that spared not even his own Son, but delivered him up for (*huper*) us all, how hath he not also, with him, given us all things?" (Rom. 8:32). To support their penal substitution theory, Calvinists argue that *huper* means "in place of." This is a stretch. *Huper* has a wide range of meanings, but the primary meaning is simply "for," such as "for the sake of," or "for the benefit of." Strong's Exhaustive Concordance does not use "in place of" in any of its definitions. Moreover, if *huper* in Romans 8:32 means "in place of," then the verse would reveal a universal salvation, since St. Paul says "for us all" (*huper hemeis pas*). The phrase "us all" is "all" inclusive.

Calvinists rebut by arguing that the "us all" in verse 32 refers to the elect of the surrounding verses (vv. 28-31, 33). It is true that St. Paul refers to the predestinated in these verses. It is also true that God delivered Christ up for the sake of the elect. However, verse 32 is not about predestination proper,

86. Protestant author John R.W. Stott cites Num. 9:13; 14:33-34; 18:22; 30:15; Ex. 28:43; Lev. 5:17; 19:8; 22:9; and 24:15 as support for the "transference of guilt" theory (*The Cross of Christ*, p. 134). However, none of these verses say that sin is transferred from one person to another nor do the verses have anything to do with the future sufferings of Christ. In fact, St. Thomas teaches that one is not punished for the sin of another (ST, Pt I-II, Q 87, Art 8) based, in part, on Ezechiel 18:20: "[T]he son shall not bear the iniquity of the father, and the father shall not bear the iniquity of the son."

but rather the atonement, which is the means by which God grants grace and predestines man. But since all men receive grace, the "for us all" of Romans 8:32 would not exclude the reprobate. This means that the *huper* of Romans 8:32 does not mean a literal "in the place of" substitution (since the reprobate would be included in that substitution but are not saved). Instead, the preposition *huper* means "for the benefit of," and it must be understood in the context of propitiation. We see this in Ephesians 5:2, where St. Paul says, "And walk in love, as Christ also hath loved us, and hath delivered himself for (*huper*) us, an oblation and a sacrifice to God for an odor of sweetness." The atonement is not a substitute sacrifice wherein Christ makes satisfaction through legal payment (in our place), but a sacrifice by which Christ propitiates the Father with an odor of sweetness (for our benefit).

Some Calvinists concede that propitiation is not the same as substitution. But the Calvinist then asks how the reprobate could be condemned if Christ fully propitiated God for their sins. Ultimately, this question goes to the heart of the mystery of predestination. But we can say a couple of things. First, because the atonement is not a penal substitution, there is not a one-to-one correspondence between the sufferings of Christ on the Cross and the sufferings of the reprobate in hell. Christ's appeasement procured sufficient grace for the reprobate but did not eliminate their ability to choose evil and be punished for their choices. Secondly, even if Christ and the reprobate suffer the same penalty (they do not), double jeopardy applies only when the *same* victim suffers twice for the same crime, not when two or more people suffer for the same crime. Further, Christ "fully propitiated" the Father for the sins of the reprobate because the propitiation is sufficient for their salvation but not efficacious for them because of the sovereign will of God.

Thus, although Scripture uses *propitiation* to describe Christ's atoning work,[87] it never uses *substitution*. Calvinists incorrectly use these terms interchangeably, but they have different meanings. If my sister pays my parents the money I stole from them, her offer is one of substitution but not propitiation. Her payment will substitute for the money I owe my parents and they will be legally made whole. But they will not be propitiated. In fact, my parents may be even angrier at me. If my sister pays off the stranger, however, he will likely be satisfied with the substitute payment. He will be happy as long as he gets his money back (with maybe some interest). Propitiation is part of personal,

87. See Rom. 3:25; Heb. 2:17; 1 John 2:2; 4:10.

intimate relationships (such as between parents and children); substitution is not.

Because Calvinists view the atonement as a legal substitution, they also say that Christ suffered the penalties of hell. Thus, they conclude that Christ's sufferings cannot apply to the reprobate because they end up in hell anyway. Once again, the Calvinist is mistaken. It is true that Christ descended into hell after His death. The Apostles' Creed says, "He descended into hell." St. Peter says that Jesus "preached to those spirits that were in prison" (1 Pet. 3:19). St. Paul reveals that Jesus "descended first into the lower parts of the earth" (Eph. 4:9). Jesus also revealed that He would be "in the heart of the earth three days and three nights" (John 12:40). However, Scripture never says that Christ suffered the penalties of hell, or equates Christ's sufferings with the pains of hell. There is also not a single Church Father or medieval theologian to advance such an idea.[88] Rather, as St. Peter says, Christ descended into hell to "preach to the spirits" by announcing their deliverance with His Resurrection.

St. Thomas further explains that the "name of hell stands for an evil of penalty, and not for an evil of guilt. Hence it was becoming that Christ should descend into hell, not as liable to punishment Himself, but to deliver them who were."[89] St. Thomas confirms that the purpose of Christ's descent into hell was to reveal the deliverance of the just: "Consequently, when Christ descended into hell, by the power of His Passion He delivered the saints from the penalty whereby they were excluded from the life of glory, so as to be unable to see God in His essence, wherein man's beatitude lies."[90] Further, St. Thomas teaches that Christ's soul did not descend into the hells of the just and the lost in the same way. With regard to the just, Christ's soul descended in essence, for "He visited them in place, according to His soul, whom He visited interiorly by grace."[91] However, with regard to the lost, His soul descended only in effect, for "He put them to shame for their unbelief and wickedness."[92]

---

88. Nicolas of Cusa (d. 1464) and Pico della Mirandola (d. 1494) were the first men to entertain this heresy. Luther and Calvin later adopted the heresy to support the theory of penal substitution. For example, Calvin says, "No wonder, then, if he is said to have descended into hell, for he suffered the death that God in his wrath had inflicted upon the wicked!" (*Institutes*, 2:16:10). While Jesus' descent into hell is mentioned in the Apostles' Creed, the Church removed it from the Nicene Creed, which reveals that the early successors to the apostles gave it little doctrinal significance.
89. ST, Pt III, Q 52, Art 1.
90. ST, Pt III, Q 52, Art 5.
91. ST, Pt III, Q 52, Art 2.
92. Ibid.

Because the atonement is about propitiation and not legal payment, its value is therefore not limited to the elect. Even Calvinists admit that Christ's sacrifice was sufficient to forgive the sins of all men. Calvin himself says the same. In fact, Calvinists would agree with St. Thomas that "Christ gave more to God than was required to compensate for the offense of the whole human race."[93] With this admission, however, the Calvinist must argue that God deliberately withholds the atonement's benefits from the reprobate.[94] In this view, God gives more than what is necessary to the elect, but gives less than what is necessary to the reprobate. As Protestant Millard Erickson says, "It is as if God, in giving a dinner, prepared far more food than was needed, yet refused to consider the possibility of inviting additional guests."[95]

On the natural level, inviting guests to dinner and then refusing to feed some of them is an injustice. Yet this analogy applies to Calvinism's view of God and the atonement of Christ. The dinner host calls his guests to dinner, and then fails to give all of them dinner. Similarly, God calls all men to salvation, but refuses to give all of them the means of salvation. Even if the Calvinist claims God doesn't call all men to salvation (which is not true), he must confess that, in his theology, God gives all men a human nature but refuses to give some of them the grace to obey the laws of nature. Of course, there is no comparison between the temporal fate of the unfed dinner guests and the eternal fate of the un-graced reprobate; the supernatural injustice is infinitely greater—and it is committed by God Himself! Calvinists correctly point out that a double payment for sin is unjust. But wouldn't God's depriving the reprobate of the grace they needed to obey Him, and then punishing them for failing to obey Him, be equally unjust?

Even though they deny that God gives the reprobate sufficient grace for salvation, many Calvinists believe in something called "common grace."[96] Common grace is a grace that God gives the reprobate to restrain them from being more evil than they already are. For example, in describing Pharao, Calvinist James White says, "His blackened sin-filled heart was constantly being reined in by God's common grace so that he was not nearly as bad as he could have

---

93. ST, Pt III, Q 48, Art 2.
94. For example, popular Calvinist R.C. Sproul asks and answers the question: "Does God give the ability to come to Jesus to all men? The Reformed view of predestination says no" (*Chosen By God*, p. 68).
95. Erickson, *Christian Theology*, p. 852.
96. Not all Calvinists believe in common grace. Reformed theologians also debate whether Calvin actually believed in common grace.

been."[97] This view causes more problems for Calvinist theology. First, with this view, the Calvinist admits that not all grace irresistibly regenerates the sinner (even though irresistible grace is one of Calvinism's Five Points). Secondly, if common grace restrains an unregenerated man's sinfulness, then unregenerated man cannot be totally depraved, since he would sin more without the grace.

Furthermore when God restrains a sinner from committing sin, it is an act of His mercy, as David says: "[M]y God, his mercy shall prevent me" (Ps. 58:11); and, "[T]he God of heaven gave them power to resist" (Jdt. 5:19). But Calvinists say that God leaves the reprobate to His justice, not His mercy. Also, if the reprobate receive *any* kind of grace from God, that means Christ died for them (or they would get no grace). That is, Christ propitiated the Father's anger against their sins insofar as the Father is willing to "prevent" them in "His mercy." Finally, this truth also highlights the fact that the atonement is not a penal substitution, since the reprobate receive grace but are not saved.

Calvinists marshal a number of scriptures to support their view of limited atonement, for example: "And she shall bring forth a son: and thou shalt call his name JESUS. For he shall save his people from their sins" (Matt. 1:21); "Husbands, love your wives, as Christ also loved the church, and delivered himself up for it" (Eph. 5:25); "I am the good shepherd. The good shepherd giveth his life for his sheep" (John 10:11); "As the Father knoweth me, and I know the Father: and I lay down my life for my sheep" (John 10:15); "Who gave himself for us, that he might redeem us from all iniquity, and might cleanse to himself a people acceptable, a pursuer of good works" (Titus 2:14); "For I delivered unto you first of all, which I also received: how that Christ died for our sins, according to the scriptures" (1 Cor. 15:3).

Of course, none of these verses says that Christ died only for the elect. In fact, none of the verses uses the word "elect." Moreover, it is a logical fallacy to conclude that Christ did not die for the reprobate just because He died for the elect. Finally, scriptures that refer to the beneficiaries of Christ's redemption (the "church," the "sheep," the "acceptable people") certainly *can* be interpreted to refer to the elect. Such an interpretation would emphasize those for whom Christ's death was efficacious. But there is no exegetical basis to exclude the reprobate from the interpretation, especially when other verses include them.

For example, St. Paul says, "For therefore we labor and are reviled, because we hope in the living God, who is the Savior of all men, especially of the

97. *The Potter's Freedom*, p. 220; cf. p. 113, 212.

faithful" (1 Tim. 4:10). In no uncertain terms, this verse says that Christ is the Savior of all, but especially of the faithful. The Greek adverb for "especially" (*malista*) means "chiefly," "most of all," or "above all." The adverb is used eleven other times in the New Testament, and it always describes a particular within a class.[98] For example, in the same epistle, St. Paul says, "But if any man have not care of his own, and especially (*malista*) of those of his house, he hath denied the faith, and is worse than an infidel" (5:8). St. Paul is exhorting us to care for all our relatives (not just some of them), but particularly those with whom we live. In Galatians 6:10, St. Paul says, "Therefore, whilst we have time, let us work good to all men, but especially (*malista*) to those who are of the household of the faith." Again, we are to work good to every single man (not just to certain men), but particularly to our brothers in the New Covenant.

As applied here, the particular in 1 Timothy 4:10 is the elect (the "faithful") and the class is all men (the elect and the reprobate). That means Christ died for all men, but especially the elect. That is because the grace from Christ's atoning death is sufficient for all, but efficacious only for the elect. Moreover, the transliteration for "all men" in 1 Timothy 4:10 is the familiar *pas anthropos*, which St. Paul uses earlier in the epistle, in 1 Timothy 2:4. This lends further support that 1 Timothy 2:4 is about God's antecedent will to save all men. As one can see, *pas anthropos* must refer to every single man, since the "faithful" is a particular within the larger class. If not, 1 Timothy 4:10 would read that Christ is the Savior of a subset of men, but especially of a subset of the subset. Such an interpretation is nonsensical.

Thus, when St. John says, "And he is the propitiation for our sins: and not for ours only, but also for those of the whole world" (1 John 2:2), he really means that Christ's sacrifice is for all men. In light of 1 Timothy 4:10, the "our sins" of 1 John 2:2 can refer to the "faithful" (elect), while "those of the whole world" can refer to "all men" (elect and reprobate).

In his second epistle, St. Peter says, "But there were also false prophets among the people, even as there shall be among you lying teachers, who shall bring in sects of perdition, and deny the Lord who bought them: bringing upon themselves swift destruction" (2:1). In this verse, St. Peter says that the Lord also "bought" unbelievers. The word for "bought" (*agorazo*) refers to the atoning death of Christ ("purchasing" our salvation; giving the "price" of His life).[99] This

---

98. See Acts 20:38; 25:26; 26:3; Gal. 6:10; Phil. 4:22; 1 Tim. 4:10; 5:8, 17; 2 Tim. 4:13; Titus 1:10; Philm. 1:16; 2 Pet. 2:10.
99. See, for example, 1 Cor. 6:20; 7:23; 1 Pet. 2:9; Apoc. 5:9; 14:3.

is demonstrated, for example, by St. Paul's discourse to the clergy at Ephesus: "Take heed to yourselves, and to the whole flock, wherein the Holy Ghost hath placed you bishops, to rule the church of God, which he hath purchased (*agorazo*) with his own blood" (Acts 20:28). While Christ especially purchased the Church (the elect) with His blood, He also purchased the lying teachers who denied Him (the reprobate).

When they see a verse like Acts 20:28, Calvinists want to limit the application of the verb *agorazo* to its object (here, "the Church"). Such an argument not only denies the plain meaning of 2 Pet. 2:1 but also ignores that the verb doesn't function with such a limitation. For example, in the Apocalypse, we read: "These are they who were not defiled with women: for they are virgins. These follow the Lamb whithersoever he goeth. These were purchased (*agorazo*) from among men, the firstfruits to God and to the Lamb" (14:4). This verse shows that "purchased" is not limited to the object of the verse (virginal men) because the elect also include *non*-virginal men. Calvinists may also argue that the heretics of 2 Pet. 2:1 were the unbelieving elect. However, this argument also fails because these unbelievers brought upon themselves "swift destruction," that is, damnation. This means that Christ purchased both the elect and the reprobate by His death on the Cross, as 2 Pet. 2:1 unmistakably teaches.

In his second letter to the Corinthians, St. Paul says, "For the charity of Christ presseth us: judging this, that if one died for all, then all were dead. And Christ died for all; that they also who live, may not now live to themselves, but unto him who died for them, and rose again" (1 Cor. 5:14-15). St. Paul plainly teaches that Christ died for *all* men because *all* men are in sin. St. Paul's use of a parallel construction (*pas apothnesko* for "all were dead" and "died for all") [100] emphasizes the exegetical parity between the group that is in sin (all men) and the group for which Christ died (all men). [101] St. Paul follows Isaias's prophecy: "All we like sheep have gone astray, every one hath turned aside into his own way: and the Lord hath laid on him the iniquity of us all" (53:6). Just as "all" went astray and died, so Christ died and bore the iniquity of "all." St. Paul also

---

100. St. Paul uses similar parallels elsewhere. For example, in 1 Cor. 15:22 and Rom. 5:18, St. Paul says "all die" and "all are made alive." Because only the elect are ultimately made alive, St. Paul in these verses is emphasizing that all who have died receive sufficient grace to be made alive. In Rom. 5:19, St. Paul says "many died" and "many are justified." Because all die and not just many, "many" in this verse also means "all"—that is, all receive sufficient grace to be justified.

101. The transliteration for "that if one died for all, then all were dead. And Christ died for all" is *hoti heis huper* pas apothnesko *ara ho* pas apothnesko *kai huper* pas apothnesko.

says, "But we see Jesus, who was made a little lower than the angels, for the suffering of death, crowned with glory and honor: that, through the grace of God, he might taste death for all" (Heb. 2:9). Jesus tasted death for all (*pas*) because all (*pas*) are in sin, but not all receive the fruits of His death.

Because Christ died for all men, He intercedes for all men before the Father in heaven. This is why St. John says, "But if any man sin, we have an advocate with the Father, Jesus Christ the just" (1 John 2:1). The Greek for "any man" (*tis*) refers to those who sin. Because all sin, Jesus is the advocate for all men, which means He died for all men. St. John says so in the next verse: "And he is the propitiation for our sins: and not for ours only, but also for those of the whole world" (v. 2). Because God loves the whole world, He sends Christ to propitiate for all the sins of the world: "For God so loved the world, as to give his only begotten Son; that whosoever believeth in him, may not perish, but may have life everlasting" (John 3:16).

Calvinist James White makes a very Catholic statement when he says, "Christ intercedes for all for whom He dies since intercession is simply the presentation of the finished work of Calvary before the Father."[102] A Catholic could not have said it much better. Christ presents His eternal sacrifice to God in His role as our High Priest and Mediator in order to forgive the sins of those who come to Him by grace. St. Paul says, "But this, for that he continueth for ever, hath an everlasting priesthood, Whereby he is able also to save for ever them that come to God by him; always living to make intercession for us" (Heb. 7:24-25). St. Paul connects Christ's ability to save with His propitiatory sacrifice. Jesus is our "faithful high priest before God, that he might be a propitiation for the sins of the people. For in that, wherein he himself hath suffered and been tempted, he is able to succor them also that are tempted" (Heb. 2:17-18).

Note that Christ intercedes for those who "come to God by Him." As we saw in John 6:44, no one comes to God unless the Father draws him. Because God draws all men to Christ in some way (John 12:31-32) and Christ's intercession is the basis for the Father's drawing, Christ must intercede for all men. Further, because not all those who the Father draws infallibly stay with Christ, Christ's intercession must include those who receive sufficient grace and resist it, and not just those who receive the efficacious grace of perseverance.[103] St.

---

102. *The Potter's Freedom*, p. 241.
103. Calvinists rely on Romans 8:34 in arguing that Christ intercedes only for the elect. While the object of Christ's intercession in this verse can certainly be interpreted as the elect (based on Rom. 8:28-33), this does not mean that Christ intercedes only for the elect. At most, it means that

Paul underscores this truth by revealing that Christ is *able* (*dunamai*) to save those who come to God, not that He infallibly saves all for whom He intercedes (see Heb. 2:18; 7:25). St. Paul does not say that Christ's intercession automatically results in salvation. We understand Christ's ability to save the reprobate in terms of sufficient grace: Christ is *able* to save the reprobate, but He lets them fall away in accord with His justice. Christ is also able to save the elect, which He actually does, in accord with His mercy.

Calvinists point out that Christ prayed specifically for the elect during His earthly ministry. For example, in His priestly prayer, Jesus says, "I pray not for the world, but for them whom thou has given me: because they are mine" (John 17:9). This does not necessarily mean that Jesus didn't pray for the reprobate. [104] He could have, insofar as He willed them sufficient grace. For example, before He raised Lazarus from the dead, Jesus prayed aloud so that the Jews who were present would believe that He was the Messiah (see John 11:42). Although "many" Jews believed in Him after the miracle, "some" Jews refused to believe (John 11:45-46). Whatever Christ intended in His prayers, we know one thing for certain: Christ willed in His prayers only what His Father willed. St. Thomas explains, "But according to the will of reason, Christ willed nothing but what He knew God to will. Wherefore every absolute will of Christ, even human, was fulfilled, because it was in conformity with God; and consequently, His every prayer was fulfilled."[105]

Thus, if Christ did pray for the reprobate, His prayers would have conformed to God's antecedent will to give them sufficient grace to be saved. When Christ prayed for the elect, His prayers conformed to God's consequent will to efficaciously save them. It is the same with the prayers of Christ's heavenly intercession. Christ's prayers always conform to the will of God, which is why Christ's prayers are always answered by God. St. Paul tells us that Christ who offered "up prayers and supplications to him that was able to save him from death, *was heard* for his reverence" (Heb. 5:7). Thus, when Jesus from the Cross said, "Father, forgive them, for they know not what they do" (Luke 23:43), He was not praying for the salvation of all of His persecutors, for it was

---

Christ's intercession secures the elect's election. As other scriptures reveal, Christ intercedes for all men (Heb. 7:24-25; John 12:32) because Christ died for all men (1 Tim. 4:10; 2 Pet. 2:1).

104. Strictly speaking, Judas Iscariot was among those "given" to Christ by the Father (John 17:12) and "chosen" by Christ Himself (John 6:71).

105. ST, Pt III, Q 21, Art 4. St. Thomas has a higher view of Christ's prayers than the Calvinists who believe that Christ could have had negative answers to His prayers. See, for example, Norman Geisler's *Chosen But Free* (p. 81) and John Gill's *The Cause of God and Truth*, 1.87-88.

not God's efficacious will to save every one of them. As St. Thomas explains, "Our Lord did not pray for all those who crucified Him, as neither did He for all those who would believe in Him; but for those only who were predestinated to obtain eternal life through Him."[106]

In the face of all the evidence against their theology, Calvinists finally resort to the emotionally charged argument for Christ's perfection: if Christ is a perfect Savior, then He didn't die for those in hell, otherwise He is a Savior who fails. Of course, the Calvinist admits that Christ would have undergone the same death to save even *one* of the elect. They also admit that Christ's death is sufficient to save all men. As we have said, this forces them, in order to preserve Christ's perfection, to admit that God deliberately *withholds* His grace (except "common grace") from the reprobate. We have already explained that such a view accuses God of the gravest of injustices and makes Him the author of the reprobate's damnation. Moreover, calling Christ's death "sufficient" to save the reprobate when no grace is offered to them is farcical. Sufficient for what? In Calvinism, Christ's death has *no* value for the reprobate. A billionaire's bank account may be sufficient to pay my bills, but it has no value to me unless he gives me access to it. In Catholic theology, Christ's death is *truly* sufficient to save the reprobate, because it provides them sufficient grace to be saved. In Calvinist theology, the reprobates are never given the offer. Christ's death is *insufficient* to save them.

Jesus Christ is a perfect Savior because He perfectly accomplishes the will of the Father through His atoning death: To propitiate the Father's wrath sufficiently for all, but efficaciously for the elect. God's consequent will is never thwarted by human beings. It is always achieved. If we are to admit that God's perfect sovereignty includes human free-will decisions (we must), then it necessarily follows that God's sovereign act of salvation is not rendered "imperfect" by human free-will decisions. Scripture never makes Christ's perfection conditioned upon man's decisions. Man's imperfection takes nothing away from Christ's perfection because God wills to permit some men to fail in their goodness.

The Council of Valence declared that Christ "does not regard the greatness and the fullness of the price."[107] St. Thomas affirms this point: "God permits the devil to deceive men by certain persons, and in times and places, according

106. Ibid.
107. Denz., 319.

to the hidden motive of His judgments; still, there is always a remedy provided through Christ's Passion, for defending themselves against the wicked snares of the demons, even in Antichrist's time. But if any man neglect to make use of this remedy, *it detracts nothing from the efficacy of Christ's Passion.*"[108]

More from the Church and St. Thomas that Christ Died for All Men

The Catholic Church has always taught that Christ died for all men and obtained for them sufficient grace to be saved. The Council of Arles (475) says:

> Also that Christ, God and Redeemer, as far as it pertained to the riches of His goodness, offered the price of death for all, and because He, who is the Savior of all, especially of the faithful, does not wish anyone to perish, rich unto all who call upon him [Rom. 10:12] . . . Christ came also for the lost, because they perished although He did not will [it]. For it is not right that the riches of His boundless goodness and His divine benefits be confined to those only who seem to have been saved. For if we say that Christ extended assistance only to those who have been redeemed, we shall seem to absolve the unredeemed, who, it is established, had to be punished for having despised redemption.[109]

The Council of Quiersy repeated the Church's teachings by condemning a Saxon monk named Gottshalk (d. 868) and his predestinarian views.[110] In chapter 4, the Council declared:

> Christ Jesus our Lord, as no man who is or has been or ever will be whose nature will not have been assumed in Him, so there is, has been, or will be no man, for whom He has not suffered; although not all will be saved by the mystery of His passion. But because all are not redeemed by the mystery of His passion, He does not regard the greatness and the fullness of the price, but He regards the part of the unfaithful ones and those not

---

108. ST, Pt III, Q 49, Art 2.
109. Denz., 160b.
110. Gottshalk's heresy was in opposition to another heresy called *preterition* (or "single predestination") whereby God elects some and simply passes others by, without giving them grace, leaving them to suffer for their sins.

believing in faith those things *which He has worked through love*" [Gal. 5:6], because the drink of human safety, which has been prepared by our infirmity and by divine strength, has indeed in itself that it may be beneficial to all; but if it is not drunk, it does not heal.[111]

Pope Clement V (1342-1352) refers to the sufficiency of Christ's Passion when he says that Christ "is known to have poured out not a little drop of blood, which however on account of the union with the Word would have been sufficient for the redemption of the whole human race."[112] The Council of Trent teaches, "But although Christ died for all [2 Cor. 5:15], yet not all receive the benefit of His death, but those only to whom the merit of His passion is communicated."[113] Pope Innocent (1644-1655) condemned the Jansenist heresy, which said, "It is Semipelagian to say that Christ died or shed His blood for all men without exception."[114] Pope Alexander VIII (1689-1691) condemned the Jansenist proposition that "Christ gave Himself for us as an oblation to God, not for the elect only, but for all the faithful only."[115] The same pope also condemned Jansen's proposition that God does not give sufficient grace to non-Christians: "Pagans, Jews, heretics and others of this kind do not receive in any way any influence from Jesus Christ, and so you will rightly infer from this that in them there is a bare and weak will without any sufficient grace."[116]

Based on the plain teaching of Scripture and the councils, St. Thomas is clear that Christ's sacrifice was sufficient to atone for the sins of all men. He says, "Christ's Passion was a sufficient and superabundant atonement for the sin and the debt of the human race,"[117] and "Christ's Passion was sufficient and superabundant satisfaction for the sins of the whole human race."[118] St. Thomas also makes a clear distinction between the efficacy of the grace of the atonement and its sufficiency: "He is the propitiation for our sins, efficaciously for some, but sufficiently for all, because the price of His blood is sufficient for the salvation of all; but it has its effect only in the elect, because of the obstacle to

---

111. Denz., 319.
112. Denz., 550.
113. Denz., 795.
114. Denz., 1096.
115. Denz., 1294. The Jansenists argued that Christ died only for Christians.
116. Denz., 1295.
117. ST, Pt III, Q 48, Art 4.
118. ST, Pt III, Q 49, Art 3.

it."[119] He also says, "The Passion of Christ is profitable to all, as far as sufficiency is concerned, both for the remission of fault and for the gaining of grace and glory, but it does not have its effect except in those who are joined to the Passion of Christ by faith and charity."[120] And again, "Christ satisfied for all human nature sufficiently, but not effectively; because not all become partakers of that satisfaction."[121]

---

119. *Commentary on 1 Tim. 2:5*, cited in Garrigou-Lagrange, *Predestination*, p. 80.
120. ST, Pt III, Q 79, Art 7.
121. III Sent. d.13, Q 2, Art 2.

5

God's Gift of Perseverance

$\mathbb{W}$e complete our study of predestination by looking at God's gift of final perseverance.[1] When we speak of final perseverance, we are referring to dying in the state of sanctifying grace. We recall that God first infuses the soul with sanctifying grace at baptism, where man's sin is washed away by the merits of Jesus Christ and he becomes an adopted son of God. As St. John teaches, man in this state of grace "hath eternal life abiding in himself" (1 John 3:15). If God efficaciously wills the person to persevere in the state of grace to the end of his life, that person will go to heaven. If God permits the person to fall out of grace through serious sin, that person will be condemned unless God restores him to grace (which God does regularly for those who repent of their sins). Because even the elect sin throughout their lives, the grace of perseverance must include the grace of repentance for their sins.

Just as God needs to preserve man in a state of grace during his life, He must give man the special grace of perseverance at his death for salvation. St. Thomas teaches that this gift is necessary for man to reach his final end: "[A] man cannot be directed to his ultimate end except by the help of divine grace, without which also no one can have those things that are necessary for tending to the ultimate end, such as faith, hope, love and *perseverance*."[2] This is why St. Paul says, "Being confident of this very thing, that he, he who hath begun

---

1. This is the last of the Five Points of Calvinism, which is called "Perseverance of the Saints." To maintain the T-U-L-I-P acrostic from a Thomist perspective, we would replace "Perseverance of the Saints" with "Preservation of the Elect," thereby emphasizing God's sovereign primacy in preserving His elect from damnation.

2. CG, 3.159 (emphasis added). See also ST, Pt I, Q 24, Art 3, where St. Thomas explains that "one is directed from two sources; namely, from predestination, which direction never fails, and from grace; for whoever has grace, by this very fact becomes fitted for eternal life. This direction fails sometimes; because some are directed, by possessing grace, to obtain eternal life, yet they fail to obtain it through mortal sin."

a good work in you, will perfect it unto the day of Christ Jesus" (Phil. 1:6). St. Peter also says, "But the God of all grace, who hath called us unto his eternal glory in Christ Jesus, after you have suffered a little, will himself perfect you, and confirm you, and establish you" (1 Pet. 5:10). David also says, "Perfect thou my goings in thy paths: that my footsteps be not moved" (Ps. 16:5).

Thus, there is a distinction between the gift of habitual grace (which causes a person to live a life of virtue) and the gift of final perseverance (which causes a person to die in a state of grace). St. Thomas is clear that "perseverance enduring until death . . . needs not only habitual grace, but also the gratuitous help of God sustaining man in good until the end of his life."[3] This is because habitual grace does not take away from the free will the power to resist sufficient grace and fall away from God. St. Thomas says that "since the free-will is changeable by its very nature, which changeableness is not taken away from it by the habitual grace bestowed in the present life, it is not in the power of the free-will, albeit repaired by grace, to abide unchangeably in the good, though it is in its power to choose this."[4] St. Thomas further explains: "The virtue of perseverance, so far as it is concerned, inclines one to persevere: yet since it is a habit, and a habit is a thing one uses at will, it does not follow that a person who has the habit of virtue uses it unchangeably until death."[5] This is why the Church says "we hope for *the grace of final perseverance and the recompense* of God their Father for the good works accomplished with his grace in communion with Jesus."[6]

In light of these truths, the Council of Trent declared: "If anyone shall say that he who is justified can either persevere in the justice received without the special assistance of God, or that with that [assistance] he cannot: let him be anathema."[7] St. Thomas also explains that "man, even when possessed of grace, needs perseverance to be given to him by God . . . And hence after anyone has been justified by grace, he still needs to beseech God for the aforesaid gift of perseverance, that he may be kept from evil till the end of his life. For to man grace is given to whom perseverance is not given."[8] Hence, we understand

3. ST, Pt II-II, Q 137, Art 4.
4. Ibid.
5. Ibid.
6. CCC 2016 (emphasis in original).
7. Denz., 832.
8. ST, Pt I-II, Q 109, Art 10. Of course, "beseeching" God is itself a grace from God.

why the Council of Trent called dying in a state of grace "the great gift of perseverance"[9] and the "special assistance" of God.[10]

GRACE VERSUS GLORY

Because many who receive grace do not persevere, there is a distinction between being predestined to grace and being predestined to glory (which also shows the distinction between sufficient and efficacious grace). By being predestined to grace, one receives the grace of baptism and becomes a child of God. By being predestined to glory, one dies in a state of grace and goes to heaven. Although, absolutely speaking, the term predestination refers to the process by which God leads a soul to heaven, Scripture distinguishes between predestination to grace and predestination to glory. For example, in Ephesians 1:5, St. Paul says that God "hath predestinated us unto the adoption of children through Jesus Christ unto himself: according to the purpose of his will." Because becoming "the adoption of children through Jesus Christ" commences at baptism, when we become "heirs" with Christ, St. Paul in this passage is referring to predestination to grace.[11] However, in Romans 8:30, St. Paul says, "And whom he predestinated, them he also called. And whom he called, them he also justified. And whom he justified, them he also glorified." In this verse, St. Paul is referring to predestination to glory, when we become "glorified" in heaven.

We see the same distinction in those verses that reveal how God chooses His people. For example, St. Paul tells the Thessalonians "that God hath chosen you firstfruits unto salvation, in sanctification of the spirit, and faith of the truth" (2 Thess. 2:12). Because St. Paul is writing to the entire Church at Thessalonica (which fell away from the faith), he is speaking of their predestination to grace. Similarly, St. Peter says, "But you are a chosen generation, a kingly priesthood, a holy nation, a purchased people: that you may declare his virtues, who hath called you out of darkness into his marvelous light" (1 Pet. 2:9). Because St. Peter is writing to all of the churches in Asia Minor (which fell away from the faith), he is speaking about their predestination to grace. Jesus also tells His apostles, "Have not I chosen you twelve; and one of you is a devil?" (John 6:71). Jesus was referring to Judas Iscariot, who was predestined to grace but not to glory. Jesus also says, "And unless the Lord had shortened the days,

---

9. Denz., 826. See also Denz., 806.
10. Denz., 832.
11. See Titus 3:7; cf. Rom. 8:17; Gal. 3:29; Eph. 3:6; Jas 2:5; 1 Pet. 3:7.

no flesh should be saved: but for the sake of the elect which he hath chosen, he hath shortened the days" (Mark 13:20). In this case, Jesus is referring to the elect's predestination to glory.

What distinguishes those who are predestined to glory from those who are not? As we have learned from Scripture, the Church, and St. Thomas, the difference is simply God's sovereign predilection for His elect. God's will is the cause of all goodness in things, and no one thing would be better than another unless God loved it more. The elect receive the grace of perseverance because God loves them more and thus gives them more assistance, even though He loves all and gives grace to all. As we learned in Romans 9, God makes this determination before we are "not yet born, nor had done any good or evil (that the purpose of God, according to election, might stand" (Rom. 9:11). The elect are better than the reprobate, not because of anything they did, but because of what God willed to give them from all eternity. The elect have nothing to boast about because they are saved by the gratuitous gift of grace, "Not of works, that no man may glory" (Eph. 2:9).

Nevertheless, as we have also learned, God gives all men sufficient grace to be saved. That means that God gives all men sufficient grace *to persevere to the end*. While God wills to infallibly save His elect and wills to permit the reprobate to be damned, St. Paul is clear that there is no injustice in God (see Rom. 9:14). The reprobate fail to persevere because they set up an impediment to God's grace, not because God wills their damnation. As. St. Thomas teaches, "but they only are deprived of grace who set up an impediment to grace in themselves; just as, when the sun illumines the world, he is charged with a fault who closes his eyes, if any evil comes of it, although he cannot see unless he first has the light of the sun."[12]

We have pointed out that reprobation may be the most mysterious aspect of the study of predestination. God could have efficaciously willed the reprobate's salvation, but instead permits them to fall away for the greater good of the universe. The justice God shows to the reprobate also "works together unto good" for the elect (see Rom. 8:28). However, God does not abandon the reprobate unless they consistently reject His sufficient graces. Even though God's grace is gratuitous, "He deprives nobody of his due."[13] Even though God decrees to permit the reprobate to fall away before foreseen demerits, He withholds the

---

12. CG, 3.159.
13. ST, Pt I, Q 23, Art 5.

grace of perseverance only because of their habitual sins. The fact that *all* men sin (both the reprobate and elect) also emphasizes the pure gratuity of God's mercy toward those He predestines to glory. In His inscrutable judgments, God restores the sinning elect to grace in His mercy, and condemns the sinning reprobate in His justice. Indeed, the grace of perseverance is "a great gift" and a "special assistance" that God gives to His elect.

We can better understand God's justice in punishing the reprobate (and, thus, withholding from them of the grace of perseverance) when we understand the profound effects of sin. Scripture teaches that "pride is the beginning of all sin" (Ecclus. 10:15). St. Thomas explains that "pride regards sin as turning away from God, to Whose commandment man refuses to be subject."[14] By turning away from God and inordinately toward temporal things, we diminish our very nature and make it more difficult to practice virtue. St. Thomas says, "Now from the very fact that a thing becomes inclined to one of two contraries, its inclination to the other contrary must needs be diminished. Wherefore as sin is opposed to virtue, from the very fact that a man sins, there results a diminution of that good of nature, which is the inclination to virtue."[15]

St. Thomas further explains that "since the inclination to the good of virtue is diminished in each individual on account of actual sin … the reason is obscured, especially in practical matters, the will hardened to evil, good actions become more difficult, and concupiscence more impetuous."[16] St. Thomas properly describes these effects as "a stain on the soul."[17] Thus, St. Thomas says that "the soul, through sinning once, is more easily inclined to sin again."[18] This means that the more man sins, the easier it is for him to resist sufficient graces. After man commits sin, St. Thomas explains that "man does not at once return to the state in which he was before, and it is necessary that his will should have a movement contrary to the previous movement."[19] St. Thomas further says that "the stain of sin cannot be removed from man, unless his will accept the order of Divine justice."[20] This is because "man is united to God by his will."[21]

However, God must move man's will to accept His justice, for "man's will

14. ST, Pt I-II, Q 84, Art 2.
15. ST, Pt I-II, Q 85, Art 1.
16. ST, Pt I-II, Q 85, Art 3.
17. ST, Pt I-II, Q 86, Art 1.
18. Ibid.
19. ST, Pt I-II, Q 86, Art 2.
20. ST, Pt I-II, Q 87, Art 6.
21. Ibid.

can only be subject to God when God draws man's will to Himself."[22] As Jesus says, "No man can come to me, except the Father, who hath sent me, draw him" (John 6:44). This means that God must draw man with the grace of repentance or he will remain in his sins. St. Thomas says, "Man by himself can no wise rise from sin without the help of grace."[23] St. Thomas is also clear that "no one can merit for himself restoration after a fall,"[24] even if he had lived a virtuous life before his fall. The Council of Trent also said that God must move man to repentance: "Those who through sin have forfeited the received grace of justification, can again be justified when, moved by God, they exert themselves to obtain through the sacrament of penance the recovery, by the merits of Christ, of the grace lost."[25] That God has no obligation to move us to repentance should make us horrified of sinning in the first place. We do not merit forgiveness, for God says, "I am, I am he that blot out thy iniquities *for my own sake*" (Isa. 43:25). We should not take for granted that we will always have the grace to repent. God would not offend justice by letting us die in our sins.

Even before God grants man the gratuitous grace of repentance, He upholds him by His grace and restrains him for a time from committing further sin. St. Thomas says that a man without grace needs "God's help to uphold him in good, since if this had been withdrawn, even his nature would have fallen back into nothingness."[26] Because of man's sinful condition, St. Thomas also says, "So, too, before man's reason, wherein is mortal sin, is restored by justifying grace, he can avoid each mortal sin, and for a time, since it is not necessary that he should be always actually sinning. But it cannot be that he remains for a long time without mortal sin."[27] St. Thomas similarly says, "But if a man, by a previous inordination, has declined to evil, it will not be entirely in his power to place no impediment to grace ... if he is left to himself for a long time, he will fall into sin, through which an impediment to grace is placed."[28] Thus, St. Thomas is clear that man is completely dependent upon God's grace, not only for good actions but also for the omission of evil actions.

God draws the reprobate with the grace of repentance (because all men sin and God gives all men the graces of salvation), but He eventually permits them

---

22. ST, Pt I-II, Q 109, Art 7.
23. Ibid.
24. ST, Pt I-II, Q 114, Art 7.
25. Denz., 807.
26. ST, Pt I-II, Q 109, Art 8.
27. Ibid.
28. CG, 3.160.

to resist His grace. With this divine permission, a reprobated person continues to sin. His reason becomes more obscured and his good actions become more difficult. Finally, as a punishment for his sins, God withholds His grace and blinds him to the truth. As with His permission to allow the reprobate to sin, God's decision to desert the reprobate must be ascribed to His plan of predestination (this makes sense, for God eternally decreed both the permission to sin and the punishment for sin, but not the sin itself). St. Thomas agrees when he says that "blindness, of its very nature, is directed to the damnation of those who are blinded; for which reason it is accounted an effect of reprobation. But through God's mercy, temporary blindness is directed medicinally to the spiritual welfare of those who are blinded. This mercy, however, is not vouchsafed to all those who are blinded, but only to the predestinated."[29] If we are tempted to ask why God deserts the reprobate, we recall St. Thomas's answer: "[W]hy He chooses some for glory, and reprobates others, has no reason, except the divine will."[30]

As we have learned, God could restore a hardened, blinded sinner through efficacious grace. As the Church, Sacred Scripture, and St. Thomas teach, if God simply wills for a man to attain His grace, man will infallibly receive it. St. Thomas says that even when a man "should not receive grace: nevertheless ... God can work beyond the order that is built into things, as He does when He gives sight to a blind man or raises a dead man."[31] Moreover, because man cannot merit the grace of perseverance, God would not violate any justice in converting an evil man on his deathbed. St. Thomas is clear about this when he says, "Now many have meritorious works, who do not obtain perseverance; nor can it be urged that this takes place because of the impediment of sin, since sin itself is opposed to perseverance; and thus if anyone were to merit perseverance, God would not permit him to fall into sin. Hence perseverance does not come under merit."[32] In other words, the grace of final perseverance, as with all grace, is a completely gratuitous gift from God.

St. Thomas also says, "Now God freely bestows the good of perseverance, on whomsoever He bestows it."[33] This reminds us of St. Paul's words: "Therefore he hath mercy on whom he will; and whom he will, he hardeneth" (Rom. 9:17-

---

29. ST, Pt I-II, Q 79, Art 4.
30. ST, Pt I, Q 23, Art 5.
31. CG, 3.161.
32. ST, Pt I-II, Q 114, Art 9.
33. Ibid.

18). This is how the Lord could reward the laborers at the eleventh hour with the same penny (symbolic for eternal life) as He rewarded those who worked the entire day (see Matt. 20:1-16).[34] As St. Thomas says, "In things which are given gratuitously a person can give more or less, just as he pleases (provided he deprives nobody of his due)."[35] Nevertheless, as St. Thomas indicates, a conversion of a hardened sinner would be "beyond the order that is built into things," and so death-bed conversions are rare.[36] In the normal order, those who live a life of virtue are saved, and those who live a life of sin are damned.

UNDERSTANDING THE SIGNS

Because we cannot merit perseverance, some may be tempted to say, "What difference does it make? If God has determined everything in advance, then why don't I live the way I want to? If I am in the elect, then I will be saved no matter what I do. If I am a reprobate, I am damned no matter what I do." This is an erroneous understanding of predestination, for a number of reasons.

First, it is erroneous because God "will render to every man according to his works" (Rom. 2:6). Because God created man as a rational creature with free will after His own image and likeness, God judges man's works because man freely chooses them and is thus responsible for them. God gives man sufficient grace to obey His commandments and do good works, and they are reprobated only "who obey not the truth, but give credit to iniquity" (Rom. 2:8).

Secondly, God will not allow His elect to persist in sin. Instead, God predestines the elect "to be made conformable to the image of his Son" (Rom. 8:29). This means the predestinated *will not live a life of sin*. Rather, God will conform them to the image of Christ. Hence, when God moves us to imitate the virtues of Christ in our lives, it is a sign of predestination. At the same time, however, we must strive by God's grace to continue in virtue. If we knew the future, we would no longer have hope, and St. Paul says "we are saved by hope" (Rom. 8:24). This means the way we live *does* matter—to God and to our eternal souls. This is why St. Peter tells us to strive to do good works to "make sure your calling and election" (2 Pet. 1:10).

---

34. Notice also that the laborers said they were unable to work until they were hired (v. 7). In other words, we can do nothing for God until He calls us, for Jesus says, "no man can come to me, unless it be given him by my Father" (John 6:66).

35. ST, Pt I, Q 23, Art 5.

36. St. Jerome believed that such conversions happen once in every 200,000 deaths.

These truths should give us great comfort in God's mercy. They should also make us resign ourselves to God's providence and be sensitive to the movements of His grace. The more God moves our wills by grace, the more docile and malleable they become to His will. As God continues to conform us to the image of His Son, He creates in us the habit of doing good and avoiding sin—more great signs of predestination. St. Thomas explains that "if the acts be multiplied a certain quality is formed in the power which is passive and moved, which quality is called a habit."[37] In fact, in times of temptation, this habitual inclination to avoid sin will help us better recognize the graces God is currently providing us to prevail over that sin. And we will also recognize that we would have to intentionally labor against the grace to commit the sin.

Thus, in describing the man of grace, St. Thomas says that "there is in him an habitual inclination to avoid sin. And so when anything presents itself to him in the form of mortal sin, out of habitual inclination he refuses it, *unless he strives in the opposite direction*."[38] Even in the face of sudden temptations, St. Thomas says, "[W]hen surprised, a man acts according to his preconceived end and his pre-existing habits ... although *with premeditation of his reason* a man may do something outside the order of his preconceived end and the inclination of his habit."[39] This means that living a life of virtue—which God has empowered all men to do—will give us great confidence that we are on the right track, lest we intentionally strive to go against the grace (God permitting). Because there is no injustice with God, He will not pull the proverbial rug out from under us. If we fall, we will know it is our own fault.

We also recall St. Thomas's teaching that "there is no distinction between what flows from free will, and what is of predestination; as there is no distinction between what flows from a secondary cause and from a first cause ... because whatsoever is in man disposing him towards salvation, is all included under the effect of predestination."[40] This means that our prayers and good works are *effects* of predestination, and not its causes. As Fr. Garrigou-Lagrange says, "before ever we ourselves decided to have recourse to prayer, it was willed by God. From all eternity God willed it to be one of the most fruitful factors in our spiritual life, a means of obtaining the graces necessary to reach the goal of

---

37. ST, Pt I-II, Q 51, Art 2.
38. *De veritate*, 24.13 (emphasis added).
39. ST, Pt I-II, Q 109, Art 8 (emphasis added).
40. ST, Pt I, Q 23, Art 5.

our life's journey."[41] Because these secondary causes (caused by God who is the First Cause) are effects of predestination, predestination is furthered by them. Thus, our salutary acts are *both* causes *and* signs from God that we are being predestined to glory. As Jesus says, "For by the fruit the tree is known" (Matt. 12:33). St. Thomas further explains:

> [P]redestination is said to be helped by the prayers of the saints, and by other good works; because providence, of which predestination is a part, does not do away with secondary causes but so provides effects, that the order of secondary causes falls also under providence. So, as natural effects are provided by God in such a way that natural causes are directed to bring about those natural effects, without which those effects would not happen; so the salvation of a person is predestined by God in such a way, that whatever helps that person towards salvation falls under the order of predestination; whether it be one's own prayers, or those of another; or other good works, and suchlike, without which one would not attain to salvation. Whence, the predestined must strive after good works and prayer; because through these means predestination is most certainly fulfilled. For this reason it is said: "Labor the more that by good works you may make sure your calling and election" (2 Pet. 1:10).[42]

How Many Persevere to the End?

Because predestination is a revealed truth of God, the number of the elect is fixed and certain. The number cannot be increased or decreased. It is certain not only because God knows all things but also because He has determined the number of the elect by His own free choice. Scripture says, "[T]he Lord knoweth who are his" (2 Tim. 2:19). Jesus says, "I know whom I have chosen" (John 13:18). Jesus also says, "My sheep hear my voice: and I know them, and they follow me" (John 10:27) and, "I am the good shepherd; and I know mine, and mine know me" (John 10:14). St. Thomas further explains: "Therefore we must say that to God the number of the predestined is certain, not only

---

41. Garrigou-Lagrange, *Providence*, p. 205.
42. ST, Pt I, Q 23, Art 8. Based on his research of the Church Fathers, Fr. Garrigou-Lagrange provides eight signs of predestination: (1) a good life; (2) a conscience free from serious sin and a willingness to die rather than offend God; (3) patience in adversities endured for love of God; (4) readiness to hear the word of God; (5) compassion for the poor; (6) love of one's enemies; (7) humility; and, (8) a special devotion to the Blessed Virgin Mary (*Predestination*, pp. 216-217).

formally, but also materially. It must, however, be observed that the number of the predestined is said to be certain to God, not only by reason of His knowledge, because, that is to say, He knows how many will be saved (for in this way the number of drops of rain and the sands of the sea are certain to God) but by reason of His deliberate choice and determination."[43]

So how many are predestined? On the one hand, Scripture suggests that the number of the elect is great. In the Apocalypse, St. John describes those in heaven: "After this I saw a great multitude, which no man could number, of all nations, and tribes, and peoples, and tongues, standing before the throne, and in sight of the Lamb, clothed with white robes, and palms in their hands" (Apoc. 7:9). On the other hand, Jesus reveals that more are damned than saved when He says, "Enter ye in at the narrow gate: for wide is the gate, and broad is the way that leadeth to destruction, and many there are who go in thereat. How narrow is the gate, and strait is the way that leadeth to life: and few there are that find it!" (Matt. 7:13-14). Jesus also says, "For many are called, but few chosen" (Matt. 20:16). Thus, although there is a great number of elect, Scripture reveals that there are more reprobates.[44]

St. Thomas believed that more men are damned than saved because more men follow their senses than their reason. He says, "In man alone does evil appear as in the greater number; because the good of man as regards the senses is not the good of man as man—that is, in regard to reason; and more men seek good in regard to the senses than good according to reason."[45] He further explains that "evil comes to pass from seeking after sensible pleasures, which are known to most men, and from forsaking the good dictated by reason, which good is known to the few."[46] And again, he says, "But in man good appears in the smaller number ... because of the corruption of man due to original sin, and the very nature of human conditions ... in which the secondary perfections that direct human actions are not innate, but either acquired or infused."[47] Consequently, St. Thomas concludes that "those who are saved are in the minority."[48]

---

43. ST, Pt I, Q 23, Art 7.

44. Most of the early Church Fathers believed the majority of men are not saved, for example, Basil, John Chrysostom, Gregory of Nazianzus, Hilary, Ambrose, Jerome, Augustine, Leo the Great, and Bernard.

45. ST, Pt I, Q 49, Art 3.

46. ST, Pt I, Q 63, Art 9.

47. I Sent, d.39, Q 2, Art 2.

48. ST, Pt I, Q 23, Art 7.

Once again, Fr. Most disagrees with St. Thomas. Because Fr. Most contends that "mercy is the greatest virtue in God,"[49] he argues that "the greatest perfection should have the greatest manifestation: therefore, according to the order of the universe, the majority should be saved. But, St. Thomas thinks the majority are lost."[50] Fr. Most also refers to St. Thomas's teaching that "[t]he order of the universe seems to require that that which is more noble in things, should exceed the less noble in quantity or number . . . Therefore it is proper that the more noble . . . be multiplied as much as possible."[51] In an apparent effort to use St. Thomas's teaching against him, Fr. Most concludes: "It is plain then, that the very order of the universe requires that the elect be more numerous than the reprobates 'as much as possible.'"[52]

Fr. Most mistakenly excludes the elect angels from his analysis. St. Thomas teaches that more angels were saved than damned. He says, "[E]vil is found as in the smaller number in the angels, because many more remained faithful than fell, and perhaps even more than all the devils and men to be condemned."[53] He also says, "More angels stood firm than sinned."[54] Scripture also symbolically reveals that only a minority of angels fell: "And his tail drew the third part of the stars of heaven, and cast them to the earth" (Apoc. 12:4).[55] Moreover, it seems evident that God created more angels than humans. Scripture reveals that God created a near countless number of angels when it says, "[T]housands of thousands ministered to him, and ten thousand times a hundred thousand stood before him" (Dan 7:10).

St. Thomas also says, "[S]ince it is the perfection of the universe that God chiefly intends in the creation of things, the more perfect some things are, in so much greater an excess are they created by God."[56] St. Thomas concludes that "the angels, even inasmuch as they are immaterial substances, exist in exceeding great number, far beyond all material multitude."[57] Therefore, if the number of the created beings in heaven includes the "elect angels" (1 Tim. 5:21), then

---

49. GPS, p. 336, ft 52. There is no one virtue in God greater than another because they are all perfect. There is nothing "more" or "less" in God. However, it is correct to say that God manifests His omnipotence most greatly by showing mercy to His creatures.
50. GPS, p. 63. cf. p. 336, ft 52.
51. CG, 2.92.
52. GPS, p. 64.
53. I Sent, d.39, Q 2, Art 2.
54. ST, Pt I, Q 63, Art 9.
55. This verse is also interpreted to refer to the consecrated souls who will perish.
56. ST, Pt I, Q 50, Art 3.
57. Ibid.

it appears that more creatures are elected than reprobated. If true, the "more noble" does exceed the "less noble" in God's creation, and Fr. Most has no reason to disagree with St. Thomas. As Scripture says, "[F]or there are more with us than with them" (4 Kg. 6:16).

ETERNAL SECURITY AND "ONCE SAVED, ALWAYS SAVED"

We complete our study by examining the Protestant doctrine of "eternal security," an idea that has a much different meaning within Catholicism. In the Catholic faith, it is true to say that the elect are eternally secure. They are guaranteed to go to heaven because God will cause them to persevere in grace to the end of their lives. God has decreed to give them the grace of final perseverance and they can never fall away. As we will see, the difference between the Catholic and Protestant view is twofold. First, in Catholicism, only God knows who are His elect. The elect do not know who they are. No one can claim that he is in the elect unless God has specially revealed it to him. Secondly, the elect are guaranteed to die in a state of sanctifying grace. The elect live a life of habitual virtue, and God preserves their election to the end.

In Protestantism, the doctrine of eternal security usually means that a person *knows* he is going to heaven (this happens once he "accepts Jesus as personal Lord and Savior").[58] If the person fails to persevere by falling into a life of sin, it means he was never saved in the first place. In other circles of Protestantism, primarily Baptist, eternal security means that the person knows he is infallibly saved after accepting Christ, even if he later falls into mortal sin or rejects the faith.[59] In this scenario, the person declares that he is "once saved, always saved." No matter which version you choose, the Protestant doctrine of eternal security, which is a relatively recent error in the history of Christianity, is one of the biggest heresies Satan has ever devised. It has given many Christians during the last 450 years a false assurance in their salvation, notwithstanding their sinful lifestyles and rebellion against God's Holy Church.

Most Protestants are unaware of the fact that not a single early Church Father or medieval theologian ever taught their notion of eternal security. The

---

58. Ironically, even though Calvinists teach eternal security, most of them admit that they do not know with infallible certainty whether they are in the elect.

59. Scripture clearly condemns such a view. For example, St. Paul teaches that fornicators, idolaters, adulterers, sodomites, thieves, drunkards, extortioners, murderers, and the like shall not inherit the kingdom of God (see 1 Cor. 6:9-10; Gal. 5:21).

heresy is also refuted by Scripture, which declares, "Man knoweth not his own end" (Eccles. 9:12). In fact, Protestants are surprised to learn that John Calvin was the first to promote this heresy. Not even Martin Luther, the lead heresiarch of the Protestant revolt, dared to teach such a thing. Instead Luther said, "Through baptism these people threw out unbelief, had their unclean way of life washed away, and entered into a pure life of faith and love. Now they fall away into unbelief and . . . soil themselves again in filth."[60] Because of the dangers of the Calvinist heresy, which lulls people into a life of indifferentism, the Council of Trent was quick to condemn it in several of its infallible canons:

Canon 15: "If anyone shall say that a man who is born again and justified is bound by faith to believe that he is assuredly in the number of the predestined: let him be anathema."[61]

Canon 16: "If anyone shall say that he will for certain with an absolute and infallible certainty have that great gift of perseverance up to the end, unless he shall have learned this by a special revelation: let him be anathema."[62]

Canon 23: "If anyone shall say that a man once justified can sin no more, nor lose grace, and that therefore he who falls and sins was never truly justified; or, on the contrary, that throughout his whole life he can avoid all sins even venial sins, except by a special privilege of God, as the Church holds in regard to the Blessed Virgin: let him be anathema."[63]

In chapter 12 on *Rash Presumption of Predestination to Be Avoided*, the Council says, "No one, moreover, so long as he lives this mortal life, ought in regard to the sacred mystery of divine predestination, so far presume as to state with absolute certainty that he is among the number of the predestined, as if it were true that the one justified either cannot sin any more, or, if he does sin, that he ought to promise himself an assured repentance. For except by special revelation, it cannot be known whom God has chosen to Himself."[64] In chapter 13 on *The Gift of Perseverance*, the Council also teaches: "So also as regards the gift of perseverance . . . let no one promise himself anything as certain with absolute certitude, although all ought to place and repose a very firm hope in God's help."[65]

It should be obvious to any Christian that creatures can fall from grace.

---

60. *Commentary on 2 Peter 2:2.*
61. Denz., 825.
62. Denz., 826.
63. Denz., 833.
64. Denz., 805.
65. Denz., 806.

After all, the angels, who were created in the empyrean heaven, fell from grace and received God's just punishment. St. Jude says, "And the angels who kept not their principality, but forsook their own habitation, he hath reserved under darkness in everlasting chains, unto the judgment of the great day" (Jude 6). The angels forsook their habitation by turning against God and rejecting their original grace-filled dignity. Lucifer, the most intelligent one of them all, led the way. Scripture says, "How art thou fallen from heaven, O Lucifer, who didst rise in the morning? how art thou fallen to the earth, that didst wound the nations?" (Isa. 14:12). St. John reveals, "And that great dragon was cast out, that old serpent, who is called the devil and Satan, who seduceth the whole world; and he was cast unto the earth, and his angels were thrown down with him" (Apoc. 9:12). Jesus also says, "I saw Satan like lightning falling from heaven" (Luke 10:18). St. Paul refers to those angels who did not fall away as the "elect angels" (1 Tim. 5:21).

We all know that Adam and Eve—whom God created in a state of grace—also fell from grace: "Wherefore as by one man sin entered into this world, and by sin death; and so death passed upon all men, in whom all have sinned" (Rom. 5:12). Here is the blow to the Protestant position: St. Paul reveals that we too can fall from grace *just like Adam and Eve*. He says, "For I am jealous of you with the jealousy of God. For I have espoused you to one husband that I may present you as a chaste virgin to Christ. But I fear lest, as the serpent seduced Eve by his subtlety, so your minds should be corrupted, and fall from the simplicity that is in Christ" (1 Cor. 11:2-3). In fact, St. Thomas says it was *more* difficult for Adam and Eve to fall from grace than it would be for us. He says, "[I]t was easier for man to persevere, with the gift of grace in the state of innocence in which the flesh was not rebellious against the spirit, than it is now. For the restoration by Christ's grace, although it is already begun in the mind, is not yet completed in the flesh, as it will be in heaven, where man will not merely be able to persevere but will be unable to sin."[66]

Before we look at the scriptures that refute eternal security, let's look at a few of the most common verses Protestants use to support their doctrine. For example, Protestants often point to Jesus' statement in John's gospel: "My sheep hear my voice: and I know them, and they follow me. And I give them life everlasting; and they shall not perish for ever, and no man shall pluck them out of my hand" (10:27-28). Of course, Jesus could be speaking about His elect. In

66. ST, Pt I-II, Q 109, Art 10.

fact, a Thomist would say this is the best interpretation of the verse. However, the verse does not say that the sheep infallibly *know* they are in the elect. The verse is about God's knowledge, not the sheep's knowledge. In fact, the verse does not have to be about the elect. We have shown in other contexts (e.g., John 6) that not all who are given to Jesus stay with Jesus to the end, but only those who are given the grace of perseverance. The words for "hear" (*akouo*) and "follow" (*akoloutheo*) are present-tense active verbs indicating continuous and ongoing actions with no guarantee that such actions will remain. We also point out that Jesus is speaking of external forces that could pluck His sheep out of His hand. Jesus in this verse does not speak to the internal forces within man that can move him to abandon Christ (which happens when man rejects sufficient grace).

In his letter to the Romans, St. Paul says, "For I am sure that neither death, nor life, nor angels, nor principalities, nor powers, nor things present, nor things to come, nor might, nor height, nor depth, nor any other creature, shall be able to separate us from the love of God, which is in Christ Jesus our Lord" (8:38-39). This is another verse that can certainly apply to the elect. Because God "hatest all the workers of iniquity" (Ps. 5:7), sin *does* separate the reprobate from the love of God (which means that God hates the reprobates in the end). But, again, the verse does not speak to the beloved's knowledge of their eternal destiny. In fact, because St. Paul is not speaking of salvation in the passage, it cannot support any notion of "eternal security." Moreover, Scripture says "man knoweth not whether he be worthy of love, or hatred" (Eccles. 9:1). St. Thomas interprets this verse to mean that man cannot know with certainty whether he is in a state of grace (although he can have a moral certitude of it if he is not conscious of grave sin).[67] If man cannot infallibly know his status with God in this life, he certainly cannot infallibly proclaim his destiny in the next life.

After St. Paul explains that God cut off most of the Jews from salvation because of their unbelief (see Rom. 11:17-25), he writes, "For the gifts and the calling of God are without repentance" (v. 29).[68] Many Protestants also see "eternal security" in this verse. But the verse speaks only about God's gifts and

---

67. The Catechism also says, "Since it belongs to the supernatural order, grace *escapes our experience* and cannot be known except by faith" (CCC 2005).

68. The Greek for "without repentance" (*ametameletos*) literally means "unregretted." It is used in only one other place in the New Testament (1 Cor. 7:10). Some Bibles incorrectly translate the word as "irrevocable." This erroneous translation has given some people the impression that the Jews have an irrevocable covenant with God independently of Jesus Christ and the New Covenant (they do not; the Jews must convert to Jesus Christ to be saved).

calling, not about man's knowledge of who gets the gifts and calling. Further, when read in context, St. Paul is simply revealing that God's offer of salvation to the Jews is unchangeable. This means that God cannot revoke His antecedent will to save the Jews, even though most of them rejected His offer. If they repent (that is, if God moves them to repentance), then they will be saved. This is why St. Paul says, "And they also, if they abide not still in unbelief, shall be grafted in: for God is able to graft them in again" (v. 23). Although most of the Jews were hardened and blinded because God had deserted them for their sins (vv. 7-10), St. Paul reveals that God *is still able* to save them (although it would be "beyond the order that is built into things"). Thus, the verse has nothing to do with the certainty or knowledge of salvation but is about what God can do.

St. Paul also says, "Who art thou that judgest another man's servant? To his own lord he standeth or falleth. And he shall stand: for God is able to make him stand" (Rom. 14:4). Of course, by efficacious grace, God is able to make man stand. God is able to cause man to persevere in grace to the end of his life. This verse says nothing about man's knowledge of his eternal fate (in fact, the verse says nothing about salvation at all). In his letter to the Colossians, St. Paul says, "Whatsoever you do, do it from the heart, as to the Lord, and not to men: Knowing that you shall receive of the Lord the reward of inheritance" (3:23-24). We know God will give us the reward of inheritance if we persevere in His grace, but we also know that He can disinherit us if we sin. This is why St. Paul warns the Colossians not to be seduced by evil men (see 2:18). Even though the Colossians "have received Jesus Christ the Lord" (2:6), St. Paul warns them to avoid the evils of the world, "Which all are unto destruction by the very use" (2:22). If the Colossians were "eternally secure," then such warnings would serve no purpose, for nothing could lead them to "destruction."

In his second letter to Timothy, St. Paul also says, "The Lord hath delivered me from every evil work: and will preserve me unto his heavenly kingdom, to whom be glory for ever and ever" (4:18). As with Romans 14:4, St. Paul is revealing what God has the power to do. St. Paul affirms that God delivers us from evil and preserves us in His grace. Salvation is the work of God, not man. The verse says nothing about how man knows he will be delivered or preserved. To the Philippians, St. Paul says, "Being confident of this very thing, that he, who hath begun a good work in you, will perfect it unto the day of Christ Jesus" (1:6). St. Paul is simply revealing that God's grace both begins (operating effect) and perfects (cooperating effect) all our good works. St. Paul repeats the same in the popular verse: "For it is God who worketh in you, both to will and to accomplish, according to his good will" (2:13). Neither of these verses speaks to man's knowledge of his salvation. As in his other letters, St. Paul warns the Philippians about "evil workers" (3:2) who can threaten their salvation. If the Philippians knew they were "eternally secure," evil workers would have no effect on them.

Protestants also see "eternal security" in St. Paul's statement to Timothy: "[T]here is laid up for me a crown of justice, which the Lord the just judge will render to me in that day, and not only to me, but to them also that love his coming" (2 Tim. 4:8). The verse does not say what Protestants claim it says. St. Paul throughout his ministry taught that man can fall from grace. In fact, St. Paul expressed uncertainty *regarding his own salvation*. To the Philippians, St. Paul says, "If by any means I may attain to the resurrection which is from the dead. Not as though I had already attained or were already perfect; but I follow after, if I may by any means apprehend" (3:11-12). In his first letter to the Corinthians, he says, "For I am not conscious to myself of any thing, yet am I not hereby justified" (4:4). St. Paul even believed he could lose his salvation when he says, "But I chastise my body, and bring it into subjection: lest perhaps, when I have preached to others, I myself should become a castaway" (9:27). The Greek word for "castaway" (*adokimos*) literally means "reprobate." Paul uses the word five other times in the New Testament, and every time it refers to the condemned.

For example, St. Paul uses *adokimos* to describe idolaters and sodomites,[69] evildoers,[70] rebels against God-given authority,[71] corrupted unbelievers,[72] and the accursed who are consigned to hell.[73] In each case, St. Paul is describing people whom God has permitted to eternally perish. Because St. Paul during his ministry thought that he also could become a reprobate, he certainly didn't believe in eternal security the way Protestants do. St. Paul never teaches that man knows whether he is saved. It is only at the end of his ministry, after a lifetime of "chastising his body and bringing it into subjection," that St. Paul expresses to Timothy a moral certitude of his salvation.[74] The verse reveals more

---

69. Rom. 1:28.
70. 1 Cor. 13:5-7.
71. 2 Tim. 3:8.
72. Tit. 1:15-16.
73. Heb. 6:8.
74. As we mentioned, God may have specially revealed to St. Paul his predestination to glory when He took him into heaven (see 1 Cor. 12:1-6).

of St. Paul's confidence in God as "judge," who will render to man according to his works, than of his confidence in himself. Of course, if God has given us the grace to live a life of virtue and sacrifice like St. Paul, then we too, at the end of our lives, can have assurance of God's heavenly reward.

To the churches in Asia Minor, St. Peter describes their heavenly inheritance as "incorruptible, and undefiled, and that can not fade, reserved in heaven for you, Who, by the power of God, are kept by faith unto salvation, ready to be revealed in the last time" (1 Pet. 1:4-5). Again, it is true that the elect "are kept by faith unto salvation" by God's efficacious grace. However, note that St. Peter says that the elect's status is *revealed in the last time* (v. 5). St. Peter does not say that the elect *know* they are eternally secure before they die. Again, the verse reveals what God does, and not what the elect knows.

It would be redundant to examine more verses. Scripture never teaches that man knows he is saved. It teaches only that God saves man according to His will. With that background, let's look at some of the many verses in Scripture demonstrating that man, like the Prodigal Son, can fall from grace (and lose his salvation). Although such a notion is anathema to Calvinist theology, there is not a clearer teaching in Sacred Scripture.

Jesus Teaches That We Must Persevere or We Will Lose Our Salvation

Jesus certainly did not teach that the elect know they will persevere to the end. Rather, He *tells* them to persevere. He says, "And you shall be hated by all men for my name's sake: but he that shall persevere unto the end, he shall be saved" (Matt. 10:22); "And because iniquity hath abounded, the charity of many shall grow cold. But he that shall persevere to the end, he shall be saved" (Matt. 24:12-13); "And you shall be hated by all men for my name's sake. But he that shall endure unto the end, he shall be saved" (Mark 13:13). Jesus conditions salvation upon perseverance (but says nothing about man's knowledge of his salvation). Moreover, because Jesus exhorts all men to persevere, God gives all men sufficient grace to do so (Jesus would not command the impossible). Nevertheless, because Jesus also teaches that no man comes to Him unless He is drawn by the Father (John 6:44), no man can persevere in Christ unless it is given to him by God. As Jesus says, "[F]or without me you can do nothing" (John 15:5).

We have referred to Jesus' parable about the good and bad soil symbolizing those who receive God's Word. Jesus says, "Now they upon the rock, are they who when they hear, receive the word with joy: and these have no roots; for they believe for a while, and in time of temptation, they fall away" (Luke 8:13). The word for "receive" is *dechomai*, a present tense verb in the middle voice that connotes an actual possession of something by an act of the will. The fact that they had "joy" from receiving the Word demonstrates the involvement of the will (we experience the highest joy when God moves our will to possess the supernatural good beheld by our intellect). We saw St. Paul use *dechomai* in 1 Corinthians 6:1 when he exhorted the Corinthians not to receive God's grace in vain. St. Luke uses the word thirteen other times in his gospel and it always refers to the actual possession of something.[75]

For example, St. Luke describes Jesus as "receiving" the people whom He cured when he says, "Which when the people knew, they followed him; and he received them, and spoke to them of the kingdom of God, and healed them who had need of healing" (9:11). Jesus also uses the verb both in regard to receiving Him as Savior and receiving children in His name when He says, "Whosoever shall receive this child in my name, receiveth me; and whosoever shall receive me, receiveth him that sent me. For he that is the lesser among you all, he is the greater" (9:48). Jesus also says, "Whosoever shall not receive the kingdom of God as a child, shall not enter into it" (18:17). At the Last Supper, when Jesus passed around the chalice of His blood, He said, "Take [receive], and divide it among you" (22:17). In these and other instances, the word "receive" (*dechomai*) always refers to something actually possessed. Thus, in the parable of the good and bad soil, those who "receive" the Word in joy truly possess the grace of God (by God willing it), and then lose God's grace (by God permitting it). In Calvinism, those who possess God's grace can never lose it.[76]

In the parable of the lazy servant, Jesus says, "Blessed is that servant, whom when his lord shall come, he shall find so doing. Verily I say to you, he will set him over all that he possesseth. But if that servant shall say in his heart: My lord is long a coming; and shall begin to strike the menservants and maidservants, and to eat and to drink and be drunk: The lord of that servant will come in the day that he hopeth not, and at the hour that he knoweth not, and shall separate him, and shall appoint him his portion with unbelievers" (Luke 12:43-46).

75. Luke 2:28; 9:5, 11, 48, 53; 10:8, 10; 16:4, 6-7, 9; 18:17; 22:17.
76. We refer to Calvinism because we have been examining its theology throughout the book. Note, however, that the error is not limited to Calvinism but is also found within other branches of Protestantism.

In this parable, Jesus reveals that a servant is capable of both doing his master's will and his own will. In other words, he can serve the master (through efficacious grace), and then fall away (by resisting sufficient grace). In Calvinism, one who serves the master can never fall away.

In the parable of the wicked servant, we learn that the servant owed his king ten thousand talents (Matt. 18:24). Because the servant couldn't immediately pay the debt, the king was about to sell off the servant, his family, and all his possessions to satisfy the obligation (v. 25). As a result, the servant fell down before the king and begged him to have patience and he would pay the debt in full (v. 26). Moved with pity, the king forgave the servant's debt (v. 27). However, that same servant would not forgive his fellow servant of a much smaller debt, even though the debtor likewise begged him for patience (vv. 28-30). On learning of this, the king reinstituted the wicked servant's debt and delivered him to the torturers until it was paid (vv. 32-34). Thus, in this parable, the servant was forgiven by his master, then did evil, and then was *un-forgiven* by his master. In other words, the servant received his master's mercy and grace, and then fell from his master's grace through his evil conduct. In Calvinism, once man is forgiven, he can never be un-forgiven and fall from grace.[77]

Jesus also says, "I am the vine: you the branches: he that abideth in me, and I in him, the same beareth much fruit: for without me you can do nothing. If any one abide not in me, he shall be cast forth as a branch, and shall wither, and they shall gather him up, and cast him into the fire, and be burneth" (John 15:5-6). In this well-known teaching, Jesus indicates that we can abide in Him in grace, and then fall away from Him by sin. As with the verb "believes" in John 3:16, the verb for "abide" (*meno*) is a present, active, nominative singular verb that requires ongoing action on the part of the subject. Man must continue to "abide" in Christ by doing His will, or he will be cast into the "fire" of hell. Further, Jesus reveals in the middle of the teaching that He is the *only reason* why man can abide ("without me you can do nothing"). In Calvinism, once man abides in the grace of Christ, he can never fall away.

Jesus also says, "Not every one that saith to me, Lord, Lord, shall enter into the kingdom of heaven: but he that doth the will of my Father who is in heaven, he shall enter into the kingdom of heaven. Many will say to me in that day: Lord, Lord, have not we prophesied in thy name, and cast out devils in

---

77. Most Calvinists would argue that the man who allegedly falls from grace never actually had grace. However, in this parable, the wicked servant did actually have grace, because he was forgiven of his debt (symbolic for his sins).

thy name, and done many miracles in thy name? And then will I profess unto them, I never knew you: depart from me, you that work iniquity" (Matt. 7:21-24). In this passage, we learn that many people are given special graces such as prophesying, casting out devils, and working miracles. However, Jesus reveals that "many" of these privileged people fall from grace and "work iniquity" (vv. 22-23). In Calvinism, those who do good works in God's name are eternally secure in their salvation and cannot fall away.

Calvinists and other Protestants often point to St. John's first epistle, where he writes, "Little children, it is the last hour; and as you have heard that Antichrist cometh, even now there are become many Antichrists: whereby we know that it is the last hour. They went out from us, but they were not of us. For if they had been of us, they would no doubt have remained with us; but that they may be manifest, that they are not all of us" (1 John 2:18-19). Because the Protestant argues that true Christians cannot lose their salvation, they use this passage to prove there is a distinction between true Christians who are saved and false Christians who were never saved. But the passage does not help the Protestant position. First, although those who "went out from us" may never have been saved, the passage simply does not require such an interpretation. In fact, St. John says that "they would no doubt have *remained* with us," which suggests that they were true Christians at some point. In other words, going "out from us" does not mean that they were "never with us."

Even if those who "went out from us" were false Christians, this doesn't mean that only false Christians leave Christ. As we have shown and will continue to demonstrate, one can be a true Christian (that is, baptized and in a state of grace) and still fall away. Further, note that St. John is writing about "Antichrists" and not average believers. An Antichrist is someone who denies the Incarnation. Thus, Protestants cannot form a general conclusion about which Christians fall away when the passage is only about Antichrists. Finally, St. John concludes by saying that "they are not *all* of us" (v. 19).[78] In other words, St. John says that *not all of them* who "went out" are "of us." That means that *some* of them who "went out" *are* "of us." That is, some of them were true Christians and still fell away. Note also that St. John says those who "went out" did not "remain" (*meno*). This is the same word ("remain") that Jesus uses ("abide") in John 15:5. This further underscores that a true commitment to Christ is an *ongoing* commitment.

---

78. The Greek transliteration is *ou eimi pas ek hemeis*.

Throughout the Apocalypse, Jesus reveals that man can fall from grace. For example, to the church at Ephesus, Jesus says, "But I have somewhat against thee, because thou hast left thy first charity. Be mindful therefore from whence thou art fallen: and do penance, and do the first works. Or else I come to thee, and will move thy candlestick out of its place, except thou do penance" (Apoc. 2:4-5). In this passage, Jesus reveals that the Ephesians had charity and had done good works. We know that they could have charity and good works only by virtue of God's efficacious grace. But Jesus also says that they have "fallen" and must do "penance." In fact, Jesus threatens that if they do not do penance, He will remove their "candlestick," which is symbolic for their eternal life. In other words, the Ephesians fell from grace. In Calvinism, it is impossible to fall from grace.

To the church at Sardis, Jesus says that there were a "few names . . . which have not defiled their garments: and they shall walk with me in white, because they are worthy. He that shall overcome, shall thus be clothed in white garments, and I will not blot out his name out of the book of life, and I will confess his name before my Father, and before his angels" (Apoc. 3:4-5). In this passage, Jesus reveals that the believers at Sardis received the white garment that is symbolic for their baptism. However, some of them "defiled their garments," which is symbolic for grave sin. For doing so, Jesus threatens to "blot out his name out of the book of life."[79] Thus, some of the believers at Sardis fell from the state of grace. In Calvinism, once a person receives his white garment of "regeneration" he cannot fall from grace or be "blotted out of the book of life."

As in the gospels, Jesus also repeatedly warns Christians to persevere to the end to be saved. For example, Jesus says, "Be thou faithful until death: and I will give thee the crown of life" (2:10). The "crown of life" is, of course, the gift of everlasting salvation in heaven.[80] However, Jesus also says, "Behold, I come quickly: hold fast that which thou hast, that no man take thy crown" (3:11). That is, if one who is in a state of grace fails to persevere, he will lose eternal

---

79. St. Thomas explains that to be "blotted out of the book of life" refers to those predestined to grace, but not to glory, for the elect are eternally secure. He says, "Therefore those who are ordained to possess eternal life through divine predestination are written down in the book of life simply, because they are written therein to have eternal life in reality; such are never blotted out from the book of life. Those, however, who are ordained to eternal life, not through divine predestination, but through grace, are said to be written in the book of life not simply, but relatively, for they are written therein not to have eternal life in itself, but in its cause only" (ST, Pt I, Q 24, Art 3).

80. See also 1 Cor. 9:25; 1 Thess. 2:19; 2 Tim. 4:8; Jas. 1:12; 1 Pet. 5:4; and Apoc. 6:2 where "crown" refers to the gift of eternal life.

life. Such a man will not blame God for not giving him efficacious grace; rather, he will blame himself and feel shameful, for he failed to keep pure his garment of grace. Jesus says, "Behold, I come as a thief. Blessed is he that watcheth, and keepeth his garments, lest he walk naked, and they see his shame" (16:15). Jesus also says, "Have in mind therefore in what manner thou hast received and heard: and observe, and do penance. If then thou shalt not watch, I will come to thee as a thief, and thou shalt not know at what hour I will come to thee" (3:3).

Jesus also continually exhorts us to "overcome" to be saved. For example, He says, "To him that overcometh, I will give the hidden manna, and will give him a white counter, and in the counter, a new name written, which no man knoweth, but he that receiveth it" (2:17); "And he that shall overcome, and keep my works unto the end, I will give him power over the nations" (2:26); "He that shall overcome, I will make him a pillar in the temple of my God" (3:12); "To him that shall overcome, I will give to sit with me in my throne: as I also have overcome, and am set down with my Father in his throne" (3:21). The word for "overcome" (*nikao*) is used seven times in the New Testament outside of the Apocalypse and it always refers to conquering evil.[81] Man must conquer temptation and sin to inherit everlasting life. Notice that Jesus never says man knows whether he will overcome or persevere to the end. He simply commands Christians to do so, and warns them of the consequences if they do not.

THE APOSTLES TEACH THAT WE MUST PERSEVERE OR WE WILL LOSE OUR SALVATION

Like their Master, the apostles also clearly teach that man can fall from grace. Scripture is replete with such warnings. Let's start with St. Paul's letter to the Romans. St. Paul describes the Romans as "brethren"[82] and "beloved"[83] and "the called of Jesus Christ" (1:6). They have been baptized (6:4), justified (5:9), sanctified (6:22), and made partakers of grace (5:2; 6:14). Thus, they have received the spirit of adoption (8:15), have the first fruits of the Spirit (8:23), and have been reconciled to God (5:11). The Romans are "dead to sin, but alive unto God, in Christ Jesus our Lord" (6:11). As the Calvinists would say, the Romans are "saved."

Nevertheless, St. Paul urges them not to allow sin to reign in their bodies or

81. Luke 11:22; John 16:33; Rom. 3:4; 12:21; 1 John 2:13, 14; 4:4; 5:4-5.
82. Rom. 1:13; 7:1, 4; 8:12, 29; 9:3; 10:1; 11:25; 12:1; 15:14-15; 16:17.
83. Rom. 1:7; 12:19.

to give in to their lust (6:12). St. Paul tells them, "Therefore, brethren, we are debtors, not to the flesh, to live according to the flesh. For if you live according to the flesh, you shall die: but if by the Spirit you mortify the deeds of the flesh, you shall live" (8:12-13). Thus, even though the Romans are partakers of grace, St. Paul warns them that they can fall from grace by living according to the flesh. These warnings cannot be for the "unbelieving elect," as Calvinists maintain, because the warnings are given to sanctified brethren who are already adopted sons of God. Neither can the warnings be for the reprobate to justly condemn them for their sins, for the same reasons.

St. Paul also warns the Romans that God can desert them for their sins, just as He deserted most of the Jews. He says, "Well: because of unbelief they were broken off. But thou standest by faith: be not highminded, but fear. For if God hath not spared the natural branches, fear lest perhaps he also spare not thee. See then the goodness and the severity of God: towards them indeed that are fallen, the severity; but towards thee, the goodness of God, if thou abide in goodness, otherwise thou also shalt be cut off" (11:20-22).[84] Of course, God will not "cut off" His elect. But Scripture never says the elect know who they are. Rather, Scripture reveals that man must "abide in goodness" or risk damnation. In the same letter, St. Paul says, "Destroy not him with thy meat, for whom Christ died" (14:15). St. Paul teaches that scandalous practices can actually destroy the faith of a believer. Note also that St. Paul says Christ died for such a person.

In his first letter to the Corinthians, St. Paul also describes the faithful as "brethren"[85] and "beloved"[86] who are already "sanctified" (1:2). St. Paul says that they "have received . . . the Spirit that is of God" (2:12) and have the Holy Ghost (6:19). Thus, the Corinthians are not lacking any grace (1:7). Nevertheless, St. Paul notes that some of them are still fornicating (5:1) and defrauding each other (6:8). St. Paul warns them: "Know you not that the unjust shall not possess the kingdom of God? Do not err: neither fornicators, nor idolaters, nor adulterers, [n]or the effeminate, nor liers with mankind, nor thieves, nor

---

84. Some Protestants argue that Rom. 11:20-22 is about the corporate election and potential rejection of the Gentiles as a group (as if such an interpretation denies the ability to fall from grace). However, Rom. 11:17 says that only "some of the branches" (in reference to the Jews) are broken off. Likewise, only some of the Gentiles would be cut off as well. The passage is about *individual* election and rejection, just like Romans 9 is about individual predestination and reprobation.

85. 1 Cor. 1:10-11, 26; 2:1; 3:1; 4:6; 6:8; 7:24, 29; 8:12; 10:1; 11:2, 33; 14:6, 20, 26; 14:39; 15:1, 31, 50, 58; 16:15.

86. 1 Cor. 10:14; 15:58.

covetous, nor drunkards, nor railers, nor extortioners, shall possess the kingdom of God" (6:9-10). Although the Calvinist might wish to say St. Paul is addressing a different group of Corinthians, St. Paul eliminates that possibility in the next verse. About these same people, he says, "[Y]ou are washed, but you are sanctified, but you are justified in the name of our Lord Jesus Christ, and the Spirit of our God" (v. 11). In other words, some of the sanctified Corinthians were committing damnable sins and risked losing the kingdom of God.

St. Paul continues to warn the Corinthians that they can lose their salvation through idolatry, fornication, and other grave sins. In referring to the condemnation of the Jews of the Old Testament, St. Paul says:

> Now these things were done in a figure of us, that we should not covet evil things as they also coveted. Neither become ye idolaters, as some of them, as it is written: The people sat down to eat and drink, and rose up to play. Neither let us commit fornication, as some of them committed fornication, and there fell in one day three and twenty thousand. Neither let us tempt Christ: as some of them tempted, and perished by the serpents. Neither do you murmur: as some of them murmured, and were destroyed by the destroyer. Now all these things happened to them in figure: and they are written for our correction, upon whom the ends of the world are come. Wherefore he that thinketh himself to stand, let him take heed lest he fall. Let no temptation take hold on you, but such as is human. And God is faithful, who will not suffer you to be tempted above that which you are able: but will make also with temptation issue, that you may be able to bear it (1 Cor. 10:6-13).

Even though the Corinthians have received the grace of God, St. Paul urges them to avoid mortal sin. St. Paul would also tell the Calvinist who holds a false presumption of his salvation to "take heed lest he fall." There is nothing about knowledge or assurance of salvation even for those who have been "regenerated" by the Holy Ghost. St. Paul also says, "Now I make known unto you, brethren, the gospel which I preached to you, which also you have received, and wherein you stand; By which also you are saved, if you hold fast after what manner I preached unto you, unless you have believed in vain" (15:1-2). Once again, the Corinthians' salvation is conditioned upon "holding fast" to the gospel, otherwise they have received God's grace in vain.

In his second letter to the Corinthians, St. Paul continues to describe them as "brethren"[87] and "beloved"[88] who have the "spirit of faith" (4:13) and "have obtained mercy" from God (4:1). St. Paul says "for in faith you stand" (2:23) and approves "the good disposition of your charity" (8:8). St. Paul even says that "Christ Jesus is in you" (13:5). Nevertheless, St. Paul prays that the Corinthians "may do no evil" (13:7). In fact, even though they have received God's grace, the Corinthians were doing evil, for St. Paul mourns "many of them that sinned before, and have not done penance for the uncleanness, and fornication, and lasciviousness, that they have committed" (12:21). This is why St. Paul exhorts them to "be reconciled to God" (5:20). St. Paul also warns them not to bear "the yoke with unbelievers" (6:14), lest their faith in Christ be jeopardized. As we have also seen, St. Paul exhorts them not to receive God's grace in vain (6:1) and fears that they can fall from grace just as Adam and Eve fell from grace (11:3). Again, there is nothing about knowing with certainty one's salvation, only warnings about losing salvation.

St. Paul also describes the Galatians as "brethren"[89] whom "Christ hath redeemed" (3:13) and who "have been baptized in Christ" and "have put on Christ" (3:27). Thus, St. Paul says, "because you are sons, God hath sent the Spirit of his Son into your hearts" (4:6). Yet St. Paul asks them, "[H]ow turn you again to the weak and needy elements, which you desire to serve again?" (4:9). Because the "saved" Galatians continued to fall, St. Paul says, "I am afraid of you, lest perhaps I have labored in vain among you" (4:11). St. Paul also says, "Stand fast, and be not held again under the yoke of bondage. Behold, I Paul tell you, that if you be circumcised, Christ shall profit you nothing. And I testify again to every man circumcising himself, that he is a debtor to the whole law. You are made void of Christ, you who are justified in the law: you are fallen from grace" (5:1-4). While St. Paul tells the Galatians they have "fallen from grace," Calvinists believe it is impossible to fall from grace. St. Paul also says "though we, or an angel from heaven" preach a false gospel, "let him be anathema" (1:8). By saying "we," St. Paul believed even the apostles were capable of preaching a perverted gospel and falling away.

St. Paul also warns the Galatians of committing grave sins: "Now the works of the flesh are manifest, which are fornication, uncleanness, immodesty, luxury, [i]dolatry, witchcrafts, enmities, contentions, emulations, wraths, quarrels, dissensions, sects, [e]nvies, murders, drunkenness, revelings, and such like. Of the

---

87. 1 Cor. 8:1; 13:11.
88. 1 Cor. 7:1; 12:19.
89. Gal. 1:11; 3:15; 4:12, 28; 5:11, 13; 6:1, 18.

which I foretell you, as I have foretold to you, that they who do such things shall not obtain the kingdom of God" (5:19-21). St. Paul also says, "Be not deceived, God is not mocked. For what things a man shall sow, those also shall he reap. For he that soweth in his flesh, of the flesh also shall reap corruption. But he that soweth in the spirit, of the spirit shall reap life everlasting" (6:7-8). Even though the Galatians have been baptized into Christ and are sons of God, St. Paul tells them that they can lose their salvation through sin. It's as if St. Paul had the Protestant heresy of eternal security in mind when he says, "Be not deceived, God is not mocked." Man is deceived, and he mocks God when he presumes his salvation and lives a life of sin.

St. Paul describes the "brethren"[90] at Ephesus as "saints" (1:1) who have been "predestinated" to grace (1:5) and "called by lot" (1:11). The Ephesians have been "signed with the holy Spirit" (1:13) and are saved by grace (2:5, 8). They are "fellow citizens with the saints" (2:19) and "members of his body" (5:30). Nevertheless, St. Paul warns them not to give "place to the devil" (4:27) and commit blasphemy (4:31) and other sins (vv. 28-31). He also tells them to "grieve not the holy Spirit of God" (4:30), which they will do if they resist grace and sin. As in his other letters, St. Paul issues a dire warning: "For know you this and understand, that no fornicator, or unclean, or covetous person (which is a serving of idols), hath inheritance in the kingdom of Christ and of God. Let no man deceive you with vain words. For because of these things cometh the anger of God upon the children of unbelief" (5:5-6). Thus, even though the Galatians were saved, St. Paul reveals that they could fall away from the faith and be damned.

St. Paul also describes the Colossians as "saints and faithful brethren" (1:2) who have been baptized into Christ (2:12). St. Paul says that God "hath made us worthy to be partakers of the lot of the saints in light: who hath delivered us from the power of darkness, and hath translated us into the kingdom of the Son of his love" (1:12-13). Clearly, the Colossians have received the grace of God. Yet St. Paul exhorts the Colossians to "continue in the faith, grounded and settled, and immoveable from the hope of the gospel" to secure their state of grace (1:23). Moreover, St. Paul warns the Colossians, "Beware lest any man cheat you by philosophy, and vain deceit; according to the traditions of men" (2:8). St. Paul also says, "Let no man seduce you" (2:18) and asks why some of them "decree as though living in the world?" (2:20). St. Paul also tells them to "[m]ortify therefore your members which are on earth" and exhorts them to

90. Eph. 5:15; 6:10, 23.

avoid the sins of "fornication, uncleanness, lust, evil concupiscence, and covet-ousness, which is the service of idols" (3:5). Again, these warnings are for saved Christians, who St. Paul says can fall from grace.

St. Paul describes the "brethren"[91] at Thessalonica as the "beloved of God" (1:4) who know their "election" (1:4) and have received the Word of God (1:6; 2:13) and the precepts of Jesus Christ (4:2). They are "followers of the churches of God" (2:14) and "children of the light" (5:5). Notwithstanding their favored position with God, St. Paul warns them to "abstain from fornication" (4:3) and the "passion of lust" (4:5) because "the Lord is the avenger of all these things" (4:6). In his second letter to the Thessalonians, St. Paul also says, "Let no man deceive you by any means" (2:3) and charges them to "withdraw yourselves from every brother walking disorderly" (3:6) so that their faith is not endan-gered (this verse shows that a "brother" can walk disorderly by sinning). Even though these Thessalonians have the "faith" (1:3), are "beloved of God" and those whom God has chosen the "firstfruits unto salvation" (2:12), St. Paul warns them to avoid sin, and never says they are eternally secure.

In his first letter to Timothy, St. Paul reveals through the Holy Ghost that "in the last times some shall depart from the faith, giving heed to spirits of error, and doctrines of devils" (4:1). St. Paul gave the same warning to the clergy at Ephesus when he says, "For I have not spared to declare unto you all the counsel of God. Take heed to yourselves, and to the whole flock, wherein the Holy Ghost hath placed you bishops, to rule the church of God, which he hath purchased with his own blood. I know that, after my departure, ravening wolves will enter in among you, not sparing the flock. And of your own selves shall arise men speaking perverse things, to draw away disciples after them" (Acts 20:27-30). Because of evil shepherds, St. Paul says, "For some are already turned aside after Satan" (5:15). These people had "a pure heart, and a good conscience, and an unfeigned faith" before "going astray" and "turned aside into vain babbling" (1:5-6).

St. Paul commends Timothy to have "faith and good conscience, which some rejecting have made shipwreck concerning the faith. Of whom is Hymeneus and Alexander" (1:19-20).[92] St. Paul also says that greed and selfishness lead a man away from the faith: "For the desire of money is the root of all evils: which some coveting have erred from the faith" (6:10); "But if any man have not care

---

91. 1 Thess. 1:4; 2:1, 9, 14, 17; 3:7; 4:1, 10, 12; 5:1, 4, 12, 14, 25. See also 2 Thess. 1:3; 2:1, 12, 14; 3:1, 6, 13.

92. Alexander may be the coppersmith St. Paul mentions in 2 Timothy 4:14 who did him "much evil."

of his own, and especially of those of his house, he hath denied the faith, and is worse than an infidel" (5:8). Those who depart from the faith do not receive "damnation" because they never had the faith, but "because they have made void *their first faith*" (5:12). At the end of the letter, St. Paul says: "O Timothy, keep that which is committed to thy trust, avoiding the profane novelties of words, and oppositions of knowledge falsely so called. Which some promising, have erred concerning the faith" (1 Tim. 6:20-21).

In his second letter to Timothy, St. Paul gives more examples when he says, "And their speech spreadeth like a canker: of whom are Hymeneus and Philetus: Who have erred from the truth, saying, that the resurrection is past already, and have subverted the faith of some" (2:17-18). St. Paul is clear that those who lost the faith actually had it. There is never any mention of "true" versus "false" faith (of course, if a faith were "false" it couldn't be "subverted").[93] St. Paul also mentions "all they who are in Asia, are turned away from me: of whom are Phigellus and Hermogenes" (2 Tim. 1:15). St. Paul further says, "For Demas hath left me, loving this world, and is gone to Thessalonica" (2 Tim. 4:9). That St. Paul specifically mentions individuals suggests that such people were never expected to fall away, since they were known to be good men. St. Paul urges Timothy to admonish such people so "they may recover themselves from the snares of the devil, by whom they are held captive at his will" (2:26). To "recover" from the snares of the devil means that they were freed from him before getting caught again.

St. Paul devotes much of his letter to the Hebrews to warnings about falling away from the faith. As in his other letters, St. Paul refers to the Hebrews as "brethren"[94] and "beloved" (6:9). St. Paul says the Hebrews are "sons of God (12:7) and "children . . . of faith to the saving of the soul" (10:39). St. Paul also says that they have been baptized into Christ (10:22) and are "partakers of the heavenly vocation" (3:1). The Hebrews "have believed" (4:3), belong to the house of God (3:6), and have been "sanctified" by the sacrifice of Christ (10:10, 14, 29). St. Paul also says that Jesus is their High Priest and Mediator.[95] In a word, the Hebrews are "saved" (or, as Calvinists would say, "regenerated"). Yet St. Paul constantly warns them about holding firm in their faith lest they fall into condemnation. To avoid redundant exegesis, we simply provide the more

---

93. St. Paul uses the term "heretic" to describe one who had the faith and lost it (see Titus 3:10). One cannot be a heretic against the faith unless one had the faith.

94. Heb. 3:1, 12; 10:19; 13:22.

95. Heb. 4:15-16; 7:25-26; 8:1-2, 6; 9:14, 24.

germane passages here. Note also that St. Paul often says "we" in these verses, which means he includes himself in the warnings:

- "Therefore ought we more diligently to observe the things which we have heard, lest perhaps we should let them slip" (2:1). In Calvinism, the faithful cannot slip and fall away.

- "For if the word, spoken by angels, became steadfast, and every transgression and disobedience received a just recompense of reward: How shall we escape if we neglect so great salvation?" (2:2-3). In Calvinism, the faithful cannot neglect salvation.

- "But Christ as the Son in his own house: which house are we, if we hold fast the confidence and glory of hope unto the end" (3:6). In Calvinism, salvation is not conditioned upon holding fast to one's confidence.

- "Take heed, brethren, lest perhaps there be in any of you an evil heart of unbelief, to depart from the living God. But exhort one another every day, whilst it is called today, that none of you be hardened through the deceitfulness of sin. For we are made partakers of Christ: yet so, if we hold the beginning of his substance firm unto the end" (3:12-14). In Calvinism, the faithful cannot depart from God, become hardened by sin, or need to hold firm unto the end to be partakers of Christ.

- "Let us fear therefore lest the promise being left of entering into his rest, any of you should be thought to be wanting" (4:1). In Calvinism, the faithful have no need to fear being wanting of the promise.

- "Let us hasten therefore to enter into that rest; lest any man fall into the same example of unbelief" (4:11). In Calvinism, the faithful cannot fall into unbelief.

- "Let us hold fast our confession" (4:14). In Calvinism, salvation is not conditioned upon holding fast to one's confession.

- "For it is impossible for those who were once illuminated, have tasted also the heavenly gift, and were made partakers of the Holy Ghost, have moreover tasted the good word of God, and the powers of the world to come, and are fallen away: to be renewed again to penance, crucifying again to themselves the Son of God, and making him a mockery" (6:4-6)[96] In Calvinism, it is impossible for a partaker of the Holy Ghost to fall away and re-crucify the Son of God.

---

96. St. Paul uses the same word for "taste" (*gneuomai*) in Heb. 2:9 when he says Christ "might taste death for all." The word connotes an actual participation with its referent. Thus, just as Christ actually tasted death, the Hebrews actually tasted the heavenly gifts and the Word of God through grace before falling away.

- "And we desire that every one of you show forth the same carefulness to the accomplishing of hope unto the end: That you become not slothful, but followers of them, who through faith and patience shall inherit the promises" (6:11-12). In Calvinism, the faithful do not need to be careful in holding hope to the end or worry about becoming slothful.
- "Let us draw near with a true heart in fulness of faith, having our hearts sprinkled from an evil conscience, and our bodies washed with clean water. Let us hold fast the confession of our hope without wavering (for he is faithful that hath promised)" (10:22-23). In Calvinism, salvation is not conditioned upon holding fast to one's confession.
- "For if we sin wilfully after having the knowledge of the truth, there is now left no sacrifice for sins, [b]ut a certain dreadful expectation of judgment, and the rage of a fire which shall consume the adversaries" (10:26-27). In Calvinism, it is impossible for one who has received the knowledge of the truth to sin willfully and lose his salvation.
- "How much more, do you think he deserveth worse punishments, who hath trodden under foot the Son of God, and hath esteemed the blood of the testament unclean, by which he was sanctified, and hath offered an affront to the Spirit of grace?" (10:29). In Calvinism, it is impossible for one who has been sanctified to reject the Son of God and deserve worse punishments than before his sanctification.
- "Do not therefore lose your confidence, which hath a great reward. For patience is necessary for you; that, doing the will of God, you may receive the promise. For yet a little and a very little while, and he that is to come, will come, and will not delay. But my just man liveth by faith; but if he withdraw himself, he shall not please my soul" (10:35-38). In Calvinism, it is impossible for the faithful to lose their confidence or withdraw themselves from God and lose the promise of salvation.
- "And therefore we also having so great a cloud of witnesses over our head, laying aside every weight and sin which surrounds us, let us run by patience to the fight proposed to us" (12:1). In Calvinism, salvation is not conditioned upon running by patience to the fight and laying aside sin.
- "Looking diligently, lest any man be wanting to the grace of God; lest any root of bitterness springing up do hinder, and by it many be defiled" (12:15). In Calvinism, it is impossible for the faithful to be wanting to the grace of God and to become hindered and defiled.
- "See that you refuse him not that speaketh. For if they escaped not who

refused him that spoke upon the earth, much more shall not we, that turn away from him that speaketh to us from heaven" (12:25). In Calvinism, it is impossible for the faithful to refuse Christ.

The Apostle James also warns his readers about falling away from the faith. Like St. Paul, St. James repeatedly refers to his audience as "brethren"[97] who have the true "faith" (1:3). Yet St. James explains to them how erring from the faith through sin can lead to death: "But every man is tempted by his own concupiscence, being drawn away and allured. Then when concupiscence hath conceived, it bringeth forth sin. But sin, when it is completed, begetteth death. Do not err, therefore, my dearest brethren" (1:14-16). In fact, St. James reveals that some of the brethren have actually committed such grave sins. He says, "From whence are wars and contentions among you? Are they not hence, from your concupiscences, which war in your members? You covet, and have not: you kill, and envy, and can not obtain. You contend and war, and you have not, because you ask not. You ask, and receive not; because you ask amiss: that you may consume it on your concupiscences" (4:1-3).

St. James also tells them to cast away "all uncleanness, and abundance of naughtiness" (1:22). He exhorts them to be "doers of the word, and not hearers only, deceiving your own selves" (1:22), otherwise their "religion is in vain" (1:26). Thus, he tells them that they must add works to their faith or their faith is dead (2:14, 20, 26). He also tells them to refrain from evil speech (3:5-10), judging their brothers (4:11) and rash swearing (5:12). St. James also says, "if any of you err from the truth, and one convert him: He must know that he who causeth a sinner to be converted from the error of his way, shall save his soul from death, and shall cover a multitude of sins" (5:19-20). Thus, St. James clearly acknowledges that one of the "saved" in his audience can "err from the truth" and be converted back again. St. James also urges his faithful to confess their sins and pray for one another, "that you may be saved" (5:16).[98]

In his first epistle, St. Peter writes to faithful Christians who are "beloved" (2:11; 4:12), whom God has "called" (1:15; 2:21), who have been "regenerated" by Christ (1:3), and who have been "redeemed" (1:18) and have the "faith" (1:7,

---

97. Jas. 1:2, 16, 19; 2:1, 5, 14; 3:1, 10, 12; 4:11; 5:7, 9-10, 12, 19.
98. St. James first urges the faithful to call upon the priests of the Church to administer the sacrament of Extreme Unction to the sick (5:14). The conjunction "therefore" (Greek, *oun*) connects verse 16 with verses 14-15, meaning that just as the faithful are to call upon the priests for the sacrament of the sick (vv. 14-15), they are to confess their sins to these same priests in the sacrament of penance (v. 16).

9, 21). St. Peter further says they have been saved in "baptism" (3:21) and "are a chosen generation, a kingly priesthood, a holy nation, a purchased people" (2:9). Nevertheless, St. Peter tells them "to refrain from carnal desires which war against the soul" (2:11). He also warns them never to become "a murderer, or a thief, or a railer, or a coveter of other men's things" (4:15). St. Peter further warns them: "Be sober and watch: because your adversary the devil, as a roaring lion, goeth about seeking whom he may devour. Whom resist ye, strong in faith: knowing that the same affliction befalls your brethren who are in the world" (5:8-9). Because of these dangers to their salvation, St. Peter reveals, "And if the just man shall scarcely be saved, where shall the ungodly and the sinner appear?" (4:18).[99]

Similarly, in his second epistle, St. Peter once again addresses the "brethren"[100] and the "beloved."[101] In fact, St. Peter says that they "have obtained equal faith with us" (1:1) and have been "purged" from their "old sins" (1:9). Yet St. Peter warns them to be "diligent that you may be found before him unspotted and blameless in peace" (3:14). Like St. Paul, St. Peter also warns that "there were also false prophets among the people, even as there shall be among you lying teachers, who shall bring in sects of perdition, and deny the Lord who bought them: bringing upon themselves swift destruction" (2 Pet. 2:1).[102] In addition to false teachers who destroyed the faith of some, others abandoned the faith and followed their passions. After mentioning lust, gluttony, adultery, and covetousness, St. Peter says, "Leaving the right way they have gone astray" (2:15). As if he were warning us of the future Protestant heresy, St. Peter declares:

> For if, flying from the pollutions of the world, through the knowledge of our Lord and Savior Jesus Christ, they be again entangled in them and overcome: their latter state is become unto them worse than the former. For it had been better for them not to have known the way of justice, than after they have known it, to turn back from that holy

99. The adverb for "scarcely" (*molis*) literally means "hardly." Thus, like Jesus, St. Peter reveals that most just men are not saved (they are predestined to grace but not to glory).

100. 2 Pet. 1:10; 3:17.

101. 2 Pet. 3:1, 8, 14.

102. St. Peter also says that many of the unlearned and unstable Christians twist the meaning of Scripture to their own destruction (see 2 Pet. 3:16). This statement, coupled with St. Peter's warning about privately interpreting Scripture in 2 Peter 1:20, should give pause to anyone who believes in *sola Scriptura*. For a thorough refutation of *sola Scriptura*, see my book *The Biblical Basis for Tradition—Why Catholics Don't Rely on Scripture Alone* (Our Sunday Visitor).

commandment which was delivered to them. For, that of the true proverb has happened to them: The dog is returned to his vomit: and, [t]he sow that was washed, to her wallowing in the mire (2:20-22).

Finally, St. John in his epistles also addresses the "brethren"[103] and the "beloved"[104] whose "sins are forgiven" (1 John 2:12). They have been "called" by God and are "sons of God" (1 John 3:1). St. John even says that they have "passed from death to life" (1 John 3:14) and have "overcome" the devil" (1 John 4:4). Yet, like Jesus, St. John makes their salvation conditioned upon continuing to abide in God's word: "As for you, let that which you have heard from the beginning, abide in you. If that abide in you, which you have heard from the beginning, you also shall abide in the Son, and in the Father" (1 John 2:24).[105] St. John also tells them not to love the world or the things in it (2:15). St. John specifically mentions "the concupiscence of the flesh, the concupiscence of the eyes, and the pride of life," which are the major temptations of the world that lead souls to ruin (2:16).

St. John also says, "These things have I written to you, concerning them that seduce you. And as for you, let the unction, which you have received from him, abide in you" (1 John 2:26-27). The obvious implication is that if the faithful turn from Christ to false teachers and worldly pleasures, they will be seduced and fall away from the faith. In addition to exhorting them to keep the commandments and love one another,[106] St. John also warns them to "let no man deceive you" (3:7) and to "try the spirits if they be of God: because many false prophets are gone out into the world" (1 John 4:1). Again, St. John is warning them that they can be deceived and fall away through the errors of false teachers. Like St. James, St. John also urges the faithful to "confess our sins" to be forgiven of them (1:9). They are not automatically forgiven by "accepting Jesus as Lord and Savior."

St. John also believed the faithful were capable of walking in darkness (1 John 1:6) and hating their brothers (1 John 2:11; 4:20). In fact, St. John reveals that a true Christian can lose his salvation through grave sin. He says, "He that knoweth his brother to sin a sin which is not to death, let him ask,

---

103. 1 John 3:13-14, 16; 3 John 1:3, 5, 10.
104. 1 John 2:7; 3:2, 21; 4:1, 7; 3 John 1:1-2, 5, 11.
105. St. John uses the same verb and tense for "abide" (*meno*) that Jesus uses in John 15:5. See also 1 John 2:6, 24, 27-28; 3:6, 17, 24; 4:13, 16; 2 John 9.
106. 1 John 2:3, 10; 3:11, 18, 22-24; 4:7, 11-12, 21; 5:2; 2 John 1:5.

and life shall be given to him, who sinneth not to death.[107] There is a sin unto
death: for that I say not that any man ask. All iniquity is sin. And there is a
sin unto death" (1 John 5:16-17).[108] Thus, St. John urges his faithful, "Look to
yourselves, that you lose not the things which you have wrought" (2 John 1:8).
Acknowledging that they could fall from the faith, St. John also says, "Whosoever revolteth, and continueth not in the doctrine of Christ, hath not God"
(2 John 1:9). Such people were living the doctrine of Christ, but did not continue living it. St. John also tells his beloved, "[F]ollow not that which is evil,
but that which is good" (3 John 1:11). Even though they were saved, St. John
reveals that they could follow evil. As with St. Paul, even though the faithful
were in God's grace, St. John says nothing about the knowledge of their "eternal security." Like St. Paul, he instead questions their security.

CLOSING COMMENTS

In this final chapter, we have seen once again that man depends upon God for
everything, including the "great gift" and "special assistance" of final perseverance. God must give man not only the gift of living in grace but also the gift of
dying in grace. God owes man nothing, and man owes God everything. God is
the cause of our being and action, and "no one thing would be better than another, if God did not will greater good for one than for another."[109] As St. James
says, "Every best gift, and every perfect gift, is from above, coming down from
the Father of lights, with whom there is no change, nor shadow of alteration"

---

107. The Church generally calls "sin unto death" *mortal sin*, and "sin which is not to death"
venial sin. Mortal sin expels sanctifying grace from the soul. Anyone who dies in mortal sin goes to
hell. Venial sin does not expel sanctifying grace from the soul, although it weakens man's will and
increases his propensity to sin. If a man dies with venial sin only (or with punishment still due for
sin), God purifies his soul in the fires of purgatory before admitting him into heaven. For a thorough treatment of this topic, see my book *The Biblical Basis for Purgatory* (Saint Benedict Press).

108. Although many Catholic apologists use 1 John 5:16-17 to support the distinction between mortal and venial sin, the passage actually seems to be distinguishing between two kinds
of *mortal* sin: sins against the faith (apostasy, heresy, or schism) vis-à-vis other mortal sins. This
is because the one who sins "not to death ... life shall be given to him," if man "asks" through
prayer. Since man does not need to be restored to grace for venial sin, this sin "not to death" must
be mortal. St. John distinguishes this sin from the "sin unto death" where no man should "ask."
St. John seems to be saying that the man who commits a mortal sin against the faith (a "sin unto
death") is rarely restored to grace through prayer, whereas a man who commits other mortal sins
("not to death") is often restored to grace through prayer. This is the distinction between a member
who is "cut off" from the Body of Christ, the Church (by mortal sin against the faith) and a "dead
member" of the Body (by mortal sin not against the faith).

109. ST, Pt I, Q 20, Art 3.

(1:17). Because eternal salvation is the "best and perfect gift" of God, man can never know whether he will receive it until God *actually gives it to him.*

Nevertheless, God gives us signs of our predestination to glory through His generous and overflowing graces. Whenever we do any good whatsoever, we know that God is working in us both to will and accomplish the good (see Phil. 2:13). As God moves us by His efficacious grace, He conforms us to the image of Christ. Through His grace, God creates in us the virtues of doing good and avoiding sin. These habits make us more aware of our dependence upon God and our confidence in God. They also make us more responsive to God's grace and better alert us to the dangers of the devil and sin. As we work out our salvation "with fear and trembling" (Phil. 2:12), we know that all of our salutary acts are gifts from God and signs of our predestination to heaven. With this assurance, "[W]e may have confidence in the day of judgment" (1 John 4:17).

While we should put our trust and confidence in God, we should never have confidence in ourselves. We should never trust ourselves or our own abilities. God alone is able to make us stand (see Rom. 14:4). God alone is able to give the increase (see 1 Cor. 3:6). God alone is able to provide the power (see 1 Cor. 4:7). God alone is able to provide the sufficiency (see 1 Cor. 9:8). As St. John the Baptist declared: "A man cannot receive any thing, unless it be given him from heaven" (John 3:27). By abandoning ourselves to God's providence and laboring under the influence of His grace, we will "make sure" our "calling and election" (2 Pet. 1:10). As St. Thomas says, "[T]he predestinated *must strive* after good works and prayer; because through these means predestination is most certainly fulfilled."[110] While our earthly lives give us only the certainty of death, we keep always in front of us the words of St. Paul:

[F]or if we be dead with him, we shall also live with him. If we suffer, we shall also reign with him. If we deny him, he will also deny us. If we believe not, he continueth faithful, he can not deny himself. Of these things put them in mind, charging them before the Lord (2 Tim. 2:11-14).

110. ST, Pt I, Q 23, Art 8 (emphasis added).

EPILOGUE

I chose to call this book *The Mystery of Predestination* for an obvious reason: to alert readers that I would most likely not be able to explain this doctrine to their complete satisfaction and contentment, for predestination is indeed one of the greatest *mysteries* of the Faith.

One always takes a risk when attempting to explain the inexplicable. I certainly recognize my own limitations in addressing this most difficult topic, and can say only that I have done my best to explain the topic using hundreds of quotes from Scripture, the teachings of the Church, and St. Thomas Aquinas. Although I believe this book faithfully presents the Thomist position, Catholics are free to disagree with my conclusions and still remain good Catholics. For although predestination is a truth of the Faith, the Church has not dogmatized any of the underlying particulars and, hence, we are free to discuss and debate them. We may never know how God's grace and man's free will work together, even in eternity.

In the book, I noted that the concepts of sufficient grace and reprobation may be the most provocative elements of the mystery. Agreeably, the average reader may have logical objections to my conclusion that sufficient grace is more than sufficient to save man, even though man must be moved by an efficacious grace to do God's will and be saved. This seems like a contradiction, and I understand and appreciate the objection. But the conclusion that God permits man to resist sufficient grace, which is truly sufficient (just as God wills man to cooperate with efficacious grace which is truly efficacious) is the logical sum of its component parts, all of which are based on divine revelation.

For example, Scripture says all good comes from God[1] and without God

---

1. See John 3:27; Jas. 1:17

man can do nothing.[2] This means if man cooperates with grace, God willed to give him the grace of cooperation, for man can do nothing without God. However, Scripture also says that God gives sufficient grace to all men,[3] and man is responsible for rejecting it.[4] This means if man rejects grace, God willed to permit him to reject it, for God is not the cause of sin, but nothing escapes His universal causality.

Similarly, Scripture says that God wills all men to be saved[5] and no one resists God's will,[6] but not all men are saved. Although we can understand these scriptural truths in isolation, we don't understand how they can be logically connected. But accepting these truths is no different from believing God is one in three persons, each of whom is God. How can three be one when three is more than one? How can sufficient grace be sufficient when efficacious grace is required? Eventually, we run out of logic and resign ourselves to letting the mystery be a mystery.

Therefore, I have resisted the temptation to abandon or compromise these divine principles, even though I don't know how they all fit together. To my finite intellect, it seems like there must be "something more to the picture." But whatever that "something" might be, it would surely surpass my understanding and ability to articulate it without appearing to desert the truths of revelation. I also know there is no injustice in God (Rom 9:14) and that our heavenly Father will judge us according to our works. To be sure, God's infinite mercy, justice, and sovereign liberty are intimately reconciled in the secret life of the Blessed Trinity, notwithstanding our inability to grasp or explain how. Nevertheless, no matter what school of thought we follow on predestination, let us recognize and boldly profess that we are incapable of any good without God, and owe all our good gifts to God, not ourselves. Then we will be light in a world darkened by secularism, where most men live as if there is no God.

---

2. See John 15:5; 1 Cor. 4:7
3. See Titus 2:11; Eph. 4:7; 1 Pet. 4:10; 2 Cor. 3:5; 9:8; 12:9.
4. See Osee 13:9
5. See Matt. 18:14; 1 Tim. 2:4; 2 Pet. 3:9; Ez. 18:23,32; 33:11; Wis. 13:1
6. See Rom. 9:19; Esth. 13:9,11; Prov. 21:1.

APPENDIX

Thomist T-U-L-I-P	*Calvinist T-U-L-I-P*
T—Total Dependence	T—Total Depravity
U—Unconditional Election	U—Unconditional Election
L—Limited Application	L—Limited Atonement
I—Intrinsically Efficacious Grace	I—Irresistible Grace
P—Preservation of the Elect	P—Perseverance of the Saints

Excerpts from the Church's Teaching on St. Thomas Aquinas

- "He alone enlightened the Church more than all other doctors; a man can derive more profit in a year from his books than from pondering all his life the teaching of others." Pope John XXII (Consistorial address, 1318).
- "But inasmuch as, by the providence of Almighty God, the power and truth of the philosophy of the Angelic Doctor ... have confounded, refuted and routed many subsequent heresies ... We order that the memory of the Doctor by whose valor the world is daily delivered from pestilential errors be cultivated more than ever before." Pope St. Pius V (*Mirabilis Deus*, 1567).
- "It is our will, and by the authority of these letters we enjoin on you, that you follow the doctrine of Blessed Thomas as true and Catholic, and strive to unfold it with your whole strength." Pope Urban V (quoted in *Aeterni Patris*, 1879).
- "His doctrine above all other doctrine, with the one exception of the Holy Scriptures, has such a propriety of words, such a method of explanation,

202 THE MYSTERY OF PREDESTINATION

such a truth of opinions, that no one who holds it will ever be found to have strayed from the path of truth; whereas anyone who has attacked it has always been suspected as to the truth." Pope Innocent VI (quoted in *Aeterni Patris*, 1879).

• "Now far above all other Scholastic Doctors towers Thomas Aquinas, their master and prince ... that rightly and deservedly he is reckoned a singular safeguard and glory of the Catholic Church." Pope Leo XIII (*Aeterni Patris*, 1879).

• "Thomas reigned as a ruler in his own kingdom. The minds of all, both teachers and hearers, with wondrous consent found rest in the guidance and authority of one Angelic Doctor." Pope Leo XIII (*Aeterni Patris*, 1879).

• "But we now come to the greatest glory of Thomas—a glory which is altogether his own, and shared with no other Catholic Doctor. In the midst of the Council of Trent, the assembled Fathers so willing it, the *Summa* of Thomas Aquinas lay open on the altar, with the Holy Scriptures and the decrees of the Supreme Pontiffs, that from it might be sought counsel and reasons and answers." Pope Leo XIII (*Aeterni Patris*, 1879).

• "... so the principles of philosophy laid down by St. Thomas Aquinas are to be religiously and inviolably observed, because they are the means of acquiring such a knowledge of creation as is most congruent with the Faith; of refuting all the errors of all the ages, and of enabling man to distinguish clearly what things are to be attributed to God and to God alone." Pope St. Pius X (*Doctoris Angelici*, 1914).

• "For ever since the happy death of the saintly Doctor, the Church has not held a single Council, but he has been present at it with the wealth of his doctrine." Pope St. Pius X (*Doctoris Angelici*, 1914).

• "We so heartily approve the magnificent tribute of praise bestowed upon this most divine genius that We consider that Thomas should be called not only the Angelic, but also the *Common* or Universal Doctor of the Church; for the Church has adopted his philosophy for her own." Pope Pius XI (*Studiorum Ducem*, 1923).

• "[I]t will be sufficient perhaps to point out that Thomas wrote under the inspiration of the supernatural spirit which animated his life and that his writings, which contain the principles of, and the laws governing, all sacred studies, must be said to possess a universal character." Pope Pius XI (*Studiorum Ducem*, 1923).

- "Sacred Studies, therefore, being directed by a triple light, undeviating reason, infused faith and the gifts of the Holy Ghost, by which the mind is brought to perfection, no one ever was more generously endowed with these than Our Saint." Pope Pius XI (*Studiorum Ducem*, 1923).

- "There can be no doubt that Aquinas raised Theology to the highest eminence, for his knowledge of divine things was absolutely perfect." Pope Pius XI (*Studiorum Ducem*, 1923).

- "Again, if we are to avoid the errors which are the sources and fountain-head of all the miseries of our time, the teaching of Aquinas must be adhered to more religiously than ever. For Thomas refutes the theories propounded by the Modernists in every sphere … It is therefore clear why Modernists are so amply justified in fearing no Doctor of the Church so much as Thomas Aquinas." Pope Pius XI (*Studiorum Ducem*, 1923).

- "And as he is, as We have said, the perfect theologian, so he gives infallible rules and precepts of life." Pope Pius XI (*Studiorum Ducem*, 1923).

- "Accordingly, just as it was said to the Egyptians of old in time of famine: 'Go to Joseph,' so that they should receive a supply of corn from him to nourish their bodies, so We now say to all such as are desirous of the truth: 'Go to Thomas,' and ask him to give you from his ample store the food of substantial doctrine wherewith to nourish your souls unto eternal life." Pope Pius XI (*Studiorum Ducem*, 1923).

- "Jesus spoke to him from the cross, saying: 'Thomas, thou hast written well about me,' and asked him: 'What reward shall I give thee for all thy labor?' the saint made answer: 'None but Thyself, O Lord!'" Pope Pius XI (*Studiorem Ducem*, 1923).[1]

- Canon 589: Religious who have already studied their humanities should devote themselves for two years at least to philosophy and for four years to theology, following the teaching of St. Thomas … in accordance with the instructions of the Holy See.[2]

- Canon 1366, 2: The study of philosophy and theology and the teaching of these sciences to their students must be accurately carried out by

1. Jesus granted St. Thomas this divine communication at the end of St. Thomas's life. Of all the private revelations recorded about Our Lord, this is the only instance where Jesus said a saint had written well of Him.
2. From the 1917 code of canon law (while the 1983 code of canon law has replaced the 1917 code, the theological and spiritual principles of the 1917 code continue to apply).

Professors (in seminaries, etc.) according to the arguments, doctrine, and principles of St. Thomas which they are inviolately to hold.[3]

Prayer of St. Thomas Aquinas

Ineffable Creator, Who out of the treasures of Thy wisdom hast appointed three hierarchies of Angels and set them in admirable order high above the heavens and hast disposed the divers portions of the universe in such marvelous array, Thou Who art called the True Source of Light and super-eminent Principle of Wisdom, be pleased to cast a beam of Thy radiance upon the darkness of my mind and dispel from me the double darkness of sin and ignorance in which I have been born.

Thou Who makest eloquent the tongues of little children, fashion my words and pour upon my lips the grace of Thy benediction. Grant me penetration to understand, capacity to retain, method and facility in study, subtlety in interpretation and abundant grace of expression.

Order the beginning, direct the progress and perfect the achievement of my work, Thou who art true God and Man and livest and reignest for ever and ever. Amen.

3. Ibid.

BIBLIOGRAPHY

Aquinas, Thomas. *Summa Theologica*. trans. Fathers of the English Dominican Province. New York: Benziger Brothers, Inc., 1947.

Augustin, Aurelius. *A Select Library of the Nicene and Post-Nicene Fathers of the Christian Church*. ed. Philip Schaff. New York: Christian Literature Co., 1886-1890; reprinted edition., Grand Rapids, MI: Eerdmans Publishing, 1974.

Calvin, John. *Institutes of the Christian Religion*. ed. John T. McNeil. Philadelphia: Westminster Press, 1960.

Catechism of the Catholic Church. United States Catholic Conference, Libera Editrice Vaticana, 1994.

Catechism of the Council of Trent. trans. John A. McHugh and Charles J. Callan. South Bend, IN: Marian Publications, Third Printing, 1978.

Denzinger, Henry. *The Sources of Catholic Dogma*. St. Louis: B. Herder Book Co., 1957.

Erickson, Millard. *Christian Theology*. Grand Rapids, MI: Baker Books, 2004.

Garrigou-Lagrange, Reginald. *Predestination*. Rockford, IL: TAN Books and Publishers, 1998. Translated from *La predestination des saints et la grace*. Belgium: Desclee, De Brouwer and Cie.

Garrigou-Lagrange, Reginald. *Providence*. Rockford, IL: TAN Books and Publishers, 1998. Translated from *La Providence et la confiance en Dieu*. Belgium: Desclee, De Brouwer and Cie.

Geisler, Norman. *Chosen But Free*. Bloomington, MN: Bethany House Publishers, 2001.

Gill, John. *The Cause of God and Truth*. Location: The Baptist Standard Bearer, 1992.

Holy Bible, Douay-Rheims Version. Rockford, IL: TAN Books and Publishers, Inc., 2000.

Houghton, S.M. *A Faith to Confess: The Baptist Confession of Faith of 1689, Rewritten in Modern English*. Leeds, UK: Carey Publications, 1986.

Hunt, Dave and White, James. *Debating Calvinism*. Colorado Springs: Multnomah Books, 2004.

Jurgens, William. *Faith of the Early Fathers*. Collegeville, MN: Liturgical Press, 1979.

Kittel, Gerhard, and Bromiley, Geoffrey. eds. *Theological Dictionary of the New Testament*. Grand Rapids, MI: Erdmans, 1964.

Kreeft, Peter. *Summa of the Summa*. San Francisco: Ignatius Press, 1990.

Luther, Martin. *The Bondage of the Will*. J.I. Packer and O.R. Johnston, eds. Westwood, NJ: Fleming H. Revill, 1957.

Luther, Martin. *Luther's Works*. ed. and trans. Jaroslav Pelikan, et. al. St. Louis: Concordia Publishing House (vols. 1-30); Philadelphia: Fortress Press (vols. 31-55), 1955-1979.

Most, William. *Grace, Predestination and the Salvific Will of God*. Front Royal, VA: Christendom Press, 1997.

Salza, John. *The Biblical Basis for the Papacy*. Huntington, IN: Our Sunday Visitor, 2007.

Salza, John. *The Biblical Basis for the Eucharist*. Huntington, IN: Our Sunday Visitor, 2008.

Salza, John. *The Biblical Basis for Purgatory*. Charlotte, NC: Saint Benedict Press, 2009.

Salza, John. *The Biblical Basis for Tradition—Why Catholics Don't Rely on Scripture Alone*. Huntington, IN: Our Sunday Visitor, 2010.

Salza, John. *Why Catholics Cannot Be Masons*. Rockford, IL: TAN Books and Publishers, 2008.

Sproul, R.C. *Chosen By God*. Wheaton, IL: Tyndale House Publishers, 1986.

Stott, John R.W. *The Cross of Christ*, Downers Grove: IL, Intervarsity Press, 1986.

Strong, James H. *The New Strong's Exhaustive Concordance of the Bible*. Nashville: Thomas Nelson, 1991.

Sungenis, Robert. *Not By Faith Alone*. Goleta, CA: Queenship, 1997.

White, James. *The Potter's Freedom*. Amityville, NY: Calvary Press Publishing, 2000.

ABOUT THE AUTHOR

John Salza is an attorney and renowned Catholic apologist, author, and speaker. He is the creator of ScriptureCatholic.com, a veritable library of over 2,000 Scripture citations and over 800 quotes from the early Church Fathers that explain and defend the Catholic faith.

Salza is the author of *Why Catholics Cannot Be Masons* (TAN Books) and *The Biblical Basis for Purgatory* (Saint Benedict Press) as well as *The Biblical Basis for the Catholic Faith*, *The Biblical Basis for the Papacy*, *The Biblical Basis for the Eucharist*, *The Biblical Basis for Tradition* (by Fall 2010) and *Masonry Unmasked* (our Sunday Visitor) and other popular apologetics titles.

Salza is also a frequent guest and host on Catholic radio shows, including Searching the Word, The Drew Mariani Show, Kresta in the Afternoon and The Voice of Catholic Radio. He has an apologetics feature on Relevant Radio called "Relevant Answers," which runs six times a day, seven days a week. He also has a daily apologetics spot on the Eternal Word Television Network's (EWTN) Global Catholic radio program called "Catholic Q&A" and has made numerous guest appearances on EWTN as well.